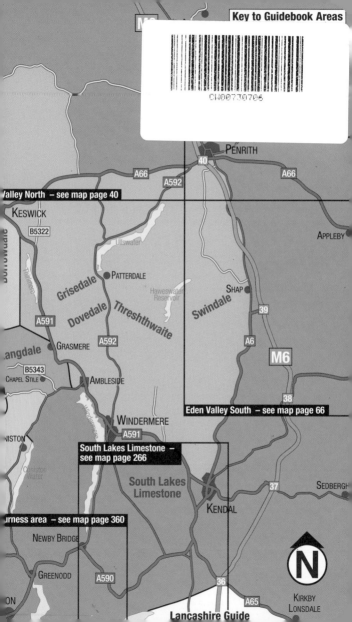

Key to Guidebook Areas

CW00730706

M6

PENRITH

40

A66

A592

A66

APPLEBY

Valley North – see map page 40

KESWICK

B5322

Ullswater

PATTERDALE

Haweswater Reservoir

SHAP

Griesedale

Dovedale

Threshthwaite

Swindale

39

A591

GRASMERE

A592

A6

M6

angdale

B5343

CHAPEL STILE

AMBLESIDE

Eden Valley South – see map page 66

38

WINDERMERE

A591

South Lakes Limestone –
see map page 266

NISTON

Coniston Water

South Lakes
Limestone

37

SEDBERGH

KENDAL

urness area – see map page 360

NEWBY BRIDGE

GREENODD

A590

36

N

ON

A65

KIRKBY
LONSDALE

Lancashire Guide

Eden Valley & South Lakes Limestone

Published by
FRCC **the Fell and Rock Climbing Club**
GUIDE **of the English Lake District**

Climbing Guides to the English Lake District

Eden Valley & South Lakes Limestone

by RJ Kenyon, N Wharton and JL Holden

Photodiagrams & Picture Research by
PC Rigby (Photographs Editor)

Maps by
A Phizacklea (Diagrams Editor)

Edited by
SJH Reid

Publishing arranged by
RJ Kenyon

FRCC GUIDE

Published by
the Fell and Rock Climbing Club of the English Lake District

The FRCC and Rock Climbing Guides to the English Lake District

Brian Davison on **W Route** (HVS), White Stone. **Photo:** Nick Wharton

The formation of the **Fell and Rock Climbing Club** was proposed at Coniston in 1906 at the instigation of Edward Scantlebury and Alan Craig, two of a "coterie of keen young mountaineers living on the southern confines of the English Lake District". Before the end of the year the club had over 40 members enrolled and was officially founded in 1907 when Ashley Abraham accepted the office of President. The first Club Journal was produced that same year and many new climbs were reported therein and in further annual volumes.

The Club published its first rock climbing guidebook in 1922 (Doe Crag by George Bower) and since that date has produced a continuous series of definitive guidebooks to Lake District climbing. These guidebooks are written and published by volunteers who update the text and check new climbs, many of which have been, and continue to be, pioneered by Club members.

The Club now has over 1200 members and owns several club huts both in the Lake District and elsewhere. Membership has always been open to applicants of either sex who can demonstrate an ongoing interest and enthusiasm for climbing in the Lake District. Enquiries regarding the FRCC and its guidebooks should be addressed to the current Club Secretary or Guidebooks Editor, whose addresses are available from the Club's website at www.frcc.co.uk or from the BMC.

This is the first FRCC definitive guide to these areas. However it is based in part on the following earlier guides:

Rock Climbers' Guide – North of England by Stewart Wilson and Ron Kenyon (Pointer Publications, 1980)

North of England Rock Climbs by Stewart Wilson (Cordee, 1992)

Rock Climbs in Lancashire and the North West by Les Ainsworth (Cicerone, 1983)

Rock Climbs in Lancashire and the North West by Phil Kelly and Dave Cronshaw (Cicerone, 1987)

Rock Climbs in the Lancashire Area edited and compiled by Geoff Milburn, Les Ainsworth and Dave Cronshaw (BMC, 1999)

British Library Cataloguing in Publication Data
  Kenyon, R.J.
  Eden Valley & South Lakes Limestone. – [9th Series] –
  (Climbing Guides to the English Lake District) –
  (FRCC Guide)

ISBN 978-0-85028-052-4

Front Cover: Yan Preston going **Up Town** (F6c), Chapel Head Scar.
Photo: Nick Wharton

Frontispiece 1: Ron Fawcett on the first ascent of **Moonchild** (E4), Chapel Head Scar in 1974. **Photo:** Al Evans

Frontispiece 2: Rob Haigh calls on all his finger strength for **Zantom Phone** (7c+), Chapel Head Scar. **Photo:** Nick Wharton

 Designed and typeset by **Vertebrate Publishing**, Sheffield, a division of **Vertebrate Graphics**. www.v-publishing.co.uk

Distributed by Cordee, Leicester. www.cordee.co.uk

Printed in China through Colorcraft Ltd, Hong Kong. www.colorcraft.com.hk

Published by The Fell and Rock Climbing Club of the English Lake District Limited
Industrial and Provident Societies Registration: 30506 R

All rights reserved. No part of this publication may be reproduced or transmitted in any form or by any means, electronic or mechanical, including photocopy, recording, or any information storage and retrieval system, without permission in writing from the FRCC.

Contents

North Cumbria & the Eden Valley 38

South Cumbria & South Lakes Limestone 259

x Contents

Introduction

This guidebook is the fifth volume in a series of definitive climbing
guides to the Lake District, one of the most popular climbing areas in
the British Isles. It deals with the far northern, eastern and southern
edge of the Lakes and indeed much of the area covered, although in
Cumbria, is not in the Lake District National Park at all. It is published
by the Fell and Rock Climbing Club of the English Lake District,
the club that has been responsible for producing definitive guides to the
Lake District since 1922. It is intended that the full Ninth Series will
eventually comprise:

1. *Lake District Winter Climbs*
   (published in conjunction with Cicerone Press)
2. *Gable & Pillar*
3. *Buttermere & St Bees*
4. *Eastern Crags*
5. *Eden Valley & South Lakes Limestone*
6. *Langdale*
7. *Dow & Slate*
8. *Duddon & Eskdale*
9. *Scafell & Wasdale*
10. *Borrowdale*
11. *Lake District Rock* (Selected Climbs)

This guide covers a large area of Cumbria that has not featured in a
definitive FRCC guide before, though two of its major crags do make an
appearance in our selected climbs guide, *Lake District Rock*. For some time
now it has seemed logical for the FRCC to extend its guidebook remit to
the whole of the county of Cumbria and indeed there was some pressure
on us to do so from the climbing community, given that the last definitive
guidebook to the Eden Valley and its surrounding areas, *North of England
Rock Climbs*, was published in 1992, and the last definitive guide to South
Lakes Limestone, *Rock Climbs in the Lancashire Area* (aka the *"Lancashire Brick"*)
was published in 1999. Both have been out of print for many years and

the FRCC is grateful to both Stewart Wilson, author and publisher of the former, and Les Ainsworth, editor of the latter, for kindly allowing use of their manuscripts and giving the project their blessing – a sadly all too rare instance of co-operation amongst rival guide producers in an age when commercial competition for plum areas seems rife.

The northern half of this guidebook area, comprising a few North Lakes Limestone quarries and Border crags, together with the far more important area of the Eden Valley, has been researched and written by Ron Kenyon who was instrumental in the early exploration of the area some forty years ago, co-authored its first ever guidebook and has continued to produce new routes there ever since, his most recent triumph being the discovery and development of Coudy Rocks in Appleby.

The most important crag in this guide though is without doubt Chapel Head Scar, a bolted limestone crag of national importance. Nick Wharton who lives in nearby Kendal, has written up this and the other crags in South-East Cumbria and on the Cartmel Peninsula that make up what is generally known as South Lakes Limestone, an area that he knows intimately. Most of the climbs he has had to research are hard sport routes and it is fortunate that Nick is more than capable of climbing the majority of them and indeed has done so. Nick was assisted by Roger Wilkinson who provided the descriptions of White Stone.

Finally to the few outcrops and quarries of the Furness Peninsula, in the area west of Chapel Head Scar, around Ulverston and Barrow – these are evening crags for John Holden. Whilst they may not be venues that many from outside the area would ever visit, there are good climbs here, worthy of record.

This is a guide that I suspect a lot of northern-based climbers will purchase, but for different reasons. Those leading the heady delights of F6c and above will buy it for South Lakes Limestone and in particular Chapel Head Scar. For the remainder, and I suspect the majority, it will be something to keep in the car for those occasions when they get rained off the major Lakeland crags and a few miles of motoring northwards, eastwards or southwards can save the day.

For whatever reason you buy this guide, I hope you enjoy it and find it easy to use – good climbing!

Stephen Reid (Editor), November 2011

Right: Andy Mitchell on the delicate yet powerful **Unrighteous Doctors** (F7c+), Chapel Head Scar. **Photo:** Nick Wharton

General Notes

Terminology

A *wall* ranges from almost vertical to slightly overhanging. A *slab* is less than vertical. A *glacis* is a very easy-angled slab. An *arête* is a sharply-angled rib or ridge. Climbs and pitches are measured in metres (m). The terms *gill* and *ghyll* (meaning stream or gully) are interchangeable. *Fell* is the Lakeland word for hill.

Grades

The standard British double-grade system is used for all except bolted routes and boulder problems. On first acquaintance this may be puzzling to visitors from overseas used to climbs having a single grade, but in fact it is relatively simple and once understood provides a great deal of information about the climbs. Many of climbs in this guide require the use of leader-placed natural protection and on any route given an adjectival grade a full rack suitable to the climb being attempted should be carried. Grades are very personal, being influenced by an individual's stature and physique, their willingness to climb above protection, and their preference for a particular style of climbing.

Adjectival Grades

These give the overall grade of the climb in good weather conditions, taking into account such factors as technical difficulty, rock quality and protection. The grades are: Moderate, Difficult, Very Difficult, Mild Severe, Severe, Hard Severe, Mild Very Severe, Very Severe, Hard Very Severe, Extremely Severe, with the standard abbreviations being used in the text. The Extremely Severe grade is open ended and is currently divided into E1, E2, through to E11.

Plus and Minus Grades

Adjectival grades have been further subdivided by use of a minus sign (-) to indicate routes that are considered easy for the grade and a plus sign (+) for those thought to be hard. This system replaces the traditional graded list and needless to say, just like a graded list, it is completely subjective.

Technical Grades

These are included for each pitch of 4a and above on routes of VS and above. This grade is an attempt to assess the pure technical difficulty encountered on each pitch and once again is open-ended. The grades to date are: 4a, 4b, 4c, 5a, 5b, 5c, 6a, 6b, 6c, 7a.

UK Adjectival Grade	UK Technical Grade (approx)	UIAA (alpine) Grade	European Equivalent	USA Equivalent	Australian Equivalent
Moderate		I, II	1	5.1, 5.2	4, 5
Difficult		II, III	1, 2, 2+	5.2, 5.3	5, 6, 7
Very Difficult		III, III+	2, 2+, 3−	5.2, 5.3, 5.4	6, 7, 8
Hard Very Difficult		III+, IV, IV+	2+, 3−, 3, 3+	5.4, 5.5, 5.6	8, 9, 10
Mild Severe		V, IV+	3−, 3, 3+	5.5, 5.6	10, 11
Severe		IV, IV+, V−	3, 3+, 4	5.5, 5.6, 5.7	10, 11, 12
Hard Severe		IV+, V−, V	3, 3+, 4, 4+	5.6, 5.7	12, 13
Mild Very Severe	4a, 4b, 4c	IV+, V−, V	3+, 4, 4+	5.6, 5.7	12, 13, 14
Very Severe	4a, 4b, 4c	V−, V, V+	4, 4+, 5	5.7, 5.8	13, 14, 15
Hard Very Severe	4c, 5a, 5b	V+, VI−, VI	4+, 5, 5+, 6a	5.8, 5.9	15, 16, 17, 18
E1	5a, 5b, 5c	VI, VI+	5+, 6a, 6a+	5.9, 5.10a	18, 19, 20
E2	5b, 5c, 6a	VI+, VII−, VII	6a+, 6b, 6b+	5.10b, 5.10c	19, 20, 21
E3	5c, 6a	VII, VII+	6b, 6b+, 6c	5.10d, 5.11a, 5.11b	20, 21, 22
E4	6a, 6b	VII−, VIII−, VIII	6c, 6c+, 7a	5.11b, 5.11c, 5.11d	22, 23
E5	6a, 6b 6c	VIII, VIII−, IX−	7a, 7a+, 7b	5.11d, 5.12a, 5.12b	23, 24, 25
E6	6b, 6c	IX−, IX, IX+	7b, 7b+, 7c, 7c+	5.12b, 5.12c, 5.12d, 5.13a	25, 26, 27, 28
E7	6c, 7a	IX+, X−, X	7c+, 8a, 8a+	5.13a, 5.13b, 5.13c	28, 29, 30
E8	6c, 7a	X, X+	8a+, 8b, 8b+	5.13c, 5.13d, 5.14a	30, 31, 32
E9	7a, 7b	XI−, X+	8b+, 8c, 8c+	5.14a, 5.14b, 5.14c	30, 31, 32

French Grades

Fully bolt-protected 'sport' routes are given French grades overall. These grades, prefixed with an 'F', are comparable with the standard French/Spanish grades of 4, 5, 6a, 6b, 6c, 7a, 7b, 7c, and 8a. They are further subdivided with a (+) symbol.

Boulder Problems

These notes are intended for those new to bouldering – regulars already understand the subtle nuances of the dark art.

The V grade system, developed in Hueco by John Sherman ('Verm' to his mates, hence the V) has been employed. This takes into account the physical challenge of the overall difficulty and not the technicality of the hardest move. Sustained traverse problems will thus often be technically easier for the given V grade. Fear and danger are not accounted for so that a decent crash mat and an alert spotter are invaluable.

For trad climbers new to bouldering, the problems can seem frustratingly perplexing at first as even the easiest problems are technically difficult. Direct comparison with trad grades is difficult; on V0 problems moves of 5a/5b can be expected, V1 to V2 and you can expect something around the 5b/5c/6a mark, V3 to V4 you can expect 6a/6b moves and after that it just gets hard.

Aid, Bolts and In Situ Protection

Only a few routes still require the use of artificial assistance and this is indicated in the description where appropriate. Aid reductions continue to be made; routes are described and graded according to the best style in which they are known to have been climbed.

The placing of bolts is a subject which has aroused much emotive discussion during recent years. In the interest of care and concern for crags and the mountain environment, and a belief that British climbing in general should continue with the principle of leader-placed removable protection, the FRCC is generally in accord with the guidelines on the use of bolts for the protection of routes as set out by the BMC. It is agreed that in the Lake District bolts are only acceptable on certain quarried crags and some agreed limestone and sandstone outcrops. Climbers are asked to adhere to this policy and only place bolts on agreed crags.

Retro-bolting has taken place on a number of routes in the Lake District but only after consultation with the first ascentionist of that route. In order to avoid any conflict, please ensure that this policy is maintained.

A number of route descriptions in this guide contain references to in situ protection including pegs, slings, bolts and wires. The history of these frequently dates back to the first ascent. There can be no guarantee that the fixed gear mentioned will still be in place when you climb the route or, more importantly, if it is there, that it will be of any use. It is well known that in situ gear will deteriorate to a fraction of its original holding power due to the elements. This can occur in a matter of months rather than years, particularly where wires or hard steel blade pegs are concerned. Therefore it is for the individual climber to assess the reliability of any in situ protection encountered. Bolts are not infallible and have been known to fail in the past. The Cumbria Bolt Fund was set up in 2008 to replace the more dodgy Cumbrian bolts, some of which are over twenty years old and of dubious safety. See www.cumbriaboltfund.com for more information.

Fixed abseil points may be found on some crags. These should be thoroughly inspected before use and, if found to be doubtful, backed up with new equipment.

Stars and Quality

The star system of indicating the quality of a climb has been established for many years in Britain and climbers have long come to expect a three star route to be something extra special, not just in terms of the particular area being described, but vis-à-vis other climbs in Great Britain as a whole. Whilst the original aim of this practice was laudable, giving only a handful of climbs three star status has brought its problems. Three star routes attract queues and queues create polish, whilst nearby almost as good two star climbs that could do with a bit of traffic often languish in obscurity and become lichenous, and so on down the scale. To remedy this many more stars are now used than previously and they are now intended to indicate quality on a much broader scale, viz:

★★★	Good climbing, on good, mainly clean rock, with purpose to the line.
★★	Mostly the above.
★	Some good climbing and a permutation of the other two factors.
	Of interest to mainly to regular visitors to the crag.

It will be seen that a three star route no longer needs to be one of the best in the country, though it will provide an entertaining (and possibly adventurous) outing.

Unrepeated Routes

Climbs that are thought not to have been repeated have their grades suffixed by a '?'. Feedback on these routes would be appreciated. It is particularly difficult to rate the quality of new or unrepeated routes: therefore, these have been given "hollow" stars as a provisional assessment. Feedback would be welcome.

FRCC Routes Archive

In order to keep the size of this guide to something that will fit in your pocket on multipitch climbs, poor or overgrown routes, and in some cases whole crags, have not been described. However, to preserve a complete history of climbing in the area, and to discourage unnecessary gardening activity, their descriptions have been preserved for posterity in the Rock Climbing section of the FRCC website, www.frcc.co.uk.

New Routes and Corrections

To aid writers of future guidebooks, please post comments, corrections, and details of all new climbs on the FRCC website www.frcc.co.uk. To do this, log in with the user name 'napesneedle' and the password '1886', go to the Rock Climbing section and follow the instructions. Several "New Routes books" exist in the area, including the Log Books in FRCC huts. However, these may not be checked regularly and first ascensionists are urged to also record their route on the website above or it may be missed. Please provide all relevant details in the usual format including grades, dates, first ascensionists and style of ascent.

Location of Crags

The location of each crag is indicated by its national grid reference. Beware those crags where the name on the map may be some way from the grid reference shown, and those where the climbers' name for a crag or other feature is different from that on the map – such instances are detailed in the text. The aspect of the main faces has been included to aid the choice of crags. The altitude given is based on a mean sea level of zero. The terms 'true left' and 'true right' are used to describe the position of a crag in a valley or gill relative to the direction of flow of the stream. The terms 'left' and 'right', unless otherwise stated, mean as the climber faces the climb.

Maps

Rather a lot of Ordnance Survey Explorer Series 1:25000 maps are needed to cover the large area described in this guide. These are OL4 (The English Lake District – North-West Area), OL5 (The English Lake District – North-East Area), OL7 (The English Lake District – South-East Area) and OL6 (The English Lake District – South-West Area), OL43 (Hadrian'sWall), OL31 (North Pennines) and OL19 (Howgill Fells & Upper Eden Valley). At 1:50000, the Ordnance Survey's Landranger maps numbers 85, 86, 90, 91, 96, 97 and 98 are required.

Photodiagrams Key

🅞 Moderate to Hard Severe

🅞 MVS to E1   🅞 F5 to F6a+

🅞 E2 to E4   🅞 F6b to F6c+

🅞 E5 and above   🅞 F7a upwards

Ⓥ Variation

1 Boulder Problem

○ Belay

Ⓐ Abseil

○ₒ Fixed lower off

∘∘∘∘∘ Footpath

∘∘∘∘→ Scramble/descent

⚠ Caution required

☠ Danger

Photodiagrams

Full colour photodiagrams of almost every crag and buttress covered have been included. The amount of work required to produce these, particularly on high remote crags, has been immense, requiring many visits and the climbing of almost every route. However it is possible that some small errors remain and if in doubt it is probably better to rely on the written description rather than the photodiagram. The symbols used should be fairly self-explanatory.

Photographs

The Editor has little sympathy for those who criticise photographs in climbing guides yet don't carry a camera themselves. Tracking down good climbing photographs for guidebooks is always a difficult task and the FRCC Guidebook Committee would like to express their gratitude to all those who submitted photographs for consideration. To those whose photographs were not selected this time, please do not be discouraged, and please keep sending them in to the Guidebook Photographs Editor, whose address, together with details of current guidebook work being undertaken, is available from the Club's website at www.frcc.co.uk.

Safety Advice

Climbing is a dangerous pastime that can seriously damage your health! Details of climbs recorded in this guidebook, together with their grades, reference to in situ or natural protection, and locations,

Above: Eden Valley stalwart Ron Kenyon getting a shot of Ben Bravington-Sim bouldering at Sandy Bay, Armathwaite. **Photo:** Michael Kenyon

are made in good faith having been compiled from first ascent or past descriptions, checked and substantiated where possible with consensus comments.

Unfortunately climbs can change; holds fall off, rock becomes dirty, in situ gear deteriorates or disappears. Even a minor alteration can have a dramatic effect on the grade or seriousness of a route. It is therefore essential that climbers judge the condition of any route before committing themselves.

The contents of this guidebook are believed to be correct. However, neither the FRCC nor its members and their friends involved with its production can be held responsible for any omissions or mistakes, nor liable for any personal or third party injuries or damage, howsoever caused, arising from its use. In this claims-conscious age, climbers are recommended to obtain suitable insurance cover. The BMC now provides third party liability cover for members and members of affiliated clubs.

Campsites, Bunkhouses, Camping Barns and Club Huts

Within the Lake District there are numerous camping barns, bunkhouses and campsites. To find out more about these contact details are given on page 386. There are also many climbing club huts, most of which are available to non-club members – contact the BMC for a list.

Wild Camping

Wild camping (ie camping outside of a proper campsite) is generally allowed on the fells above the 300 metre contour as long as one is above the final (intake) wall and not within 100 metres of habitation. Any campsite used should be left as it was found and all litter cleared (whether yours or not!).

Right: Dan Robinson on **Cadillac** (F6c+), Mill Side Scar. **Photo:** Nick Wharton

Geological Notes

by Dave Bodecott

Most of the central Lake District crags are part of the Borrowdale Volcanic Group, formed 460-450 Ma (million years ago). Some time after the Borrowdale Volcanic period, the area was uplifted by the Caledonian mountain-building phase (about 400 Ma). Erosion of the Caledonide mountains enabled shallow tropical seas and accompanying limestone sedimentation to extend across the area during the Carboniferous era (350-300 Ma). The older rocks progressively underlie this cover of Carboniferous limestones and sandstones, which form the escarpments of Caldbeck (Head End Quarry), Berrier Hill, Shap, Orton and Ravenstonedale. These units in turn dip eastwards under the Permian and Triassic red rocks (300-200 Ma) of the Eden Valley. The Pennine fault bounds the red rocks to the east and again brings the Carboniferous limestones and sandstones to the surface where some good outcrops like Cumrew, Windmore End and Brough Scar develop along the west-facing escarpment.

The Great Scar and Melmerby Scar limestones are the main units of massive grey limestones that form the popular climbing crags of the Pennine escarpment. Sandier units are present as at King's Meaburn. In total, the Carboniferous limestones are part of a package about 400-1000 metres in thickness. The Permian age Whin Sill (295 Ma) is intruded into the limestones and forms impressive dolerite cliffs at High Cup Nick, although the rock is loose and broken.

In the Kendal area, Chapel Head Scar, White Scar, Scout Scar and Humphrey Head are formed by prominent fault blocks and escarpments created by later tectonic uplift. Of the several major limestone units in the area, the Urswick limestone is one of the most prominent in forming climbing crags.

Further uplift occurred during the Hercynian mountain building phase (300 Ma), and continental drift brought the then landmass into the northern hemisphere trade winds, which led to the onset of desert conditions during the Permian and Triassic periods. These Appleby group desert sediments underlie the Eden Valley, which developed west of the Pennine and Dent fault system.

The Appleby Group consists of the Penrith Sandstone, 100-275 metres in thickness, the Eden Shales, then the overlying St. Bees Sandstones. Obviously, the Penrith Sandstone forms the climbing interest, though rounded in character and often with poor natural protection. These sandstones were largely formed as desert sand dunes, often cross-bedded, as can be seen at Cowraik (or Cowrake), Armathwaite, Lazonby and Scratchmere – all crags noted for their difficult problems – and at the unprotectable Coudy Rocks at Appleby which have recently been bolted. Unusual brockrams (a breccia of cemented limestone and sandstone fragments dating from the Permian period) up to 150 metres thick develop in places e.g. at the Hoff. Triassic braided river sandstones (200 Ma) also occur at Dufton.

No rocks younger than the Triassic are preserved across the area due to the erosional effects of the early Tertiary tectonic uplift (ca. 65 Ma).

Finally, these earthquakes have been recorded: 1786-7, 1867, 1885, 1901, 1911, 1979/1980, 1988, 2011. That is once every 28 years on average, so climbers beware!

Acknowledgements
British Geological Survey.
www.bgs.ac.uk
Cumberland Geological Society.
www.cumberland-geol-soc.org.uk
Dr. Andrew Bell, Open University.

Above: Grand outlook: **Scout Scar** with the Kentmere Fells in the distance. **Photo:** Phil Rigby

Access & Conservation

by Simon Webb & Peter Davies

Access

Access to the crags described in this guide will be taken for granted by the majority of users but in fact in some cases it may have been achieved only through years of patient negotiation. The National Trust, Forestry Commission, United Utilities, or other private owners who are broadly sympathetic to climbers, own most of the crags in the Lake District itself but unfortunately this situation does not pertain on the margins of the area where access is generally at the whim of private landowners. In this guide there are many crags where climbing is currently banned and repeated negotiations to change this situation have failed. Full descriptions of these crags have been included to preserve the historical record but no right of access is implied. Also, in a few cases where access is currently permitted, the situation remains delicate and increasing numbers of climbers are only likely to make it more so. Here is an area in which we can all help, not only by cherishing this region in the manner it deserves, parking thoughtfully, co-operating with farmers and landowners, following the country code, observing bird restrictions, picking up litter at crags and so on, but by ensuring that others do the same. Outsiders look on climbers as a group and inconsiderate behaviour by a few will be seen, rightly or wrongly, as a reflection upon us all. The onus is on all of us to make certain that it doesn't happen in the first place.

Bird Restrictions

Three species of bird nesting on the crags described in this guidebook are of particular note – these are the **peregrine**, **raven** and **ring ouzel**. All use crags as nesting sites as a strategy to avoid predators. In addition, ground-nesting upland **waders** (such as curlew and golden plover) frequent the Pennine hills and Border moors.

Peregrine and Raven

Many climbers will be familiar with the iconic birds of the Cumbrian uplands, peregrines and ravens.
Peregrines are stocky, broad-winged birds of prey, which swoop at lightning speed from above

Photo: RSPB

onto unfortunate medium-sized birds such as pigeons. Their call is a piercing shriek which, if they are disturbed, will be repeated for long periods. They nearly always nest on coastal cliffs or inland crags but their nest will not be obvious – just a shallow depression in the soil or grass. White bird droppings can sometimes mark the location but could equally just be a roost or perching site. Cumbria has an exceptionally high density of nesting peregrine with some 60 pairs breeding in a good year. This core population is important in conservation terms as birds from here will spread out and re-colonise other areas in the UK.

Ravens are very large black birds, much bigger and more thick set than a crow. Their calls are a distinctive "cronk" and "pruck-pruck". Also distinctive is their acrobatic flight with characteristic tumbling and inverted flying. The birds seem to delight in this and appear to be playing in the air. Ravens' nests are large piles of twigs, often on a crag.

Photo: RSPB

Both raven and peregrine are vulnerable to disturbance but the peregrine receives stronger (Schedule 1) legal protection on account of the shooting, poisoning, egg and chick theft that they have been subjected to over the years. Voluntary **Bird Restrictions** to protect both birds are put in place annually on various crags across Cumbria (raven: 15th February to 31st May, peregrine: 1st March to 30th June). Crags that have been restricted regularly in the past are indicated in the text. Usually, restricted crags will be signed, but this may not always be the case and all climbers should acquaint themselves with the latest known details which can be found on the BMC website at www.thebmc.co.uk or on the FRCC website at www.frcc.co.uk. It may be that only some parts of the crag are restricted, so other routes can be climbed. If this is the case it will be indicated on the signs. These bird restrictions generally only apply to the more popular crags but this does not mean that it is acceptable to climb on all other crags in the nesting season. On crags where there are no formal restrictions you will need to keep an eye out for birds and nests and make judgements about your impact. Where birds have not nested in any particular year, the ban may be lifted early. It is important that climbers follow some basic guidance in order to prevent disturbance as well as to make sure they are not breaking the law. Apart from possible prosecution, the police may arrest you and confiscate your climbing equipment as evidence to present at your trial – which may take a long time to come to court! The law states that it is an offence to intentionally or recklessly disturb a Schedule 1 bird at, on, or near the nest. It is also an offence to recklessly or intentionally disturb dependent fledged young. These fledglings are young birds that have just moved away from the nest but are still dependent to some extent on their parents for food and protection. As you walk in to the crag keep a look out for peregrines and other birds. Peregrines in particular may be calling as they fly about the area. When you arrive they may be disturbed but this is a normal response. Try and move out of their line of sight as quickly as you can and then wait and see if they settle down. Try to spot where they originate. This will enable you to decide whether there is a nest site that is being used near the route that you are hoping to do. The birds will probably be disturbed if they can see you so don't climb next to the nest but find a route that is not within their line of sight. If you do this, and the crucial early period of egg incubation is past, then you might find that the birds calm down quickly and climbing will not move them off the nest. However, if the birds continue to appear aggressive and agitated and are staying away from the nest, to continue climbing will cause damaging disturbance by keeping the parents off the nest for too long. In such circumstances you should find another climb either on another part of the crag further away from the nest or even on another crag.

There are no hard and fast rules to determine when you might be too close as so much depends upon the tolerance of the individual bird. If the crag is very popular with climbers, then any nesting birds may be habituated to climbers' presence. Such peregrines may be able to accept climbing in quite close proximity, as long as it is around the other side of an arête or on a separate buttress. But you can always be sure that climbing very close or directly onto the nest will cause damaging disturbance. At crags in remote areas where there is little climbing activity, birds may be disturbed even at some distance. Of particular importance is the line of sight. The best policy is to err upon the side of caution and if in any doubt retreat. For this reason it is not possible to set firm guidelines about how far away you need to be to avoid disturbance or whether you will be breaking the law or not.

There is increasing conservation concern about the ring ouzel.
Photo: RSPB

Ring Ouzel

The ring ouzel is closely related to the blackbird and looks similar. Adult males are all black except for a white crescent on the breast and a yellow bill. The male sings its loud and mournful song from trees or rocks, although if disturbed near the nest they make a harsh "chack chack" call. The female is similar but duller, and young birds often lack the breast crescent. The ring ouzel is migratory, spending winter in Spain and Africa, but breeds in the Pennines and Lake District, in gullies, rocky areas or scree slopes above the 250 metre contour line. They usually nest in mature heather or occasionally under bracken, but very often on rock ledges or steep slopes, laying several eggs in a neat cup-shaped nest. More than half the UK population of ring ouzels have been lost between 1988 and 1999 and this has led to its recent (2002) red listing as a bird of conservation concern. It is thus extremely important that crags with heather or bilberry covered ledges are safeguarded from crag clean ups or gardening. If you encounter a chack-chack call from the bird it would be sensible to retreat and help this threatened bird maintain breeding success in Cumbria.

Breeding Waders

The blanket bogs and heather moorlands of the Pennines and Border moors are known for their breeding wader populations. Curlews, golden plover and dunlin breed here, together with red grouse. These birds, which are almost absent from the central Lake District, are ground nesting and are sensitive to disturbance. Advice to climbers is simple: do not take a dog to the crag in these areas during spring and early summer, but if you must, then keep it on a short lead.

Rare Plants, the Climber and "Gardening"

The most impressive English examples of upland vegetation are found amongst the high fells of the Lake District and North Pennines where there is steep craggy ground that sheep can't reach, with specialised soils and climatic conditions that are favoured by upland plants. In the valleys and the lowlands, agriculture has led to a loss of ecological diversity, with grasslands ploughed up and fertilised and natural vegetation only surviving on the crags. Although we often think of the fells and mountains as natural or wild, the vegetation is in general highly modified and man is responsible. In particular the impact of increased sheep numbers over the past fifty years has led to a huge reduction in the area of heathland vegetation in Cumbria. Crag vegetation is therefore particularly important as it provides a reservoir of rare flora that can re-colonise the uplands now that conservation organisations are negotiating lower sheep numbers. But for now, only climbers experience and enjoy these stands of wild plants, which have been lost or degraded elsewhere.

Climbers will also notice that there are more trees on the crags than on gentler fell-sides. Sheep are once again the culprits and only on the steeper slopes (or where grazing pressure is very low) can trees get beyond the seedling stage. Some of the upland trees are rare and specialised - juniper is probably the most well known of these. A scrubby evergreen and rather prickly native conifer, its berries smell strongly of gin when they are purple and ripe. A specialist dwarf type of juniper inhabits the crags above 500 metres. A more natural landscape would have a greater woodland cover and junipers and willows would grow high on the open fells.

Left: Lancastrian whitebeam, which is only found on the limestone crags of the southern Lake District. **Right:** Spiked speedwell; confined to the cliff-top grasslands of South Lakes Limestone. **Photos:** Simon Webb

The vegetation described below needs protection across its whole range. It really is so rare and vulnerable that it is vitally important to conserve any fragments that are left. What follows describes the most extensive and richest areas that we know about but if a place is not mentioned it does not mean that it is unimportant nor that it does not matter.

In the **Borders Area** in the far north-east of Cumbria, there are gritty sandstone edges and tors amongst the blanket bogs and peatlands of the moors. These are lonely crags, where bog mosses and cotton grass dominate the open ground. Millions of tonnes of carbon are locked up in these upland peat bogs and restoring and protecting the hydrology of this landscape is becoming increasingly important in slowing climate change. Further south, in the **Eden Valley**, the Eden sandstones are younger rocks and are infrequently visible because this broad valley has a deep cover of glacial till, though here and there the River Eden has exposed pocketed and fretted red sandstone crags in deep wooded gorges – on these the vegetation of the crags has much in common with the surrounding woodlands. Higher up the Eden Valley the geology changes to limestone or brockram (a type of breccia of cemented limestone and sandstone fragments) and the crags are low scars adjacent to the upper tributaries of the river. In the headwaters, upstream of Brough, wooded limestone ravines such as the Argill and Augill have small isolated crags which are surrounded by colourful tall herbs and orchids. High above the Eden Valley, the escarpment of the Northern Pennines exhibits bands of alternating limestone and sandstone which are set amidst blanket bogs in a similar fashion to the Border moors. Vegetation on the small limestone crags (such as Murton and Brough Scar) is quite rich with hoary whitlowgrass, northern bedstraw and alpine cinquefoil, whilst the Whin Sill (a basaltic dolerite intrusion) outcropping at High Cup Nick, is high enough to support rare montane vegetation, including one of only three English locations for alpine saxifrage. The western scarp of the Pennines has been grazed for centuries, at times quite heavily, and only on the crags is a richer vegetation found. Key sites at High Cup Nick, Helbeck, Brough Scar and Murton Scar are climbed on but many other outcrops and broken scars are also important refuges of this type of vegetation.

In the **South Lakes**, the Morecambe Bay limestones are in a lowland setting of ash woodland, hazel coppice, limestone pavements, scree, juniper scrub, and colourful limestone grassland, the whole landscape being botanically rich. The crags at Whitbarrow, Scout Scar, Farleton Knott, Hutton Roof and Humphrey Head are particularly important because they are the only place in the world for Lancastrian whitebeam, a tree with pale-backed leaves, which favours crag edges. The trees on the crags also include ancient yews and counting the annual growth rings of these has established that even small trees can be thousands of years old. Cliff-top grasslands are botanically rich with plants like hoary rock-rose and spiked speedwell confined to this area. Bolts and lower-offs help protect this habitat, whilst topping out could cause serious damage.

The Law on Wild Plants and Birds

Natural vegetation and birds are an important part of our heritage and Government has enacted strict laws to protect them. These laws apply to both landowners and those enjoying outdoor recreation. This legal framework is part of the UK's national and international obligations towards conservation.

Much of the upland landscape is within Sites of Special Scientific Interest (SSSIs). Although there is much of interest to conserve outside these sites, SSSIs do form the central core of the statutory conservation system in the UK. This wildlife law doesn't just give powers to designate and protect special sites, it also provide for many positive initiatives to conserve our wildlife including mechanisms for grants, management agreements and action plans as well as open access provision.

In general terms all wild birds and their nests and eggs are protected by law with heavy penalties (a fine of up to £5000 and/or six months' imprisonment) for disturbance.

Natural vegetation is also protected by legislation both within SSSIs and beyond. Reckless damage to an SSSI carries severe penalties with a £20,000 maximum fine. In addition to general protection many of the rarer plants and animals receive additional protection.

These laws are tough but if you take time to find out about the birds and natural vegetation it is unlikely that there will be conflicts. Following the code of conduct is always a better alternative to court cases or permanent climbing bans.

Code of Conduct

Climbers (and others involved in outdoor recreation) are not generally responsible for the decline in the extent and quality of wildlife habitats in the UK. However the nature of the sport is that it takes you to the most sensitive parts of the landscape, to the refuges unaffected by grazing pressure and to the places best suited to rare plants and nesting birds. Climbers need to be aware that they are going to these special places and must take extra care not to damage or disturb them.

Take care not to damage the crag flora. Route preparation (or "gardening") is a significant threat to rare upland vegetation. If new route preparation will result in the destruction of upland vegetation or bird habitat then it should not go ahead. Gone are the days when it was acceptable to dig routes out of the hillsides, the environmental price is far too high. More detail on this subject can be found in the *Lake District Green Climbing Guide* (BMC, 2006).

Any trees growing above the 600 metre contour are likely to be really important ecologically or a rare species or both – these are not good places for runners, belays, lower-offs or abseils. On lowland crags trees are equally important – they may be rare whitebeams or ancient yews and they were there centuries before climbers.

Adhere to the negotiated restrictions to protect nesting birds. These protect the birds from disturbance and the climber from accidentally breaking the law. If you experience obvious 'alarm-calling birds' then retreat from the area, even if there is no bird ban in place. In some locations (see above) ground-nesting waders are extremely vulnerable to disturbance by dogs in spring or summer. Please do not let your dog threaten successful bird breeding. A short lead will happily resolve the conflict.

Conclusions

Climbers (in both summer and winter) can play an important role in protecting the natural environment. The best places for climbing are often the most important locations of natural vegetation, home to rare plants, trees and ferns and they also provide nesting locations for a range of vulnerable bird species. These places are sensitive and climbers must take extra care to minimise their impact. Climbing and nature conservation can happily co-exist if the code of conduct described above is followed.

Simon Webb (Natural England, www.naturalengland.org.uk) &
Peter Davies (Cumbria Bird Club, www.cumbriabirdclub.org.uk)

Acknowledgements

North Cumbria & The Eden Valley

Firstly, I must acknowledge the work done by Stewart Wilson in producing the previous guidebooks to the Eden Valley, and the times we have been out climbing and developing these crags together, going back now some 40 years!

I would like to thank those who have been involved over the years in the development of the crags and new routes and in particular Alan Greig, Phil Rigby, Tom Foster, Karl Lunt, Paul Carling, Steve Crowe, Len Garnett, Jim Greave, John Kettle and Dom Bush. I would also like to thank John Simpson, Dennis Hodgson and John Workman for their initial forays into finding the crags at Lazonby and King's Meaburn and giving us the inspiration to explore by revealing what was hidden away in the Eden Valley.

I would especially like to acknowledge members of the Eden Valley Mountaineering Club with whom I have climbed in the Eden Valley over the last 35 years – in particular Alan Beatty, Tim Dale, Alan Davis, Alan Stark, Alan Hewison, Gary Baum, Alan Dougherty, Eric Parker, Jonathan Farnworth, Peter Simpson and especially Chris King.

I would also like us all to remember Jeff Lamb, Mike Hetherington, Peter Day and Dave Bowen who put a lot into their climbing, much of it in the Eden Valley, but are now sadly no longer with us.

Lastly I would like record my appreciation of my long-suffering family, Chris, Michael and Catherine, and apologise for dragging them off far too often to obscure parts of the Eden Valley. I promise it will only be exotic foreign holidays from now on.

Photo: Michael Kenyon

Ron Kenyon, May 2011

South Cumbria & South Lakes Limestone

As this is the first time that the FRCC has produced a guidebook covering the limestone crags of the South Lakes, much reliance was placed on the hard work of the previous guidebook producers, and this must be recognised. In particular I want to thank Les Ainsworth and the rest of the BMC Guidebook Committee. Without their work this would have been a much harder task. Karl Lunt has provided valuable information, particularly for Slape Scar and Hebblethwaite Hall Gill, both of which were "discovered" and initially developed by him and his pals, and Roger Wilkinson has done a great job of writing the White Stone section.

Thanks are also due to those friends and climbing partners who have put up with the endless repeat visits to the same crags for the sake of checking routes, helping with the confirmation of grades as well as taking and posing for photos: Ian Cooksey, Neil Cooper, Brian Davison, John Freeman, Chris Gore, Graham Iles, Rob Knight, Mick Lovatt (TPM), Dave Nicholl, Keith Phizacklea, Tim Whiteley, Cherrie Whiteley, Stuart Wood and of course the rest of the "Barrow Lads".

My family have played more than their fair share in the production of this volume: my daughter Flora has helped check approach descriptions and Karen, my wife, has put up with the all-consuming effort that goes into creating a guidebook.

I think it is also appropriate to thank the wardens of the Lake District National Park, in particular Dave Pickup, who have adopted a positive, balanced attitude regarding bird restrictions at Chapel Head Scar.

Photo: Flora Wharton

Nick Wharton, June 2011

In checking and writing up The Furness Peninsula, I would echo Nick's comments above concerning previous guidebook writers. I'm also fortunate to have Al Phizacklea as a climbing partner. We've been guidebook checking for over 20 years and the enthusiasm was still there to sort out the Furness area, even though it doesn't have quite the same cachet as Scafell.

Thanks are also due to my wife Val and family. They have all been incredibly supportive and understanding when I've gone out climbing on yet another beautiful day.

Photo: Val Holden

John Holden, November 2011

Editorial

We are indebted to Stew Wilson for allowing his long out of print and much sought after guide, *North of England Rock Climbs* (1992), to be used as the basis for the Eden Valley section and for passing on details of all the new routes he had received. South Lakes Limestone and the Cartmel and Furness Peninsula sections were written with the blessing of Les Ainsworth and Lancashire Guidebook Committee who kindly agreed to us "taking over" all the crags in South Cumbria (with the exception of

Farleton and Hutton Roof): these had previously been covered in various Lancashire guides over the years.

Phil Rigby has again laboured long into the night to produce all the fantastic photodiagrams and has also collated an excellent collection of action and historical photographs. Al Phizacklea's maps once again get us to the crags with a minimum of dither and Eric Shaw has gone the extra mile to supply crag photos for many diagrams (even including a visit to far off Christianbury Crag!).

Numerous other climbers have contributed photographs; some of these are professionals who would normally charge for their work but have been happy to forgo their usual fee to support a good cause – the continuance of club-published definitive guidebooks: their names are recorded in the text and we are grateful to them all. We would encourage all climbers to consider carrying (and using!) a camera when they climb in the Lakes – good results can be sent to the Photographs Editor who can be contacted via the FRCC website.

We are grateful to Simon Webb and Peter Davies for the chapter on the climber and the environment, a reminder that there are other things that appreciate the crags even more than climbers. The geological section was written by Dave Bodecott, and Ron Kenyon has compiled all the information sections at the rear of the book with the exception of the advice on mountain accidents which was written by Dr John Ellerton, and the crag guide which was the work of Max Biden. Proof reading was again kindly undertaken by Max Biden, Al Davis and Sally Baxendale – some people are puttons for glunishment! Vertebrate Graphics, and in particular Jane Beagley, have again done wonders with the layout and Colorcraft have converted the whole caboodle into a useful guidebook that is small enough to live in the pocket of your rucksack, or indeed your trousers, while also being resistant to the vagaries of the Cumbrian weather.

Stephen Reid, November 2011

Historical

North Cumbria & the Eden Valley

Dubbed in a promotional poster some years ago "Cumbria's Best Kept Secret", the Eden Valley is very much in the shadow of the Lake District and, though many climbers over the years will have passed through it, either en route to the Lakes, or to or from Scotland, few will have realised that it sports an interesting collection of crags useful both to locals as evening venues and as a low-lying quick-drying alternative to the mountain crags when the weather does its worst.

By the 1960s Cowraik Quarry, Headend Quarry and Windmore End had all been climbed on though little was fully recorded in those early days. However in 1969 John Simpson discovered the climbing potential of Lazonby Crag, a stunning crag in a spectacular situation in the Eden Gorge, and paid a visit with John Workman, Alan Beatty and Dennis Hodgson – the results being Merry Monk and Gadzowt. A second visit by John Workman, accompanied by a youthful Ron Kenyon, kindled the interest of the latter who returned with Beatty, Tim Dale, Phil Rigby and others from the Penrith area to start serious development of the crag. Of particular note were Silicosis and Pneumoconiosis by Barry Dixon and Beatty. Dixon's pal Tom Proctor paid a visit in 1974 to make the first free ascent of Cobweb, which was recorded as a "photoclimb" in the magazine *Rocksport*. Just downstream from Lazonby, the outcrops of Armathwaite were discovered in 1973 by Stew Wilson and Dale and more or less simultaneously developed with the ascent of numerous climbs including Glenwillie Groove, Codpiece, Flasherman, The Monkeyhanger and Time and Motion Man. The team involved in developing both crags was based around Penrith and, though it had contact with climbers in Carlisle and the Carlisle MC, it managed to keep both venues secret for some time.

Eventually, at the end of 1973, the cat was let out of the bag and this led to an explosion of interest, especially at Armathwaite, with the

Left: Alan Greig cleaning off a new route in the early days at Armathwaite (right of **Paper Moon**) watched by Pete Whillance. **Photo:** Ron Kenyon

likes of Pete Whillance, Pete Botterill, Jeff Lamb, Dave Armstrong, Mike Hetherington and Alan Greig all getting stuck in – a dedicated team which had trained on the makeshift climbing wall at Trinity School and could from then on regularly be found at Armathwaite, especially in the Sandy Bay and Hetherington's Bay areas. This period saw a change of ethics in new routeing from the previous ground up approach to pre-inspection, cleaning and top-roping prior to the first lead. A tremendous collection of routes followed with The Exorcist, Dome Slab, Free and Easy and Wafer Thin to name but a few. At this time in the early 1970s, this group of climbers started to make its mark, not just in the Eden Valley, but throughout England, Scotland and Wales and also the world – with routes like The Gates of Delirium (E4) on Raven Crag, Incantations (E6) on the Napes, The Naked Ape (E5) at Creag an Dubh Loch, The Risk Business (E5) at Creag a'Bhancair, A Midsummer Night's Dream (E6) on Clogwyn du'r Arddu and many others, which were established due, in no small part, to the intensive climbing regime based around Armathwaite.

In 1973, Simpson, Workman and Hodgson opened up a new crag with an aided ascent of Marik at Jackdaw Scar, near King's Meaburn. The Dale, Rigby, Beatty and Kenyon team then worked away at the crag with numerous routes including a free ascent of Marik, The Gebbeth and Phall. Whillance showed up and claimed Maid Marian Way and Lamb led the nearby Trilogy.

In 1975 the climbing fraternity in Penrith formed the Eden Valley

Above: Barrie Dixon on the first ascent of **Phred** (VS Aid), Lazonby, in 1972. **Photo:** Ron Kenyon

Mountaineering Club which published a guide to Lazonby and Armathwaite, *Interim Guide to Rock Climbs in the Eden Valley*, written by Wilson and Kenyon, and which helped to promote and popularise the crags.

Windmore had been climbed on by Peter Day and friends from Kirkby Stephen in the 1960s and then by Kelvin Neal who produced a guide to the crag which was developed further during the 1970s and right up to the present day. A great little crag with something for everyone – well not quite that good for multi-pitch routes!

During the 1970s further crags along the valley and in the nearby areas of outlying Cumbria were developed, principally by members of Eden Valley MC. These included The Hoff, Murton Scar, Cumrew Crag, Scratchmere Scar, Seat Quarry (originally called Caldbeck Moor Quarry), Spadeadam Crag, Aisgill, Augill Beck and Argill Beck.

In the early 1980s a small group of young climbers from Appleby, spearheaded by Robin Curley and including Chris Thwaites and Noel Stansfield, were developing both their talents and some impressively steep routes, in particular at Murton Scar and Brough Scar. Many of their climbs were protected by threads but the cord decayed over time and the routes became neglected. All the threads were replaced in 2009 and it is hoped that this will encourage interest in these excellent venues – or should they be bolted?! The buttresses are relatively short but the routes have bite.

North of England (Pointer Publications, 1981), written by Wilson and Kenyon, bought the latest Eden Valley area developments to wider notice.

Armathwaite stalwarts Alan Greig, (left) and Dave Armstrong on the finger traverse below **Dome Slab**, Armathwaite, in the early '70s.
Photo: Dave Armstrong Collection

Jeff Lamb on the first ascent of **The Exorcist** (E4), at Armathwaite in 1974. **Photo:** Ron Kenyon

Above left: Karl Lunt on the first ascent of **The Fearful Void** (E3), Lazonby, in 1987. **Photo:** Andy Kay **Above right:** Paul Ross and Pete Greenwood on the first ascent of **Whelpo Way** (HS), Seat Quarry, around 1980. **Photo:** Chris Bonington

In particular, Karl Lunt, a Lancastrian "exiled" in Carlisle in the mid to late 1980s, left his mark on various crags right along the valley from Aisgill to Spadeadam Crag and especially at Lazonby, where he was the undoubted local expert and systematically blitzed the crag, dispensing with aid points, leading previously top-roped problems and creating superb and committing new routes.

Routes continued to be discovered at Armathwaite; of particular note, One Hand Clapping was an audacious solo by Geoff Brown in 1987 and a number of the Armathwaite "Not Leds" attracted the attention of Chris King who set to on his local outcrop resulting in the first leads of Soft Touch, Beyond the Thunder Dome and Mellow.

In the early 1990s Paul Ross, Chris Bonington, Pete Greenwood and friends climbed a great number of routes at Seat Quarry but no details were recorded apart from a photo of Paul Ross leading Whelpo Way with Pete Greenwood coming out of retirement to belay and climb. However, amongst others they also appear to have climbed Creepers Keepers, Rattle Up, Angerton and Warnell Way.

In 1992 Stewart Wilson produced the second edition of *North of England* (Cordee), which expanded its area over the 1981 guide. This was the last guide to the area and has formed the basis for the book you hold in your hand.

Not all has been sweetness and light however. A large rockfall at King's Meaburn (the sandstone base of the Main Wall) highlighted the instability

Left: Tom Phillips on an early ascent of **Simulator** (HVS), Windmore End. **Photo:** Karl Lunt.

of the crag. A number of routes, including Gont and The Windeye and to a lesser extent Windkey, were affected by this – but all were reclimbed (and soloed) by local lad Leo Houlding whose most notable contribution was Leo's Line (though more notable lines elsewhere were to follow!).

Unfortunately, after a protracted legal case concerning access along the path to the Armathwaite Crag and along the west side of the River Eden below Lazonby Crag, access has been withdrawn for Lazonby Crag. It is very unfortunate that such a superb crag in a magical situation should not be available to climb on. There has also been a number of other access issues, most notably at the Hoff, Helbeck Wood Crag, Parkhead Quarry and the left side of Windmore End. Hopefully the landowners concerned will change their minds about access in due course, even if this means climbers having to accept some controls being put in place. On the plus side, all climbers should appreciate the landscape and access to crags which they are able to enjoy.

The number of new routes had diminished with the new millennium. However with a new guide in the making, there was a revival of enthusiasm all along the valley and in particular with a new crag at Coudy Rocks and the introduction of the bolt to the area (bolts had been previously been placed on The Helm at Windmore End by persons unknown but were removed after complaints from both the first ascentionist and the land owner).

The Eden Valley has always been a backwater compared to the Lake District but contains a wide selection of outcrops. For a backwater it has produced quite a variety of routes and some impressive lines. It has been a playground for some of the country's leading climbers and hopefully this guide will maintain interest in this beautiful area.

Ron Kenyon, 2011

South Cumbria & South Lakes Limestone

The history of climbing on the limestone outcrops of the South Lakes gives a good insight into the shifting attitudes and ethics of the times. Much early activity was probably not recorded. If, in the early days, the Lakeland crags were seen as mere training for alpine routes and the Greater Ranges, then the "insignificant" limestone outcrops scattered round the southern edge of the Lakes would have been seen as practice grounds for "real" rock climbing in the Lakes, or beyond, and their routes, as such, would not have been seen as being worthy of recording.

The first concerted effort towards development for the sake of itself came in the early '70s when routes, often employing a point or two of aid, started appearing and previously aided routes had their aid whittled away. Through the '70s and into the '80s harder (and bolder) routes were added and it is worth bearing in mind how poor much of the protection was on the compact, featureless limestone. Protection often consisted of threads (some of which were drilled) and pegs – in other words, very poor quality fixed protection. It was not until the mid 1980s that a few brave individuals, no doubt inspired by similar activity elsewhere in the country, had the foresight to go beyond the accepted norms of the day and start to place more worthwhile and trustworthy fixed protection by the use of drilled bolts. Whilst many saw this as heresy (and some still do) and the end of climbing as it was then known, this bold step allowed the next phase of inspired routes to be pioneered. Subsequently many of the old and overlooked routes of the past have had bolts added, thus encouraging a transformation from overgrown choss to cleaned-up and now highly popular excursions. The eventual recognition by the majority that these limestone outcrops are, in the main, sport climbing venues, was long overdue but greatly appreciated. For those few remaining dissenters, there is still the whole of the Lake District in which to frighten yourself.

Chapel Head Scar

The original development here took place on the Lower Crag which unfortunately saw an access ban several years later on ecological grounds. 1974 saw the first significant development on the Main Crag with Les Ainsworth and Dave Cronshaw picking the obvious natural lines of The Veil, Starshine and Sun God. Word of this amazing crag soon spread and the mighty Ron Fawcett paid a visit to produce Moonchild, followed shortly after by the other leading man of the time, Pete Livesey, who matched Fawcett's route with his own Lunatic. In the following year Ed Cleasby added Cyborg, Half Life and Atomic Bong. Fawcett returned to add the wandering War of the Worlds. The most significant breakthrough came in 1979 when Cleasby found a way up the Great Buttress to give Android (although this did include a point of aid – duly dispatched later that year by Dave Knighton). Around the same time Cronshaw and Knighton produced the excellent Interstellar Overdrive. The 1980s saw a succession of developments; The Route of All Evil by George Smith and Al Phizacklea opened up the full potential of this superb wall. A direct finish, The True Path (since incorporated into Eraser Head), was added soon after by Martin "Basher" Atkinson. In 1985 Gary Gibson paid a flying visit and recorded Up Town, a route that spurred the locals into a frenzy of activity as Gibson was renowned for monopolizing new route activity when he saw an opportunity. Al Phizacklea quickly completed a long-standing project to produce Wargames – probably still the best

route on the crag and originally protected by drilled threads, whereas Paul Cornforth did the decent thing and placed a proper bolt to protect the crux of his Perverse Pépère. Finally the modern age had arrived and this opened the floodgates to new development. Cornforth led the way with Super Dupont and Driller Killer and the following year with La Mangoustine Scatouflange, Super Duper Dupont and Maboulisme Merveilleux – just a hint of continental influence here? At the same time Paul Ingham was creating first Phantom Zone and then Zantom Phone (later straightened out by John Gaskins) and Tony Mitchell produced the powerful Electric Warrior plus Cosmic Dancer and Flight Path – another variation finish on the Route of All Evil Wall. Steve Hubbard climbed Stan Pulsar, an excellent direct line up the middle of War of the Worlds. Throughout the '80s development continued with most of the action from the same teams.

Jim Bird, having finished with Scout Scar, added the fine Cement Head and an independent lower section on the Route of All Evil Wall to link with The True Path finish to create Eraser Head. Andy Hyslop added yet another right-hand finish on this wall giving Mid-Air Collision. Dave Birkett stamped his mark on the crag with the impressive Unrighteous Doctors in 1991 and the following year, showing some rather pessimistic foresight, climbed the alternative access route onto Great Buttress: For When the Tree Falls – ready for when the tree falls!

In 1992 Stuart Wood and Keith Phizacklea (two of Barrow's finest) filled a significant gap underneath the traverse of Atomic Bong with Gilbert Cardigan and Shades of Mediocrity whilst Tony Burnell found it all Tufa King Hard. In the same year John Gaskins emerged from his garage for long enough to add the short but hard Surfing with the Alien, squeezed in next to Phantom Zone.

In 1994 Steve Crowe and Andrew Earl made a tough right-to-left girdle of Great Buttress to produce Le Grand Traverse. Then in 1997 another large gap was filled by Keith Phizacklea and Steve Whittall. Keith producing 62 West Wallaby Street and next to it Stevie, fresh back from operations on the front line, added War Hero.

The occasional gap continues to be filled; as recently as 2006 Al Towse added Witherslack Alice. In 2008 the finishing groove of War of the Worlds was equipped thereby extending the excellent Phantom Zone to the top of the crag in a consistent style. This also paved the way for a link up of this groove with the start of Cement Head, which has come to be known as Combat Plumber. In 2011 John Freeman, one of the local up and coming hot-shots, linked the start of Unrighteous Doctors with the finish to Prime Evil giving a hard direct line, Doctor Evil, at 8a.

Left: Paul Cornforth on the first ascent of **Maboulisme Merveilleux** (F7c+), Chapel Head.
Photo: Al Phizacklea

Humphrey Head

The early work at this delightful seaside venue was led by Mick Goff in the late '60s. Sadly, many of the early developments, particularly those to the left of the descent path succumbed to the unstoppable forces of nature and became overgrown. However many of the early routes on the Main Crag still exist – Virility, Noda, Fusion, Hammerlock, and have subsequently had their aid points dispensed with. Some time in the early '70s Tony Greenbank added the good looking, though now somewhat overgrown, Sunflake. In 1978 Pat McVey and Mark Danson produced the excellent Triggerfinger – still one of the best routes on offer.

Above: Al Phizacklea taking a flyer onto a skyhook runner on the first ascent of **Firing Squad** (F7b+), Humphrey Head. **Photo:** Bob Wightman

It was in 1984 that a new era dawned when Al Phizacklea and Rob Knight turned up armed with a bolt gun to produce The Firing Squad, an act of desecration that excited considerable comment in the climbing press of the day. Two years later, after the furore had died down, Phizacklea returned with an electric generator and drill and added a whole load of top belays, and a long list of new routes was created starting with Shot by Both Sides by John Topping. Paul Cornforth duly arrived, having heard (as was rumoured at the time) the noise of the drill from the bar of the Golden Rule in Ambleside! He proceeded to add the crag's hardest route at the time, Humphrey Hymen. 1989, in particular, saw another surge of activity with Rick Graham, Ken Forsythe, Andy Hyslop, Ted Rogers, Luke Steer and Mark Radtke all doing their bit. The early '90s saw the big figure of John Dunne free the aid route out of Edgar's Arch, and Iain Greenwood filled the major gap in the crag with Humphrey Dumphrey. Towards the end of the '90s, while working on the guidebook, Les Ainsworth and Dave Cronshaw filled more gaps around January to produce the now overgrown Wolfman and the cleaner Adela, at the time eschewing the logical step of placing bolts and preferring to dice with death (or at least serious injury). A couple of bolts have subsequently been placed which greatly improves the climbing experience on this lovely piece of clean rock. Sadly, apart from John Gaskins adding the desperate Head Like a Hole in Edgar's Arch in 2005 (F8b+ and currently the hardest route on South Lakes Limestone), the past decade has seen little activity and as a result much of the crag is becoming overgrown – and it would appear, far more so than ever before – bring back acid rain!

Scout Scar

Far off to the east, away from the idyllic sea-washed pastures of the Furness Peninsula, another group of climbers (actually it was mainly the same ones) was making the most of what they had on their doorstep. For those in the mighty metropolis of Kendal this meant Scout Scar. Once again the early '60s saw members of the local climbing club practising their skills, and no doubt a number of routes, mostly with varying degrees of aid, would have been climbed and dismissed as not worthy of writing up – a few individuals nowadays could learn a thing or two from that ethic! Most notable was the creation of Born Free by a young Frankie Booth, and at some point the pegging of Ivy League.

The mid '70s saw the old aid routes starting to be climbed free as well as new free routes appearing. And, as was occurring on the other crags, the mid '80s saw the bolt gun brought into use. Here the leading architect was Jim Bird; others joining the fun included Dave Seddon, Paul Carling and Glen Suttcliffe. Tony Mitchell put in an appearance with his Vision of Things Gone Wild in 1986. Additional slots were filled in the early '90s by Mark Lardner, Andy Hyslop, Andy Tilney and Stuart Halford.

White Scar

Back on Whitbarrow, the most obvious challenge always had to be the imposing White Scar. Standing over the main road from the civilised world to Barrow, it looks awesome – back in the '50s and '60s it must have reminded climbers of the mighty faces of the Dolomites and provided a tempting practice ground. Once again the early pioneers turned up with their pegs, hammers and etriers, put in their practice, got terrified and returned to the relative safety of working in a 1950s' shipyard, without recording what they had done. At some point in this period the obvious central challenge of The Book of Invasions was ascended. The early '70s saw the ever-route-hungry duo of Ainsworth and Cronshaw claim Stride Pinnacle (way off to the left), then, several years later, Puppy Dog Pie (off to the right) thus neatly avoiding the obvious big bit in the middle! Cronshaw and Knighton got closer to the main challenge in 1978 when they climbed Aqualung on the left flank of Space Buttress. They followed this with a full-frontal assault producing an almost-free ascent of The Book of Invasions and the equally good looking Prometheus Crisis, which shared the same remaining aid-point. The same pair also found a relatively easy way up Space Buttress with TMA, as well as the routes on the left wing. A couple of years later Ed Cleasby cleaned up the aid on The Book of Invasions/Prometheus Crisis.

The next major breakthrough came in 1988 when good looking super-star Mick Lovatt forced a major new line up the wall left of the The Book of Invasions to create Introducing the Hardline. In 1996 Brian Davison teamed up with Nick Green to add the sort of route that is ideally suited to Brian's worrying sense of adventure – Sidewinder is a girdle traverse of the

Above: Mick Lovatt, the perfect man, on the first ascent of **Zona Norte** (F7b), White Scar.
Photo: Steve Wilcock

whole crag. Ten years after his first campaign that man Lovatt was back –
just as good looking and even stronger, to finish what he had started, by
producing the tremendous Zona Norte, Ten Years After and Men at Work
with Tim Whiteley and Steve Wilcocks. Sadly, it was shortly after this that
certain individuals went too far in trying to improve access to the base of

the climbs – much to the displeasure of the landowners and English Nature (now Natural England), resulting in a long-standing climbing ban on this impressive crag. Hopefully this will soon be resolved, if for no other reason but to allow Davison to finish off his girdle by linking it to Millside Scar.

Millside Scar

Just along the escarpment from White Scar, Millside Scar is very much the lesser relation. The crag was first climbed on, apparently after defeat at the hands of White Scar, by that dynamic duo Cronshaw and Ainsworth who ascended Pioneer's Cave – a striking feature and the most obvious line. The first really significant ascent though, and still the best route on the crag, was Cadillac by Ed Cleasby and Al Phizacklea in 1982. Others added routes over the next few years, culminating in the other main attraction of the crag, Countach, a fine, if harder companion to Cadillac. Pathfinder, an earlier aid route, was freed at the same time by Lakeland legend Pete Botterill. The mid-'90s saw a blitz of new routes by local hero Keith Phizacklea (the better looking, but more follically challenged of the two phamous Phizackleas) with Firebird and The Green Route, and with a special appearance by the Italian stallion – Dom Donnini, resulting in Integrali.

Slape Scar

It has been said that David Livingstone had less problem finding Victoria Falls, and Christopher Columbus – well that was just easy! Slape Scar on the other hand is a different proposition. An initial expedition was mounted by members of an earlier civilisation. Max Biden and Frank Booth ventured into the heartland of Whitbarrow in March 1972 and climbed four routes. However they considered the place too remote to be of interest to others so did not report them and it's now so long ago that they cannot remember where they went. It is probable that these initial routes have been subsequently re-climbed and re-claimed. The next intrepid band of explorers, Karl Lunt, John Shepherd, Indiana Jones and Andrew Hinton rediscovered this hidden gem within the Lost World of Whitbarrow. Their first batch of routes was produced during the end of '91 through to mid-'92. Several years later two others eventually found their way to the crag – guess who? – Ainsworth and Cronshaw of course. Bob Larkin and Philip Osborne also had a couple of visits in '99. Brian Davison, who must have found the rock far too solid and stable for his liking, also added a few routes on a number of occasions. Most remarkably, John Gaskins visited in 2000 to produce Axiom, a jaw-dropping, bolt-protected, extended boulder problem over the large central roof, the hardest route on South Lakes limestone at the time.

Nick Wharton, 2011

North Cumbria & the Eden Valley

The area described in this section extends north and east of that covered by the FRCC Eastern Crags guide to the county boundary. It includes a few limestone quarries just north of the Northern Fells, a few isolated crags on the border with Scotland and Northumbria and rather more extensive sandstone and limestone climbing in the Eden Valley.

Few if any of these crags can really be considered major venues but they provide potential for climbing when clag envelops the fells and have saved many a day out for climbers visiting from the North-East, and of course they are important evening crags for climbers based around Carlisle, Penrith, Appleby, Brough and Kirkby Stephen.

Above: Andy Ross admires a fine sunset over the Solway after an evening's climbing at Head End Quarry. **Photo:** Ian Grimshaw

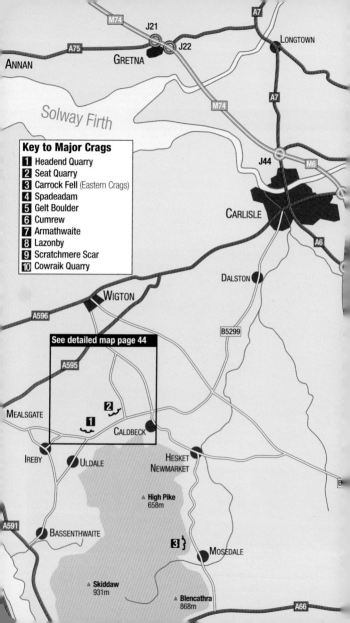

Key to Major Crags

1. Headend Quarry
2. Seat Quarry
3. Carrock Fell (Eastern Crags)
4. Spadeadam
5. Gelt Boulder
6. Cumrew
7. Armathwaite
8. Lazonby
9. Scratchmere Scar
10. Cowraik Quarry

See detailed map page 44

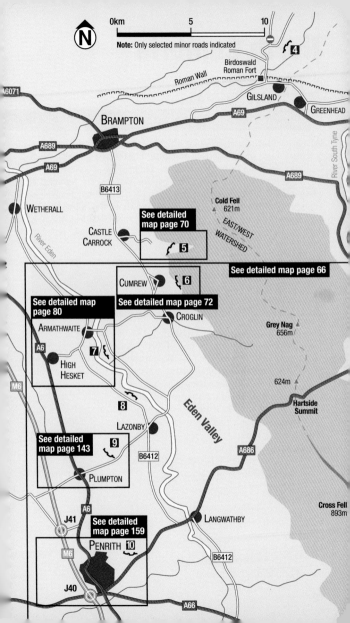

0km 5 10

Note: Only selected minor roads indicated

N

4

Birdoswald
Roman Fort

Roman Wall

GILSLAND

GREENHEAD

A6071

A69

River South Tyne

BRAMPTON

A689

A69

A689

B6413

Cold Fell
△ 621m

WETHERALL

EAST/WEST
WATERSHED

River Eden

CASTLE
CARROCK

**See detailed
map page 70**

5

See detailed map page 66

CUMREW

6

See detailed map page 72

CROGLIN

Grey Nag △
656m

**See detailed map
page 80**

ARMATHWAITE

A6

7

HIGH
HESKET

624m △

M6

Hartside
Summit

8

Eden Valley

LAZONBY

**See detailed
map page 143**

9

A686

B6412

PLUMPTON

Cross Fell
893m

J41

A6

**See detailed
map page 159**

M6

PENRITH **10**

LANGWATHBY

B6412

J40

A66

North Cumbria Limestone

Along the northern and eastern fringes of the Lake District there are a scattering of small limestone outcrops and disused quarries. Most of these are either poor venues or are blighted by access problems. Of the remainder, *Head End Quarry* has for many years provided a pleasant location for group instruction – unfortunately this is reflected (literally in some cases) by the polish on the holds. Nearby *Seat Quarry* is generally steeper and looser than *Head End* but it is hoped that further development there may take some of the pressure away from *Head End*.

Head End Quarry

Grid Reference: **NY 249 408**   Altitude: **295m**
Faces: **South**   Approach: **2 mins**

Also known as **Sandale**. Whilst *Head End Quarry* itself does not have much of an outlook, the top of the climbs command extensive views across the Solway Firth in one direction and a fine aspect of Skiddaw and the Northern Fells in the other. Catching all the available sunshine (and wind), these faces of carboniferous limestone dry very quickly and provide a good year round venue.

The quarry is about 40 metres long and up to 10 metres high. It has good landings and the rock is generally sound, but care should be taken at the top. The climbs tend to be on steep slabs and walls and holds are generally positive, though the popularity of the crag has meant that many holds are polished, particularly on easier routes. Protection is not always good on the harder routes and the use of a bouldering mat is recommended.

Approach:
The quarry is near the summit of Catlands Hill (spot height 304m). From the south follow the B5299 from Caldbeck towards Boltongate. About 2km before Boltongate turn right for Sandale and then beyond Sandale, on an ascending road, the quarry entrance will be seen on the right, just before the road bends sharply to drop down the other side of the hill. Vehicles should be parked sensibly on the roadside.

Head End Quarry Left Side

1	Novices' Route	VD
2	Catlands Wall	MVS *
3	West End Groove	VD *
4	West End Direct	S *
5	Dodgy Neck	VS

6	Diogenes	S
7	Controlled Gurning	VS
8	Headend Chimney	MS
9	Kamikaze	HVS *
10	Nippo Crack	VS *
11	Letter-Box Direct	MVS *
12	Divine Wind	VS *

13	Letter-Box	MVS **
14	Bird's Nest Direct	D *
v1	Variation	D
15	Bilberry	VD
16	Bloodhound	E1 **

17	Crusthound	HVS *

Photo: Ron Kenyon

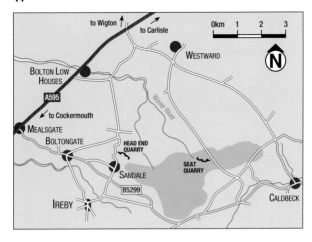

There are belay stakes at the top of the crag but these are of unknown origin and age and should, as always, be treated with caution. If top-roping, please extend your belay system over the edge of the crag to limit erosion.

Descend to the left.

The routes are described from **left** to **right**.

West End Wall

This can be identified by three steps in its left-hand arête and a chockstone corner/crack at its junction with *Suicide Wall*.

1	**Novices' Route**	8m	VD		

Climb a crack, just right of the arête, then directly to the top.

2	**Catlands Wall**	7m	MVS	★	

(4c). Climb the wall.

3	**West End Groove**	8m	VD	★	

A good and popular though polished route.

Climb the shallow cracked groove on good holds until a step right can be made on smaller polished holds to gain the top.

| 4 | **West End Direct** | 8m | S | ★ | |

Climb the steep face on small worn holds.

| 5 | **Dodgy Neck** | 8m | VS | | |

Serious with interesting rock and moves.

(4c). Gain a pedestal ledge then climb the face direct to finish on some unusual calcite holds.

| 6 | **Diogenes** | 8m | S | | |

A good companion climb to, and starting as for, *Dodgy Neck*.

(4b). Climb directly up the vertical cracks to finish up the middle of the fluted top block.

| 7 | **Controlled Gurning** | 8m | VS | | |

(5a). A pleasant and thought-provoking route climbing the wall up to and over a bulge.

| 8 | **Headend Chimney** | 8m | MS | | |

More a crack than a chimney and thoroughly insecure – a truly nightmare experience!

Climb the crack awkwardly but with good jams.

Suicide Wall

A steep wall of excellent rock bounded on its right by an arête of protruding blocks taken by *Bird's Nest Direct*.

| 9 | **Kamikaze** | 8m | HVS | ★ | |

(5a). A fingery exercise with bold moves and suspect holds directly up the wall.

| 10 | **Nippo Crack** | 8m | VS | ★ | |

(4c). Climb the crack and groove on the left to finish.

| 11 | **Letter-Box Direct** | 8m | MVS | ★ | |

(4b). Follow cracks diagonally rightwards.

| 12 | **Divine Wind** | 7m | VS | ★ | |

(4c). Fine climbing up the non-independent line just right of *Letter-Box Direct*.

| 13 | **Letter-Box** | 8m | MVS | ★★ | |

(4b). Start one metre left of the arête and climb onto the slot-like ledge of the *Letter-Box*, then follow good holds to finish up two thin cracks.

| 14 Bird's Nest Direct | 7m | D | ★ | |

Follow the blocky right-hand arête on good holds to below a steep crack. Climb this or move right to an awkward mantelshelf finish.

Summit Face

The most impressive face, consisting of a steep narrow pillar with a bulging finish. Further right the face has a footledge at half-height and is less steep at the top.

| 15 **Bilberry** | 10m | VD | | |

Climb the grassy crack.

| 16 **Bloodhound** | 10m | E1- | ★★ | |

Start below a crack which cuts through the left-hand side of the top bulge of the pillar.

(5b). Climb directly up and gain the crack with interest and ascend it in a fine position.

| 17 **Crusthound** | 10m | HVS+ | ★ | |

The grade is height dependant with the interest reserved for the top.

(5a – 5c). Climb up to the prominent crack in the bulge with difficulty and climb it with even more difficulty.

| 18 **Soap Gut** | 10m | S | | |

Climb the corner just right of the bulging pillar, then the crack above.

| 19 **Snail Wall** | 10m | S | | |

Barely independent.

(4a). Climb the corner and white wall to gain a good ledge. Finish up the finger-wide flake-crack above, taking care with the rock.

| 20 **Fossil Arête** | 10m | HS | | 2004 |

(4a). The cracked grey wall with the steep arête above is climbed on the right of the arête using this for the left-hand. Harder if the bulge at half-height and arête are climbed direct (VS 4c).

| 21 **Devil's Kneecap** | 10m | S | ★ | |

(4a). Climb the steep wall (bold) by means of widely-spaced but good holds to the obvious ledge. Finish up the pleasant wall above.

| 22 **Mollusc** | 10m | MVS | | |

(4c). Climb the chest-high roof and rib direct.

Head End Quarry Right Side

15	Bilberry	VD
16	Bloodhound	E1 **
17	Crusthound	HVS *
18	Soapgut	S
19	Snail Wall	HS
20	Fossil Arête	S *
21	Devil's Kneecap	MVS
22	Mollusc	S
23	Blah	
24	Crystal Cruise	VS *
25	Crystal Wall Direct	MS **
26	Dids	VS *
27	W.A.C.	VS **
28	The Butcher's Dog	HVS *
29	Nut Smasher Crack	VD *
30	Terrace Stairway	M *
31	Terraza	M
32	Piggy Malone	S
33	Bobtail	HS
		D *

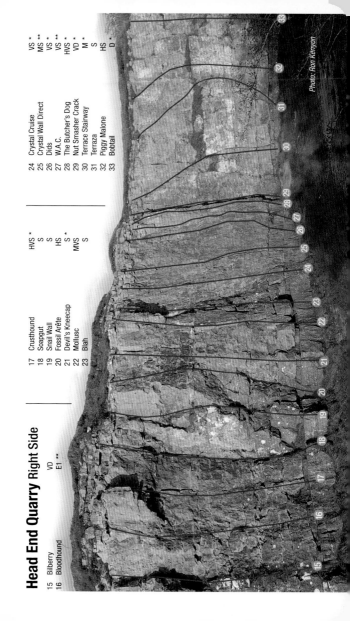

Photo: Ron Kenyon

Above: Ian Grimshaw and Anna Blackburn soak up the evening sunshine on **Mollusc** (MVS), Head End Quarry. **Photo:** Stephen Reid

Crystal Wall

This is the attractive steep slab characterised by excellent rock with, in places, a veneer of calcite which gives the wall some good but fragile holds and its name.

23 **Blah**	8m	S		

(4b). Climb the twin cracks which run up to a bulge until a jam and a long reach lead to an awkward finish.

24 **Crystal Cruise**	8m	VS	★	

(4c). Gain and climb the slab direct.

25 **Crystal Wall Direct**	8m	MS	★ ★	

(4a). Follow the fine thin crack in the centre of the slab on good holds to a long reach for the top break. Pull over the top with care.

26 **Dids**	8m	VS	★	

(5a). Ascend the wall keeping out of the central crack.

27 **W.A.C.**	8m	VS	★★

A sustained climb with a difficult start. Start about one metre left of the bounding arête.

(5a). Climb the overlap on small holds. Delicate climbing follows up a shallow scoop and then, either move right onto the prow, or finish direct, taking care with the rock.

28 **The Butcher's Dog**	8m	HVS	★

(5a). Climb the arête to the top – blinkers required.

Terrace Wall

The final wall of good rock is split by a grassy ledge (the *Terrace*) at half-height.

29 **Nut Smasher Crack**	8m	VD	★

Climb directly up the crack which forms the angle.

30 **Terrace Stairway**	8m	M	★

A good little climb with a fair degree of interest.

Climb a crack to the *Terrace*, then follow the interesting left-slanting staircase to the top.

31 **Terraza**	8m	S	

The ledgy wall is climbed to the *Terrace* and followed by a stiff pull up the tiny groove on the left. The steep wall just right gives a harder finish.

32 **Piggy Malone**	8m	HS	

Climb the steep face between two slanting cracks, without using the cracks, and mantelshelf onto the *Terrace*. Finish up the left-slanting scoop which is awkward to start.

33 **Bobtail**	8m	D	★

A route for rabbits which follows the easiest line up the wall right of *Piggy Malone*.

Heads or Tails		V1	

An amusing low level traverse of the whole crag – can be climbed either way – ad infinitum.

Seat Quarry Main Wall

1	Faulds	S
2	Hang In There	E1
3	Lynedraw	S
4	Dunbeath	MVS
5	Midget Gem	E2
6	Creepers Keepers	MVS
7	Time and Away	VS
8	Aughertree	S
9	Rattle Up	MVS
10	Rattlebeck	HS
11	Suck It and See	Not Led
12	Mighty Midget	E1

Photo: Ron Kenyon

Seat Quarry

Grid Reference: NY 283 402
Faces: East

Altitude: 310m
Approach: 5 mins

This disused limestone quarry (also known as *Caldbeck Moor Quarry*) lies high on the fells, about 4km north-west of Caldbeck, with marvellous views over the northern Lake District fells and towards Scotland. Unfortunately the views are the best thing about it; the rock is friable and loose holds abound – so far, climbs are located only on the more stable sections though that is not saying much. With the shortness of the routes, a bouldering mat is useful in case of simultaneous departure of all your foot and handholds. However, an optimistic view is that increased traffic will result in some more solid rock being unearthed.

In 2009, following a meeting of local Outdoor Centres, arrangements were put in place for the controlled development of the crags, starting with belay systems at the top of the routes – to date though nothing has been done about this and anyone visiting would be advised to come armed with some stakes and a sledge hammer to set up belays. Any belay stakes in place should be carefully checked before use. On no account should belays be taken on the drystone wall at the top of the crag, nor should the wall be crossed.

13	Snittlegarth	HS
14	Layaway Kenny	HVS
15	Angerton	HS
16	Rash Raiser	VS
17	Willy Knott	HVS
18	Clea Crack	HS
19	Paddigill	HVS

20	Whelpo Way	HS
21	Young At Heart	HVS
22	Cowslaw	HS
23	Cleamire	HS
24	Thistlebottom	VS
25	Warnell Way	E1
26	Biggards	HVS

Approach:

The quarry is located near the road running north from just above Faulds (see map on page 44), on the Caldbeck Moor to Westward road. It can be seen to the west, at the high point of the road and at the end of a gated track. The quarry belongs to the local council and access has been arranged through the Lake District National Park – please park sensibly on the verge adjacent to the road.

Main Wall

This is directly opposite to the entrance to the quarry.

Descent is via a grassy ramp towards the left end of the wall but take care in the wet.

The routes are described from **left** to **right**.

| 1 | **Faulds** | | 6m | S | | 1970s |

Start below a wide crack 15 metres right of the descent ramp and climb the wide crack and the loose V-groove above.

| 2 | **Hang in There** | | 7m | E1- | | |

(5a). Serious climbing up the interesting, steep and committing wall.

3	**Lynedraw**	7m	S		1970s

Climb the obvious but pretty awful corner.

4	**Dunbeath**	8m	MVS		1970s

(4c). Climb the thought-provoking square-cut arête.

5	**Midget Gem**	8m	E2		2010

(5c). Two different desperate starts can be used to gain a horizontal crack-line then climb more easily, but with interest, to the top.

6	**Creepers Keepers**	8m	MVS		Early '90s

(4a). Climb the crack on the right of the wall.

7	**Time and Away**	8m	VS		

(4c). Gain the ramp and climb the wall.

8	**Aughertree**	8m	S		1970s

Climb the wall left of the twin V-cracks to reach the left-hand crack at mid-height. Follow this to the top.

9	**Rattle Up**	8m	MVS		Early '90s

(4c). Climb a short crack over an overlap and continue up the centre of the wall to the top.

10	**Rattlebeck**	8m	HS		

Start as for *Rattle Up* and follow the crack-line.

11	**Suck it and See**	8m			Not Led

(5c). Gains and climbs a slanting groove, then moves right and up the wall to the top.

12	**Mighty Midget**	8m	E1-		2007

(5a). Climb the faint groove to gain a crack-line, then climb this and leftwards to the top.

13	**Snittlegarth**	8m	HS		1970s

Climb the crescent-shaped crack.

14	**Layaway Kenny**	8m	HVS		2007

(5a). Layaway up the steep lower wall and finish up the upper wall with continued interest.

Right: Steve Prior and Johnny Wilson battle the **Mighty Midget** (E1), Seat Quarry.
Photo: Stephen Reid

15 Angerton	8m	HS		Early '90s

Climb the steep crack.

16 **Rash Raiser**	9m	VS+		1970s

(4b). Climb the arête.

17 **Willy Knott**	9m	HVS		

(5a). Climb the interesting wall.

18 Clea Crack	9m	HS		

Climb the crooked crack-line.

19 **Paddigill**	9m	HVS		2007

(5a). Climb the wall with continued interest to the top.

20 **Whelpo Way**	9m	HS		1970s

Climb the thin crooked crack up the centre of the buttress.

21 **Young at Heart**	9m	HVS		Early '90s

(5a). Climb the wall (peg for protection).

Above: One way to combat loose rock at Seat Quarry! Stephen Reid takes sensible precautions on **Snittlegarth** (HS). **Photo:** Ron Kenyon

22 **Cowslaw**	9m	HS		

Climb the broken crack-line.

23 **Cleamire**	9m	HS		

Gain and climb the slanting crack-line.

24 **Thistlebottom**	10m	VS		1970s

(4b). Follow a right-slanting crack to its end then move left to finish up a slab.

25 **Warnell Way**	9m	E1-		Early '90s

(5a). Climb the wall left of *Biggards*.

26 **Biggards**	9m	HVS		1970s

(5a). Climb the curving right-hand crack that runs the full height of the wall.

The Lonning		V1		

A lower traverse of the *Main Wall* starting at *Faulds* and finishing at *Biggards*.

Arch Buttress

This is the section of rock with an obvious arch 14 metres right of *Biggards*.

27 **Cumdivock**	9m	VS-		

(4b). Start as for *Arch Psychic* and climb the wall above.

28 **Arch Psychic**	10m	VS-		

(4c). Start just left of the arch and ascend rightwards to finish up the wall above.

Seat Quarry
Arch Buttress

27	Cumdivock	VS
28	Arch Psychic	VS
29	Cunningarth	VS
30	Chalkside	MVS
31	Steady as she Goes	MVS

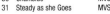

Photo: Ron Kenyon

Seat Quarry Right Wall

32	Seat Arête	S
33	Twin Airwaves	VS

34	The Unseen Message	HVS
35	Pow Crack	VS
36	Seat of Power	HVS
37	Ramp and Away	VD

Photo: Ron Kenyon

29 **Cunningarth**	9m	VS	

(4c). Climb up to and over the right-end of the arch then finish up the wall above.

30 **Chalkside**	9m	MVS	

(4a). Climb the crack-line on the right of the arch.

31 **Steady as She Goes**	9m	MVS	

(4b). Climb the wall.

Right Wall

An area of solid rock towards the right of the back wall of the quarry.

32 **Seat Arête**	9m	S	

Climb the interesting square arête and easier rock to the top.

33 **Twin Airwaves**	9m	VS+	

(4c). Start up the crack-line in the lower wall and gain a broken ledge, then finish up the wall with interest.

34 **The Unseen Message**	9m	HVS		2007

(5a). Intricate climbing up the lower wall is followed by easier but still interesting climbing to the top.

Spadeadam Crag Main Buttress

1	Snakelet	HVS
2	Back and Biting	HVS **
3	Viper	MVS *
4	Serpent	VS *
5	The Mamba	S
6	Snake Charmer	HS *

7	Wiley Sike	MS **
v1	Extended Traverse	VS *
8	Sidewinder	VS *
9	Anaconda	VS *
10	Venom	E3 *
11	Hissing Sid Vicious	E1 *
12	Krait	VS *
13	Black Adder	E1 *
14	Slow Worm	MVS

Photo: Eric Shaw

Just downstream of here is a fine waterfall, Crammel Linn, which is well worth a visit and has a fabulous pool for a dip on a hot summer's day.

Descend to the left.

The climbs are described from **left** to **right**.

Main Buttress

1	**Snakelet**	7m	HVS+		1988

The extreme left side of the buttress has a cracked overlap at the top.
(5a). Climb the bulging wall and finish directly over the overlap.

2	**Back and Biting**	8m	HVS	★★	1988

(5b). Start below a steep scooped slab and make a hard move to gain the slab, with a chockstone on the right. Finish directly or, more easily, step left at the top.

3	**Viper**	8m	MVS	★	1970s

(4c). Climb the corner, surmounting a block at mid-height and climbing the groove above this (crux) to a fine finish.

| 4 | **Serpent** | 8m | VS | ★ | 1970s |

(4c). Climb to and ascend a large flake then continue to the top, finishing as for *Viper*.

| 5 | **The Mamba** | 8m | S | | 1970s |

Start to the left of a broken section of rock and climb a curving corner, passing a tree at mid-height.

| 6 | **Snake Charmer** | 8m | HS | ★ | 1988 |

Climb the easy-looking (but not) rib to finish at a tree.

| 7 | **Wiley Sike** | 8m | MS | ★ ★ | 1970s |

Start below a pedestal ledge which gives access to a face broken by three cracks.

Gain the pedestal and either finish straight up the left-hand crack or step right and finish up the centre crack or, better, move out right to the slanting right-hand crack, and finish via the fine arête.

v1   *Extended Traverse*   12m   VS   ★   2011

Exposed climbing on perfect rock that can be used as a variation finish to *Wiley Sike*, *Sidewinder* or *Anaconda*.

(4c). Follow *Wiley Sike* to the arête via the right-hand crack, step across the offwidth crack of *Anaconda* and foot traverse onto the undercut buttress on the right until almost under a block. Climb up rightwards to the block to exit.

| 8 | **Sidewinder** | 8m | VS | ★ | 2006 |

(5a). Follow the crack of *Anaconda* until a strenuous hand-traverse can be made out left onto the nose. Pull up to a ledge and follow the right-hand side of the arete to an easier finish.

| 9 | **Anaconda** | 8m | VS | ★ | 1970s |

(4c). Climb the obvious wide crack. An extra large Friend helps. Another one giving you a good leg up from below would help even more!

| 10 | **Venom** | 10m | E3 | ★ ★ | 1988 |

(5c). A strenuous but pleasing line. Start below an obvious flake under the roof and climb to the flake, jam round its left-hand side, pull onto the wall above and climb it direct.

| 11 | **Hissing Sid Vicious** | 10m | E1 | ★ | 1988 |

(5b). Climb the parallel cracks to the roof, pull through this onto the wall above and step left to finish at some jutting blocks.

| 12 **Krait** | 9m | VS+ | ★ | 1970s |

(4c). A very exciting climb with great exposure. Gain a sloping ledge and follow a crack-line up to and through a break in the overhangs, stepping out right onto a hanging ledge. Move right again to a fine rib and finish up this. The climb was originally finished direct but this is very overgrown.

| 13 **Black Adder** | 9m | E1 | ★ | 1988 |

(5c). Climb the clean rib with an undercut and difficult start.

| 14 **Slow Worm** | 9m | MVS | | 1970s |

Start below a ledge with a tree stump at the right-hand end of the buttress.
(4c). Climb a short slanting corner on the right to reach the tree, or the steep cracked corner on the left (5a), then follow a groove above to the top.

Right-Hand Buttress

This is the buttress with the conspicuous overhanging arête, 50 metres right of Main Buttress.

Spadeadam Crag
Right-Hand Buttress

15	Indian Rope Trick	VS *
16	Backstreet Crawler	E3 **
17	Cobra	HS

Photo: Eric Shaw

Left: Rick Armitage trying to avoid getting bitten by **Hissing Sid Vicious** (E1), Spadeadam Crag. **Photo:** Stephen Reid

Above: Rick Armitage conjures up some magic on **Indian Rope Trick** (VS), Spadeadam Crag.
Photo: Stephen Reid

15 **Indian Rope Trick**	8m	VS-	★	2006

An indifferent start leads to a spectacularly positioned finish.
(4b). Gain a footledge at the foot of a short groove and climb the groove to a bilberry ledge. Move up right (crucial cam in pocket) and hand-traverse rightwards to the arête, then finish up the steep wall on jugs.

16 **Backstreet Crawler**	8m	E3	★ ★	1988

The overhanging arête – start just left of the arête. A selection of cams is useful.
(5b). Climb the short groove, then hand-traverse right onto the edge. Continue direct on large well-spaced holds.

17 **Cobra**	9m	HS		1970s

Climb the crack and V-groove. Take care with blocks at the top of the groove.

Scrapyard Challenge	8m	VS		2012

(4c). Climb the groove right of *Cobra*, exiting leftwards via a hanging platform.

Christianbury Crags (NY 577 823) is composed of a number of small tors of fell sandstone in an extremely remote location. It is best approached from The Flatt, north of Bewcastle. Many routes have been climbed but none recorded. Recently Dan Varian has shown his considerable talents with a number of boulder problems here.

Top: Christianbury Crags in the middle of nowhere! **Photo:** Eric Shaw   **Above:** Dan Varian stretching out on **Beaching the Whales** (V8), Christianbury Crags. **Photo:** Dan Varian Collection

Black Stantling (NY 594 799) is a small crag of absolutely superb fell sandstone up to 10 metres high. If it was not for its remoteness it would be a popular bouldering venue – a mountain bike helps with the approach.

Comb Crag (NY 591 649) is tiny but of good quality sandstone with about six routes (4c – 5c).

Leap Quarry (NY 594 650) is quite impressive and may be worth a look.

Bishop Hill Quarry (NY 613 588) has attracted attention but has not produced any recorded routes – with some effort it might result in some reasonable climbs.

Lodges Quarry (NY 591 632) was developed in the 1980s by members of Carlisle Mountaineering Club, notably Dave Armstrong and Pete Whillance, despite which it has not gained popularity.

The Eden Valley

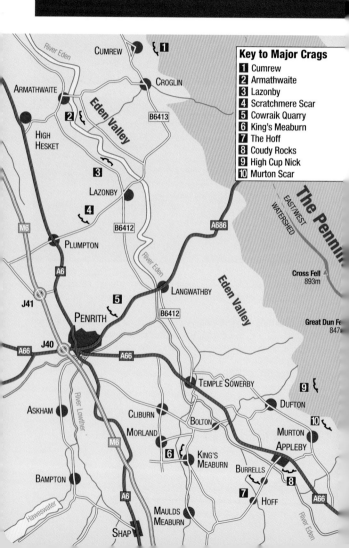

Key to Major Crags

1. Cumrew
2. Armathwaite
3. Lazonby
4. Scratchmere Scar
5. Cowraik Quarry
6. King's Meaburn
7. The Hoff
8. Coudy Rocks
9. High Cup Nick
10. Murton Scar

To the east of the Lake District lies the long valley of the River Eden, which starts at Mallerstang on the Yorkshire border and meanders leisurely to the Solway Firth. More than once described as "Cumbria's best kept secret", it is still often overlooked in the headlong rush to the Lake District or the Scottish Highlands.

Though none of its outcrops compare with the major crags of the Lake District, they give very accessible climbs that are often dry throughout the year and, lying in the lee of the main massif, provide good wet weather alternatives on those rare days when clag shrouds the Lakeland fells. The main crag of interest is *Armathwaite*, set in the delightful Eden Gorge, facing south and with a wide mixture of routes and boulder problems. *Lazonby Crag* is one of the most spectacular sandstone crags in the country but unfortunately access is currently banned. *Scratchmere Scar* is small but has a wide selection of routes on immaculate fell sandstone and magnificent views towards the Lake District. *Jackdaw Scar* at King's Meaburn is in a delightful situation and is well worth a visit early in the year before vegetation has run riot, though the stability of the crag remains questionable. Nearby, the *Hoff* (the crag in the meadow) is set in a low lying sunny location and resembles an outdoor climbing wall though the downside of this was that you might end up sharing it with an outdoor ed group – unfortunately, with a recent change of ownership, access is currently denied. The newly developed crag of *Coudy Rocks*, set in the heart of Appleby, has been transformed with bolts. On the flank of the Pennines, *Cumrew Crag*, gives a friendly and pleasant venue, whereas *Murton Scar* and *Brough Scar* provide much sterner stuff. *Windmore End* is a long edge in a fine location and gives innumerable short routes, many of them quite testing, and all within easy access of the A66 near Brough - worth putting on the radar for a few hours climbing.

The Gelt Boulder

The *Gelt Boulder* or *Geltstone* is situated on the side of the River Gelt in the fabulously remote Northern Pennines. The boulder is about 6 metres high and is composed of fine-grained Quartzite. An added attraction is an excellent natural swimming pool just downstream.

Gelt Boulder

1	Too Many Gelts	V0
2	Over the Gelts and Far Away	V0 *
3	Give Him a Big Gelt	V2 *
4	Gelt Arête	V1 *
5	A Gelt Too Far	V2 *
6	Gelt Up	V0 *
7	Gelt Crack	V0 *
8	A Fistful of Gelts	V0
9	Traverse of the Gelts	V0 *
10	Lower Traverse of the Gelts	V1 *

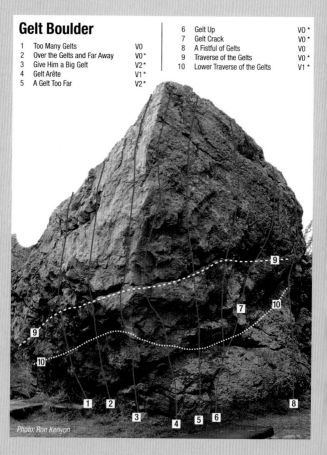

Photo: Ron Kenyon

Above: Michael Kenyon on **Gelt Arete** (V1), The Gelt Boulder. **Photo:** Ron Kenyon

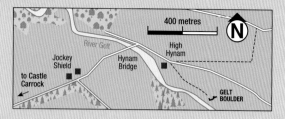

Approach:

Castle Carrock is located on the side of the Pennines about 9km south of Brampton. From the centre of the village a road leads past the two pubs and then uphill to Geltsdale. Park on the obvious right-hand bend at Jockey Shield Cottages. Follow a track downhill, crossing the river at Hynam Bridge and then turn right along the bank. Where the main track turns up the hillside, bear right to the cottage of High Hynam, continue on a small path, and after approximately 300 metres the fine natural swimming pool complete with waterfall is reached. Continue upstream for a further 200 metres to the *Boulder*.

River Face

This has a couple of longer routes on loose rock (both VD).

Upstream Face

1	**Too Many Gelts**		V0-		

Climb up the centre of the wall.

2	**Over the Gelts and Far Away**		V0	★	

Climb up just right of the centre of the wall.

3	**Give Him a Big Gelt**		V2	★	

Climb up just left of the arête – using the arête.

Main Face

4	**Gelt Arête**		V1	★	

Climb up just right of the arête – using the arête.

5	**A Gelt Too Far**		V2	★	

Climb the wall right of the arête – without using the arête.

6	**Gelt Up**		V0 -	★	

Start as for *Gelt Crack* and climb directly up on inviting holds.

7	**Gelt Crack**		VO –	★	

Climb the obvious crack-line.

8	**A Fistful of Gelts**		VO -		

Climb the arête without using the crack of *Gelt Crack*.

9	**Traverse of the Gelts**		VO -	★	

Takes the upper traverse crack-line – slightly harder from right to left.

10	**Lower Traverse of the Gelts**		V1	★	

Easier if you are short.

Start at the left and climb just below the upper traverse to the arête, then move down to the obvious horizontal crack-line.

Middle Gelt Quarry (NY 542563) is about 6 metres high and of reasonable rock with three recorded routes.

Low Gelt Quarries (NY 528586) are situated in the picturesque and popular Gelt Woods. There are various crags in the woods including a huge quarried face which has been attacked with bolts, pegs and top ropes.

Cumrew Crag

Grid Reference: **NY 562 504**   Altitude: **350m**
Faces: **West**   Approach: **15 mins**

Cumrew is a small part-quarried outcrop of generally compact lime-stone in a fine position on the west side of Cumrew Fell, above the village of Newbiggin. Its superb outlook makes up for the shortness of the climbs and the fact that many of them are rather squeezed in between the few natural lines. As a bonus, the rock is quick to dry, even in winter. Aside from the climbing it is also an excellent place for a spot of bouldering or just as a place to take the family for a day out. In situ belay stakes should be treated with caution.

Approach:
The crag is approached from Newbiggin, just south of the village of Cumrew on the B6413 Plumpton to Brampton road. Follow the minor road into the village and towards the fell. After passing the last bungalow on the left a track will be seen going up the fellside alongside a wood. Park here and follow the track until, after passing the third gate, the drystone wall on the left soon curves to the left. Follow a track beside this wall until another gate is reached. Continue on the grassy track through the gate, passing

Cumrew Main Crag

1	Cryptic Crack	HS
2	Starsky	VS *
3	Kojak	VS
4	Hutch	VS *
5	The Lollypop	HS *

Photo: Ron Kenyon

under small outcrops. *Cumrew Crag* is directly behind the ruined limekiln at the end of the track. The crag is on Access Land - however dogs are not permitted.

To the left of the main crag are several bouldering areas, the one nearest being the best. The small natural edge further left has some immense loose blocks - routes have been climbed here but not recorded.

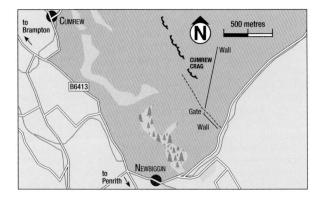

6	The Wand	V1
7	Stoney Butts	S
8	White Magic	V5 **
9	Creepshow	VS *
10	Black Magic	MS
11	Cauldron Wall	MS *
12	Grey Malkin	E1
13	Toil and Trouble	E2 *
14	The Cauldron	VD
15	Grey Yaud	D *
16	Tabby	S **
17	Black Cat	E1 *
18	White Spirits	E2 *
19	The Croglin Vampire	VS **
20	Phantom	E2 *
21	The Renwick Bat	HVS *
22	The Fenny Thing	S

Bat Wall ⟶

Amphitheatre Wall

On the left of the main crag, above a low grass-covered ridge of spoil, is a series of walls with poorly defined ribs.

1	**Cryptic Crack**	7m	HS		1970s

Climb the steep crack.

2	**Starsky**	9m	VS	★	1970s

A bold little climb. Start below and left of a white-streaked overlap.
(4c). Climb a short awkward wall to a good ledge below the overlap. Pull over this rightwards and continue directly to the top.

3	**Kojak**	15m	VS		1985

(4c). Climb *Hutch* to the bulge, then make a delicate rising traverse to reach a white ledge. Continue left to finish at the top of *Cryptic Crack*.

4	**Hutch**	9m	VS	★	1970s

Start below a shallow left-facing little groove.
(4c). Gain and climb the little groove direct with limited protection. Step onto the arête at the top of the groove and finish directly.

| 5 **The Lollypop** | | 9m | HS | ★ | |

Climb the broken walls and finish up the wall above.

| 6 **The Wand** | | | V1 | | 1985 |

Climb the steep rib.

| 7 **Stoney Butts** | | 9m | S | | 1970s |

(4a). Start immediately right of the steep rib and climb the break in the steep wall to gain the ledge by a delicate step left. Finish up the broken groove.

| 8 **White Magic** | | | V5 | ★★ | 1970s |

An excellent fingery problem.

Climb the centre of the steep smooth wall gaining holds above a slight slab. Finish up and left.

| 9 **Creepshow** | | 9m | VS | ★ | 1985 |

(5a). Climb the corner/groove which leads steeply to a good ledge. Finish up the short wall above to the right of a prominent groove.

| 10 **Black Magic** | | 13m | MS | | 1970s |

Climb the wall, past a jammed block, to a good ledge. Move left to finish up the steep prominent groove.

| 11 **Cauldron Wall** | | 9m | MS | ★ | 1970s |

Climb the wall leftwards on good holds to a fine horizontal break. Pull out left onto a ledge then climb the tall detached block and easy upper groove.

| 12 **Grey Malkin** | | 9m | E1 | | 1985 |

(5b). Start as for *Cauldron Wall* and climb directly to the horizontal break, passing between two saplings, then climb the wall above.

| 13 **Toil and Trouble** | | 9m | E2 | ★ | 1985 |

(6a). Climb the steep calcified wall, passing the break (crux), then trend slightly rightwards up the wall above.

| 14 **The Cauldron** | | 9m | VD | | 1970s |

Climb the chimney/crack over chockstones to the top – this is a very prickly affair with a thornbush in the way!

Left: Jonathan Farnworth and Johnny Wilson get to grips with **Hutch** (VS), Cumrew.
Photo: Ron Kenyon

Main Wall

Main Wall is split by several obvious thin crack-lines.

| 15 **Grey Yaud** | 9m | D | ★ | 1970s |

Interesting and pleasant.
> Climb a short slabby wall on sloping holds to a ledge and finish up the curving flake-crack.

| 16 **Tabby** | 9m | S | ★★ | 1970s |

> Climb the thin right-trending crack then move left to follow the small corner.

| 17 **Black Cat** | 9m | E1+ | ★ | 1985 |

> (5b). Climb a thin crack past a pothole to the overlap. Finish with difficulty up the steep wall above, just left of the thin crack.

| 18 **White Spirits** | 9m | E2 - | ★ | 1985 |

> (5b). Climb the wall via the white streak. Gain good footholds above the overlap and finish directly up the wall on small holds.

| 19 **The Croglin Vampire** | 9m | VS + | ★★ | 1970s |

The classic of the crag; steep and fingery with adequate protection.
> (5a). Climb the thin crack on poor holds to a horizontal break. Power over the overlap on excellent holds and enjoy the steep upper wall.

| 20 **Phantom** | 9m | E2 - | ★ | 1985 |

> (5b). Climb the wall to the overlap (runners) then follow the small V-groove and the wall above direct.

| 21 **The Renwick Bat** | 9m | HVS - | ★ | 1970s |

More serious than the *The Croglin Vampire* with a large block of dubious stability in the upper section.
> (4c). Climb the corner to the horizontal break. The overlap above has a crack going left and up. So must you, to finish as for *Phantom*.

| 22 **The Fenny Thing** | 9m | S | | 1970s |

> Climb the rib to a ledge, then move right and finish up the short wall.

Right: Paula Hamilton-Gibson takes on **The Croglin Vampire** (VS), Cumrew Crag.
Photo: Ron Kenyon

Cumrew Bat Wall

1	Bats the Way	V0 ★	4	Bat Out of Hell	V0	
2	Batty	V0	5	Batting for England	V2 ★★	
3	Bat Crack	V0 ★	6	Bats in the Belfry	V1 ★	
			7	Bat on a Tin Roof	V0	

Photo: Ron Kenyon

Bat Wall

A short wall providing some interesting short problems – sit down starts increase the interest.

1	**Bats the Way**	V0 -	★	

Climb the wall on magic holds.

2	**Batty**	V0 -		

The wall and the left-hand of the twin cracks on the left of the wall.

3	**Bat Crack**	V0 -	★	

The right-hand twin crack.

4	**Bat out of Hell**	V0		

Climb the wall without using the crack.

5	**Batting for England**	V2	★ ★	

Start at the white mark and climb the wall with interest.

6	**Bats in the Belfry**	V1	★	

Climb the wall just left of the faint crack.

7	Bat on a Tin Roof		VO -

With a sit start, climb the faint crack.

Climbs have been recorded at **St Constantine's Cells Crag** (NY 467 534) in Wetheral Woods. The rock is soft and the climbs are serious.

Low Holm Gill (NY 510 499) is an impressive bluff of sandstone on a spur of land. Several easier routes have been done on the slab on the right and a steep crack (VS) on an isolated buttress across the river.

Armathwaite Quarry (NY 508 465) enjoyed a brief burst of fame whilst all the new routes were being done; a notice stating "Danger – No Tipping – Keep Out" does not encourage visits.

Armathwaite

Grid Reference: **NY 505 452**   Altitude: **50m**
Faces: **South-West**   Approach: **10 mins**

This outcrop of excellent quality sandstone, properly called **Coombs Crag**, is situated on the east bank of the River Eden upstream of the bridge at Armathwaite and is in a beautiful woodland location with climbing from bouldering to two pitch routes at a good range of grades. It provides a good wet weather alternative to the Lakes, though is best in the winter and spring when there is limited foliage on the trees.

The crag is composed of Penrith sandstone and, because of its windborne origin, cross-bedding is evident everywhere. Differential weathering of these beds and the ubiquitous "Armathwaite Pockets" are responsible for the best of the harder routes. The character of the crag changes as one moves from section to section. Protection on the majority of hard routes is often absent or illusory and many of the first ascents, especially of the hardest climbs, involved pre-inspection. This should be borne in mind by anyone considering an 'on sight' lead. Also included in this section are a few "not led" problems which have nevertheless been named and graded. The FRCC would not normally record such unled "routes" but, due the unprotectable nature of some of the rock, there has been a strong tradition of doing so at Armathwaite. There has equally been a strong tradition of whittling down their numbers and it is to be hoped that by recording them this exemplary trend will continue.

The relative softness of the rock has meant that erosion is a problem but this can be limited with care. When top roping, careful rigging and a long sling should be used. Wire brushing of routes is a definite no-no and please avoid abseiling down the line of delicate routes. Only soft shoes (no vibrams, tricounis or crampons) should be used for climbing and groups under instruction should consider alternative venues.

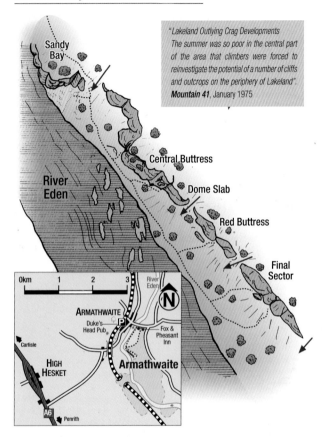

"Lakeland Outlying Crag Developments
The summer was so poor in the central part
of the area that climbers were forced to
reinvestigate the potential of a number of cliffs
and outcrops on the periphery of Lakeland".
Mountain 41, January 1975

Sandy Bay

Central Buttress

River Eden

Dome Slab

Red Buttress

Final Sector

0km 1 2 3

River Eden

N

ARMATHWAITE

Duke's Head Pub

Fox & Pheasant Inn

Carlisle

HIGH HESKET

Armathwaite

A6

Penrith

Approach:

From Armathwaite (which is 5km east of the A6 between Carlisle and Penrith), cross to the east side of the bridge over the River Eden and park near the Fox and Pheasant Inn (but not in their car park!). A squeeze stile in the parapet of the downstream side of the bridge, and a short flight of steps, leads to a path under the bridge and upstream along the bank of the river. After 800 metres the path forks above an impressive natural weir where the Eden crosses the Armathwaite Dyke - a spectacular quartz–dolerite intrusion. In order to reach the *Faces Section*, take the right fork to the river and continue upstream to the crag. To reach the *Main Cliff,* continue along the left fork for 200 metres, over the top of the *Faces Section*, to a steep descent via rocky steps to river level. As one faces the river, *Sandy Bay* is to the right whilst the *Main Cliff* is upstream to the left.

An alternative approach is via a footpath from the front of the Fox and Pheasant Inn through woods to a stile over a fence. Cross the stile, turn right and descend to the *Main Cliff* path, just past the fork. The track going straight ahead from the stile passes along the top of the crags and can provide a useful approach or return from the upstream areas of the crag.

The woods are owned by Forest Enterprise, though sporting rights have been retained by the previous owner. It is essential that climbers observe the usual courtesies with regard to other land-users, particularly anglers and game-shooters. Shooting takes place about three or four times in the season in Coombs Wood, usually on a Friday or Saturday - it is safer to stay near the crag on these days!

Faces Section

The main features of this section are two bays which can be reached, river level permitting, by traversing from the sides or by abseil. The left-hand downstream bay is *Botany Bay* whilst the right-hand bay, *Faces Bay*, is remarkable for the strange and rare carvings on its walls of faces and a salmon with, high up, a beautifully executed inscription, a quotation from Isaac Walton's "Compleat Angler": "O the fisher's gentle life etc...". Nearby, at the start of *A Big Hand*, is an inscription which may be of much greater antiquity, possibly Roman in origin. The carvings and the later inscriptions are almost certainly the work of William Mounsey, scholar, traveller and local gentleman of the 18th century.

Above: Carved faces at Armathwaite. **Photo:** Josephine Keen

Armathwaite Faces Buttress

1	FBSJ	VD
2	Blank's Expression	VS
3	Boomerang	VS
4	Aborigine	HVS
5	Cook's Left Hand	VS *
v1	Cook's Apron	VS *
6	Cook's Crack	VS *
7	Cook's Tour	NL
8	Blockbuster	HS
9	A Big Hand	S
10	Kingfisher	VD **
11	Kaleidoscope Eyes	E2 *

Not all routes shown.

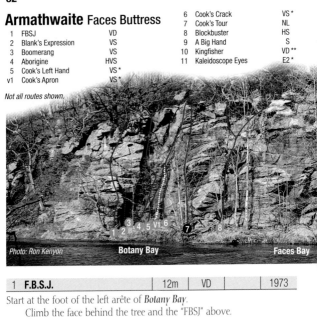

Photo: Ron Kenyon   **Botany Bay**   **Faces Bay**

1	**F.B.S.J.**	12m	VD		1973

Start at the foot of the left arête of *Botany Bay*.
Climb the face behind the tree and the "FBSJ" above.

2	**Blank's Expression**	12m	VS		1985

(5a). Start at some roots and climb the difficult left-curving groove to join and climb *Boomerang*.

3	**Boomerang**	12m	VS		1975

(4b). Climb the shallow right-slanting groove and then hand-traverse left and finish up the arête.

4	**Aborigine**	12m	HVS		1975

Start at a slightly overhanging scoop, a few metres below a small cave.
(4c). Climb to the cave, then left into a chimney, which is followed until moves right lead into a groove and the top.

5	**Cook's Left Hand**	12m	VS	★	1975

(4b). Climb the right-slanting crack to a hard move into a deep groove and follow this to the top.

Sandy Bay

v1   *Cook's Apron*   12m   VS   ★   1986

(4c). Climb the centre of the face between the cracks and finish up *Cook's Left Hand*.

| 6 | **Cook's Crack** | 12m | VS | ★ | 1975 |

(4b). Climb the steep crack, then move left into the groove of *Cook's Left Hand* and finish as for that climb.

| 7 | **Cook's Tour** | | | | Not Led |

(5b) A top-rope problem up the centre of the impressive wall to the right of *Cook's Crack*.

| 8 | **Blockbuster** | 12m | HS | | 1974 |

Start below a corner just left of the carved salmon.

(4a). Climb the steep corner past a large dubious block then move right into another groove. From a ledge below a roof, either move right and climb to the top on unstable rock or, safer, go to the left of the roof and climb to the top on better rock. Not an outstanding route!

A route called **The Scroll** (1975) has been climbed up the face to the left of the fine inscription but as it utilises the inscribed area climbers should avoid it.

Armathwaite Sandy Bay

8	Blockbuster	HS
9	A Big Hand	S
10	King Fisher	VD **
11	Kaleidoscope Eyes	E2 *
12	Grey Duster	E3 **
13	The Arête	E3 **
14	Time and Motion Man	E1 **
15	The Orbit	E4 *
16	Blue Lugs	E5 *

17	The Exorcist	E4 ***
18	Blast Off	E4 *
19	Glenwillie Grooves Direct	MVS *
20	Glenwillie Grooves	HS **
21	Harry's Arête	E1
22	Harry's Groove	HS

Faces Bay

Photo: Ron Kenyon

9	**A Big Hand**		12m	S-		1973

A very pleasant but dirty slab with a lack of protection, starting at the back corner of *Faces Bay*.

> Layback up the corner passing a small 'neb' to a ledge. Climb up until an obvious short traverse rightwards leads one to the trailing branches of a large oak and the top.

Sandy Bay

This popular area, which is the upstream end of the *Faces Section*, consists of an overhanging wall of rock to the left of the prominent

slanting corner of *Glenwillie Grooves*. To the right of this corner is a wall bounded on its right by some pleasant slabs and right of the slabs the stone steps of the approach. The area is notable for its many boulder problems.

10 **Kingfisher**	16m	VD	★★	1973

Steep and satisfying, with big holds and deep water soloing potential.

From the *Sandy Bay* traverse left just above the river and climb up to the left of the tree which guards access to the open groove. An easy corner is followed to either an awkward move over an overlap and up to the top, or alternatively move left and up an awkward slab to finish.

The following three routes are extended boulder problems that gain the ledge near the top of *Time and Motion Man*. Either finish up *Time and Motion Man* or jump into the river!

11 **Kaleidoscope Eyes**	15m	E2	★	1986

(5b). Start from the top of the sawn stump at the left-hand end of *Sandy Bay*. Move up and leftwards to a step below the steep arête and climb this direct to finish on the ledge.

12 **Grey Duster**	15m	E3	★ ★	1975

An entertaining climb with a steep start 2 metres right of the sawn stump.

(6a). Climb the centre of the bulging wall on finger-caressing edges and layaways into a very shallow groove. A good hold on the left enables the final crack to be first viewed and then climbed. Finish up the groove to the ledge.

13 **The Arête**	15m	E3+	★ ★	

A slap happy problem which should guarantee hours of fun! Start below the overhung rib.

(6b). Levitate up the slopers to a conspicuous little blackened pocket at 3 metres. Continue on better holds to finish directly up the upper continuation of the arête to the ledge.

Above: Ben Bravington-Sim going for the undercuts on **Time and Motion Man** (E1+), Armathwaite. **Photo:** Ron Kenyon

Armathwaite Sandy Bay

11	Kaleidoscope Eyes	E2 *
12	Grey Duster	E3 **
13	The Arête	E3 **
14	Time and Motion Man	E1 **
15	The Orbit	E4 *
16	Blue Lugs	E5 *
17	The Exorcist	E4 ***
18	Blast Off	E4 *
19	Glenwillie Grooves Direct	MVS *

Photo: Ron Kenyon

| 14 **Time and Motion Man** | 16m | E1+ | ★ ★ | 1973 |

Once graded VS, but the start of this route has become much harder with the erosion of the sand level at its base. Start in the damp alcove just right of the undercut rib.

(6a). Either dyno to a good hold or move up and leftwards with great difficulty and some contortions onto a very narrow gangway under some small square-cut overhangs. Better holds lead to jugs below a little bulge guarding a fine groove. Enter the groove with some relief and then exit on its left wall to gain a good ledge. Move left and climb a slight groove to an awkward finish. It is also possible to finish straight up the slim corner just to the right.

| 15 **The Orbit** | 25m | E4 | ★ | 1977 |

A committing and serious route which girdles the wall from bottom left to top right. Start as for *Time and Motion Man*.

(5c/6a). Climb into the prominent groove at 5 metres (runners can be arranged on the ledge of *Time and Motion Man* above left). Move out across the right wall of the groove onto ever-steepening rock until one can make an ascending traverse to the good ledge which crosses the face at two-thirds height (junction with *The Exorcist*). From this ledge, traverse right, moving down slightly (protection from a sling over a flat-topped spike above and to the right), until a hand-traverse leads down into the fine corner of *Glenwillie Grooves*. Finish up this.

| 16 **Blue Lugs** | 18m | E5 | ★ | 1975 |

Start below the painted initials WT.

(5c). Climb the bulge strenuously on good holds to reach and follow the obvious hairline fault. At the top overhangs, move out left with difficulty to a strenuous exit. Poorly protected.

| 17 **The Exorcist** | 18m | E4 | ★ ★ ★ | 1974 |

The route that puts the "arm" in Armathwaite! An excellent line, steep and compelling on good clean rock. Start at the base of *Glenwillie Grooves Direct*.

(6a). A hard pull onto a ledge leads up to a peg at 5 metres. Move out with trepidation to a pocket on the right. A sequence of strenuous and technical moves leads back left then straight up. Rising doubts as to the peg's solidity urge one upwards to a good ledge. From the sanctuary of the ledge a bulge is climbed into the top groove, which is best exited on the left.

Right: Michael Kenyon bouldering around the start to **The Exorcist** (E4) in Sandy Bay, Armathwaite. **Photo:** Ron Kenyon

| 18 **Blast Off** | 20m | E4 | ★ | 1977 |

Steep situations, indifferent protection and suspicious rock make this climb a very serious undertaking. Start immediately right of *The Exorcist*.

(5c). Ascend the pleasant corner for about 3 metres until the impending crack on its left wall can be climbed. From the top of the crack traverse left into a shallow niche. The bulging rock above leads to a ledge common with *The Exorcist*. Move up and right to a roof conspicuous by an eroded hole on its underside. Climb out steeply using this hole and continue steeply to better holds. Finish via a jutting prow on the left.

| 19 **Glenwillie Grooves Direct** | 16m | MVS | ★ | 1973 |

(4b). Follow the corner/groove direct starting just left of *Glenwillie Grooves*.

| 20 **Glenwillie Grooves** | 18m | HS | ★★ | 1973 |

The crux of the route is at the top which is short and sharp but very safe. Start from a tar-spattered ledge 3 metres right of the corner.

Climb the wall just right of a thin crack until a good ledge is gained on the left. The slab on the right leads delicately to a foothold next to a sheaf of saplings. Climb the wall to the left to gain another ledge below the final corner. This is climbed with an interesting layback, then follow the ledge above with care to the tree belay.

Above: Tom Foster on the as yet unled **Full Frontal** (6a). **Photo:** Phil Rigby
Left: A young Leo Houlding cutting his teeth on **The Exorcist** (E4), in 1994. **Photo:** Phil Rigby

Sandy Bay Bouldering

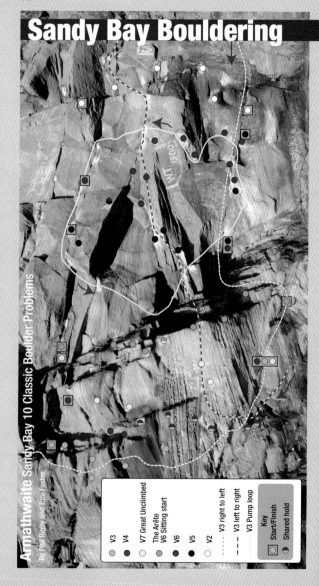

Armathwaite Sandy Bay 10 Classic Boulder Problems

By Phil Rigby and Tom Foster

- ● V3
- ● V4
- ○ V7 Great Unclimbed
- ● The Arête
- ● V6 Sitting start
- ● V6
- ● V5
- ○ V2

- ······· V3 right to left
- – – – V3 left to right
- ——— V3 Pump loop

Key
- ▢ Start/Finish
- ● Shared hold

Top: Sam Duff on **The Arête** (V6 sit start), Sandy Bay, Armathwaite. **Photo:** Ron Kenyon **Above left:** Mark Hetherington bouldering in the Sandy Bay, Armathwaite. **Photo:** Mark Hetherington Collection **Above right:** Tom Foster on the **Great Unclimbed** (V7), Sandy Bay, Armathwaite. **Photo:** Phil Rigby

Armathwaite Harry's Groove Area

21	Harry's Arête	E1		23	Smiling Faces	VS *
22	Harry's Groove	HS		24	The Thirty-Nine Steps	VD *

Photo: Ron Kenyon

To the right of *Glenwillie Grooves* the rock is less attractive.

21 **Harry's Arête**	16m	E1		1978

(5b). Climb the narrow groove just right of *Glenwillie Grooves* and, from a large foothold, swing awkwardly left onto the arête, where a move around it leads onto an easier-angled slab which is followed to finish as for *Harry's Groove*.

22 **Harry's Groove**	16m	HS		1975

Start below the main right-sloping groove.

Climb the groove to a loose break in a bulge. Move over this into a heathery recess, then up left along a ledge and layback the stepped corner.

23 **Smiling Faces**	16m	VS	★	1986

(4b). Climb the blunt arête on the right of the wall on small but good holds until a hard move gains a slab. Follow this to a ledge then finish as for *The Thirty-Nine Steps*, following the short slab rightwards until steep moves lead up to finish at a solid tree.

Armathwaite Stinkhorn Buttress

25	Ducking Drop	E1 *
26	Herbie	HVS
27	Meat is Murder	E2 **
28	Astral Wall	NL
29	Stinkhorn	S

Photo: Ron Kenyon

| 24 **The Thirty-Nine Steps** | 13m | VD | ★ | 1980 |

Start below a steep slab.

> Climb the slab using small ledges to a triangular ledge. Gain a higher bigger ledge, then ascend the short slab rightwards until steep moves up the wall above lead to a satisfying pull out at a solid tree.

The descent steps now divide the crag. To the right of these lies the *Main Cliff* which is divided into several buttresses.

Stinkhorn Buttress

This is just to the right of the descent steps. A short scramble up an easy rake leads to a ledge below the obvious wide crack of *Stinkhorn* at the right-hand end of this steep face.

| 25 **Ducking Drop** | 10m | E1 | ★ | 1998 |

Start on the front of the buttress 3 metres left of *Herbie*.

> (5a). Trend up rightwards to a good crack one and a half metres left of the arête, then go over the bulge above to the top.

| 26 **Herbie** | 10m | HVS | | 1973 |

(4c). Climb the bulge just left of the crack of *Stinkhorn* until a comforting flake can be gained. Move leftwards until it is possible to ascend slightly leftwards. Move back right and finish at trees.

| 27 **Meat Is Murder** | 10m | E2 | ★ ★ | 1998 |

An impressively steep climb though it avoids the real issue of the prominent arête.

(5b). Climb the steep crack of *Stinkhorn* until holds on the left wall can be used to gain the arête at a sharp flake. Climb the rippled bulge above the flake and move up and left around the corner and gain a ledge.

| 28 **Astral Wall** | | | | Not Led |

(5c). Follow the crack as for *Stinkhorn*, then embark onto the steep wall and climb it just right of the arête.

| 29 **Stinkhorn** | 10m | S | | 1973 |

Climb the obvious bulging crack to a good ledge. The continuation is disappointing.

Hetherington's Bay

This popular little hollow lies at the foot of the crag just above the path and comprises the left side of the large and complex *Central Buttress*. The bay is named after the late Mike Hetherington who spent many hours here – even at night with a Tilly lamp for illumination. High above the vertical right–hand wall is the overhanging *Cally Crack* which finishes on a spacious ledge known as *Heugh Chare*.

The bay is a popular bouldering area. There are particularly good traverses across its lower walls, whilst interesting problems find their way through the slim grooves to the left of the start of *Joe Soap's Corner*.

| 30 **Petit Mal** | 10m | VD | ★ | 1980 |

Start at the left-hand end of the *Bay*, about one metre left of the flat rock ledge bearing shot holes.

Climb the groove by the line of least resistance to gain and climb a flake to the belay ledge of *Joe Soap's Corner*.

| 31 **Nosescratcher** | 16m | HS | | 1973 |

Lack of protection makes this a somewhat serious climb. Start at a low ledge with a shot hole.

Step up and right onto the slab then climb rightwards across the slab to a blunt arête and follow this on poor rock to a ledge. Belay up to the left as for *Joe Soap's Corner*.

Armathwaite Hetherington's Bay

Heugh Chare

Long Ledge

Hand traverse with overhanging loop

Photo: Phil Rigby

32 **Indian's Revenge**				★	Not Led

A fine steep top rope problem starting below the V-groove 5 metres left of *Joe Soap's Corner*.

(6b) Gain the groove directly and follow it to the overhanging upper wall. Climb this, initially with good but widely spaced holds, then with more difficulty, to gain the less steep upper wall. Finish up a short groove.

33 **Joe Soap's Corner**		32m	VS	★	1973

A good line but there is some poor rock. Start in the main corner of the *Bay*.

1   16m (4b). Climb straight up the corner then continue with care up the left-slanting line to reach a belay ledge.

2   16m (4a). Ascend the corner above and move leftwards up a flaky wall. Continue up the steep wall above, just left of a block, and finish up easy rocks. Alternatively it is possible to scramble left to below *Stinkhorn Buttress*.

34 **Cally Crack**		12m	E2	★ ★	1973

A steep and intimidating climb – originally graded HVS!
(5b). Climb *Joe Soap's Corner* until moves can be made out right past a dubious block to the foot of the crack – climb it!

35 **Jeff's Wall**			V4	★	1975

A highball boulder problem, which climbs the centre of the steep wall right of *Joe Soap's Corner*.

Central Buttress

This is the complex buttress just above the riverside path. At 13 metres there is the grassy *Long Ledge* which has a big oak on its right end. Above the left-hand end of *Long Ledge* and 5 metres higher is another ledge, *Heugh Chare*. On the right of the buttress are three well-defined grooves providing some excellent climbs, including the classic *Flasherman*.

Descents: There is a narrow path along the top of the buttress – this can be slippery when wet. This path can be followed leftwards to join the approach path above the descent steps leading down to the crag. Alternatively follow the path rightwards to descend the steep earthy gully to the right of *Dome Slab*.

36 **Princess Anne's New Ring**		26m	VS -	★	1973

Start at the foot of the little slab in the arête on the right of *Hetherington's Bay*.

1   13m (4a). Climb the slab for 3 metres then move diagonally leftwards on shelving rock to a point below the oak tree on the *Heugh Chare* ledge above. From here, bear right then back left and surmount the final wall to the oak.

2   13m (4b). Climb the corner at the back of the ledge gymnastically to a deep groove. Swing out left to a good ledge and finish up the corner above.

v1   *Hooked Up*   E3   10m   2010
Start at the popular large bouldering roof at the right side of *Hetherington's Bay*.
(5c). Pull up and over the roof with great care and follow the obvious ledge up leftwards. Gear can be placed behind a suspect block before attacking a second roof, right of *Cally Crack*.

Armathwaite Heugh Chare Area

34	Cally Crack	E2 **
v1	Hooked Up	E3
36	Princess Anne's New Ring	VS *
37	The Monkeyhanger	HVS **

38	The Schnuck	VS *
41	Savage Simian	HVS **
42	Janet of the Apes	VS *

Heugh Chare

Photo: Ron Kenyon

37 **The Monkeyhanger**	35m	HVS	★ ★	1973

An excellent climb with a serious top pitch in a fine position. Start as for *Princess Anne's New Ring*.

1   16m (4a). Climb the slab for 3 metres then move right onto a wall of good rock, past a small beech, to the end of the long grassy ledge. Climb the steep wide crack on fantastic holds to a tree belay on *Heugh Chare*.

2   19m (4c). Either climb the short overhanging wall at the back of the ledge to gain a shelf, then traverse right for about 4 metres to the right arête, or traverse right from the ledge to near the arête, then climb up in an exposed position to the ledge above. Continue up to a second ledge, more exposure. Move slightly right, over an overlap, to gain and finish up a delicate and unprotected slab - not a good place to be in damp conditions!

38 **The Schnuck**	14m	VS	★	1973

A good steep alternative last pitch to either *Princess Anne's New Ring* or *The Monkeyhanger*. Start on *Heugh Chare*.

2   (4c). Climb the steep wall to gain the flat shelf as for *The Monkeyhanger*. Continue up on flat holds to gain and climb a groove leading to a small ledge on the left and a tree belay above.

Oak Tree at top of Pitch 1 of Bullgine Run.

Photo: Ron Keny

39 **The Bullgine Run**	30m	VD	★★	1973

The lower reaches can be mossy but the top pitch, following the big rightward-slanting slab in the upper part of the buttress, is superb. Start at the toe of the buttress at a break which gives access to a right-slanting ledge leading to below the big oak on *Long Ledge*. This is just right of the start of *Princess Anne's New Ring*.

1   10m. Gain the ledge and follow this rightwards to just below the oak and either ascend up a series of small flakes, or move rightwards and then sidle back left and up to the tree.

2   20m. The obvious juggy slab, starting to the left of and running up behind the tree, is now followed easily up and rightwards. Climb a short crack to gain a detached horizontal block - the *Plank*. Walk the *Plank* and continue moving rightwards, until an easy gully leads to the top.

40 **Wildcat on the Swallowtail Line**	23m	HS	★★	1973

Start at an undercut corner just right of *The Bullgine Run*.

1   7m. Climb up using flat holds to gain the ramp of *The Bullgine Run* then continue up an obvious crack to gain *Long Ledge* and move right to belay on the tree.

2   16m. Follow the groove behind the belay tree rightwards to a ledge. Join *The Bullgine Run* and climb the short crack to gain the *Plank*. Above is a crack through the roof; overcome this and continue up the crack to the top.

The following five routes start at the top of pitch 1 of *The Bullgine Run*.

41 **Savage Simian**	27m	HVS	★★	2004

A mini-adventure taking a line running left to right across the roof above *The Bullgine Run*. Protection is reasonable where it matters.

Above: Eric Parker following **Savage Simian** (HVS), Armathwaite. **Photo:** Ron Kenyon

(5a). Climb the arête directly behind the beech, on the left of the juggy slab of *The Bullgine Run*, on good but suspect holds and no protection, to gain a ledge and a broken block on the right. Move leftwards off the block to gain good holds over the overhanging arête (as for *Janet of the Apes*) and pull over onto a ledge. Move out rightwards on small footholds across the top of the roof above *The Bullgine Run*, pull into the bird-limed V-groove and gain a spike. Continue for 3 metres to a recess then finish rightwards up a crack-line.

42 **Janet of the Apes**	20m	VS+	★	2004

A bold and exciting eliminate line between *The Monkeyhanger* and *The Bullgine Run*.

(4c). Climb the juggy slab of *The Bullgine Run* to below a triangular recess. Move out left by exciting moves on good holds to a broken block. Move further left slightly, then off the block to gain good holds over the overhanging arete. Pull over with some difficulty onto a ledge. Move slightly right, over an overlap, to gain and finish up a delicate and unprotected slab as for *The Monkeyhanger*.

43 **Victory V**	18m	E2	★	1975

Climbing in an impressive position - a direct version of *Janet of the Apes*.

(5b). Follow *Janet of the Apes* to gain the ledge with the broken block. Continue right past the roof and climb the V-groove above to finish just to the right of *Janet of the Apes*.

Armathwaite Central Buttress Area

46	Ituna	S *
47	Douber	HS
48	Flasherman	VS ***
49	Flasherman Direct	HVS *
50	Erection	E1 ***
51	Viennese Oyster	E3 **
52	Soft Touch	E4 **
53	Nurts Way	HVS

See inset

Photos: Ron Kenyon and Phil Rigby

---

44 The Overhanging Crack Finish | 16m | E2 |

(5b). The obvious overhanging crack above the traverse on *The Bullgine Run*.

---

45 Zephyr | 22m | VD | ★ | 1973

Traverse right along *Long Ledge*. Climb a corner-crack then gain a smooth slab on the right. Climb this diagonally rightwards until it abuts against a break in the steep wall above. Climb the wall delicately to a ledge on the right. Broken rock above leads to a final steep wall which provides a pleasant but avoidable finish.

46 **Ituna**		30m	S	★	1973

The ancient name for the River Eden. A much better climb than appearances would suggest. It follows a fine gangway slab to the left of and parallel with *Flasherman*. Start 7 metres right of *The Bullgine Run* at an embedded block below a shallow corner with a smooth right wall.

Bridge up the corner and traverse right to a ledge on the arête. Continue up the corner to an awkward finish on a good ledge. Move right and follow the fine slabby gangway to finish at the same point as *Flasherman*.

47 **Douber**		25m	HS		1973

Start at the foot of the blunt rib, 4 metres right of the corner of *Ituna*, and climb this to an awkward finish at the junction with *Ituna*. Follow the left-slanting cracked groove up the buttress.

On the right side of the buttress, and at a higher level, is a very open and interesting face which is remarkable for its fine rock architecture, a fine towering arête on the right and a gigantic block overhang to the left of the arête, whose appearance has everything to do with the choice of route names in this area.

48 **Flasherman**		30m	VS -	★ ★ ★	1973

Plenty of exposure on the runout crux ensures an adventurous experience for middle-grade climbers. A classic! Start in a cave under an overhang below the big open-book corner.

(4b). Climb diagonally right up a slab and pull over the bulge on big holds to a block. Move up and enter the corner and follow it to the large flake at its top. Step right and climb boldly up the shallow groove to good holds then move left to finish past the downward pointing oak (as for *Ituna*).

49 **Flasherman Direct**		25m	HVS -	★	1975

(5a). From the top of the big corner, climb the steep continuation corner direct to gain a good ledge. Now climb up and rightwards to finish.

50 **Erection**		26m	E1	★ ★ ★	1974

A stiff undertaking heightened further by a lack of protection near the top - another fantastic experience. Start at a steep wall directly in line with the prominent block overhang.

(5a). Climb the wall with much interest and then more easily move up to the overhanging block. Follow the horizontal undercut flake rightwards and gain its top awkwardly. The shallow scoop in the steep wall above is climbed with trepidation in a wonderful position.

51 **Viennese Oyster**	27m	E3	★ ★	1987

A juicy little number taking an intimidating line and giving varied climbing in superb situations. The in situ piton is not as young as it was in 1987. Start as for *Erection*.

(5c). Climb the steep wall and slab to below the block overhangs where a high runner in the horizontal flake-crack is recommended. From the level of the lower block overhangs, traverse right to an obvious jug on the bulge. Pull strenuously over the bulge, then step left and move over a small triangular roof: peg runner in situ on the right. Either reach high and right for good holds, then traverse steeply right round the arête and climb to the top, or climb directly up the wall above.

52 **Soft Touch**	22m	E4	★ ★	1997

Start beneath the steep broken wall just right of the arête and below the gully.

(5c). Climb the centre of the wall and from the top of the broken wall move out left to gain a flake and pocket. Follow the steep arête and finish, either up the arête, or by the wall on the right (as for *Viennese Oyster*).

Erection Arête ★ ★ Not Led

A good problem.

(5c). Instead of moving left to gain the base of the arête, move up a crack until a left-slanting underclimb crack can be followed towards the arête and finish as for *Soft Touch*.

Full Frontal ★ ★ Not Led

(6a). A direct start to *Erection Arête* which takes the three-stepped roof below the arête. Climb the obvious sandy slab rightwards. Pull left below the first roof and climb directly through the overhangs on snappy holds to gain the arête.

53 **Nurts Way**	22m	HVS		1979

A poor route. Start at the foot of the steep wall below the gully (as for *Soft Touch*).

(5a). Climb the wall and scramble up the gully to below the steep right-slanting crack on the left wall. Climb this to finish at an oak tree.

Left: Catherine Kenyon starting the high groove on **Flasherman** (VS). **Photo:** Ron Kenyon

Armathwaite Dome Slab

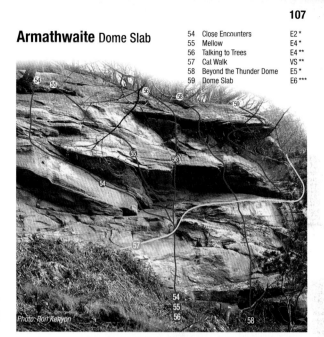

Photo: Ron Kenyon

Dome Slab

This is the clean buttress of pale yellow rock separated from *Erection Arête* by a steep dirty wall and gully. *Dome Slab* consists of slabs and walls sandwiched between roofs and overhangs and hosts a bevy of quite fearsome climbs.

Descent is by a gully on the right of the buttress – this is often slippery but tree branches can be used for aid.

| 54 **Close Encounters** | 10m | E2 | ★ | 1970s |

A contrived route. Start towards the left side of the buttress below the right-hand end of the first barrier of overhangs.

(5c). Climb easily up rightwards to a weakness in the overhang and then leftwards to gain and follow the *Finger Traverse* leftwards until an easing and jugs. A hard move up leads to a fine flake hold and the final step to a tree.

Left: Graham Everett gets to grips with **Erection** (E1), Armathwaite. **Photo:** Ron Kenyon

Extension

From the jugs, continue the traverse into *Nurts Way*. This reduces overall grade to **E2 (5b)**.

Direct E2

(6a). The left end of the traverse can be gained directly over the roof.

55 **Mellow**	14m	E4	★	1995

(5c). Start as for *Close Encounters* and move easily up to the second tier of overhangs which is breached by a left-slanting break. Follow this and attain with difficulty a standing position above the traverse of *Close Encounters* then move diagonally leftwards up the slab to finish at a tree.

56 **Talking To Trees**	14m	E4	★ ★	1975

(5c). Start at the same point as *Close Encounters* and then continue easily to the overhang which is breached by a vertical fluted runnel. Reach a large triangular block below the top overhang (runners at the top of the block) and pull over the bulge awkwardly to continue up past a thin flake-crack to gain the top.

57 **Catwalk**	25m	VS	★ ★	2009

An amazing traverse across the buttress at a reasonable grade following a slab sandwiched between overhangs. Take a full selection of cams and start as for *Close Encounters*.

(4c). From a small ledge gain the slab by a short crack, then traverse right on amazing holds to an awkward step just before the right arête. From the arête, either continue rightwards to a step down to belay at a tree, or follow a crack to a precarious finish.

58 **Beyond The Thunder Dome**	14m	E5	★	1997

Start below a block lying poised on the lower slab 4 metres right of *Close Encounters*.

(6b). Climb past the block and move up diagonally rightwards to the next break through the second tier of overhangs. Surmount the overhang and climb directly to the final overhang which is overcome by desperate moves rightwards up a shallow slanting flange.

59 **Dome Slab**	14m	E6	★ ★ ★	1974

Hard, serious and intimidating. The crux calls on reserves of strength and determination not usually brought into play and retreat from it could prove to be a nasty experience. Protection of some kind can be arranged in the block below the finish of *Talking To Trees* and also in the main roof and on the (now small) spike on the lip. Start directly beneath the widest point of the top roof.

(6a). Ascend pleasantly up the gradually steepening line of shelves and shallow corners to just below the roof. An extended move up brings a thin crack to hand which is used to reach out left to the prominent right-trending flange on the lip. Use this and good but low-placed holds to make the depressingly difficult crank onto the slab above and reaffirm your faith in Divine Providence.

Red Buttress

Extending rightwards from *Dome Slab* is the *Red Buttress*, which consists of a steep wall of soft rock on the left (below which the *Split Boulder* provides some good bouldering) and, further right, a slab seamed with wrinkles and overlaps.

Descent is either down the gully to the left next to *Dome Slab* or by the shallow gully with tree roots on the right next to the *Final Section*.

Good Dog Glen	6m	VS		2000

(4c). Start 8 metres left of *Red Monkey* behind a multi-stemmed tree. Climb the corner-crack above then move right to finish up a short corner.

Split Boulder

Photo: Ron Kenyon

Armathwaite
Red Buttress

60	Red Spider	E2
61	Red Monkey	E1 **
62	Red Lion	HVS

60 **Red Spider**	16m	E2		1974

A horrible route that might be best avoided. Start on top of the *Split Boulder*. (5b). Climb out of a little corner and move up and right on reasonable rock to a ledge below the prominent V-shaped recess of *Red Monkey*. Follow the best and soundest line up and leftwards to reach a tree overhanging the face. A good nut runner on *Red Monkey* is recommended.

61 **Red Monkey**	16m	E1	★★	1974

(5b). Pull over the small bulge on excellent holds and climb the fine little wall to an easing below the recess. Enter the recess and exit via hard moves on the right wall to gain the obvious prow – this can be well protected.

62 **Red Lion**	14m	HVS -		1974

The old name of the Fox and Pheasant Inn in Armathwaite. (5a). Follow *Red Monkey* but move rightwards up a lower diagonal break to join and finish up *Coombs Crack*.

Fox and Pheasant	13m	HVS -		2009

(5a). Start just left of *Coombs Crack* and climb up and left to gain the ledge of *Red Lion*. Follow the diagonal break of *Red Lion* rightwards, keeping to the right of the arête, until it is possible to move left onto the arête - finish with care. The arête direct still awaits an ascent.

63 **Coombs Crack**	13m	VS		1974

(4c). An esoteric experience up the corner-crack.

The buttress now changes character and becomes a steep slab of excellent rock.

64 **Wafer Thin**	13m	E5	★★	1974

An exacting lead. The crux involves excruciating footwork and body placements that would do justice to the Royal Ballet. Start below a steep blunt rib.

(6b). Climb the rib on undercuts until small flakes on the left can be used to gain access to the slab. A series of moves up and slightly leftwards enable one to reach up right to the top break and finish above.

Direct Finish 1975
   Climb directly up the slab from the top of the blunt rib - slightly harder than the original way but not as fine.

Right: Pete Gunn belayed by Davina Mouat on the classic layback flake of **Paper Moon** (E3).
Photo: Nick Halbert

Armathwaite Paper Moon Area

63	Coombs Crack	VS
64	Wafer Thin	E5 **
65	Paper Moon	E3 ***

v1	Bad Moon Rising	NL *
66	Devil Moon	NL *
67	New Moon	E5 *
68	Moondance	E1 *

Photo: Ron Kenyon

65 **Paper Moon**	13m	E3+	★ ★ ★	1974

A magnificent climb providing continuous interest and difficulty on good rock. It follows the prominent overlap to a finely-placed crux right at the end. Originally graded HVS!

(5c). Climb up and slightly leftwards to gain the start of the overlap. Follow this rightwards to an intriguing finish which makes good use of a vertical crack to the right to gain a ledge above the overlap.

Two variations have been top-roped but still await a led ascent:

v1 **Bad Moon Rising** ★ Not Led

(6b). Starting as for *Paper Moon*, gain the overlap and make a couple of moves up before moving left to climb the slab above by a series of hard moves.

66 **Devil Moon**			★	Not Led

(6b/c). Starting as for *Paper Moon*, after moving right to an arch, use this to move right again to reach a right-facing flake edge. A finish is made up the crack to the right of the finish of *Paper Moon*.

Armathwaite Free 'n' Easy Wall

69	Moving Pictures	NL *
70	One Hand Clapping	E6 **
71	Free 'n' Easy	E5 ***
72	Plain Sailing	NL **
73	Sailing Shoes	NL **
74	Mr Bundy's Best Friend	NL *
75	The Crescent	E3 **
76	Jelly Terror	E1 **

Photo: Ron Kenyon

67 **New Moon**	10m	E5	★	1975

Another desperately hard problem.

(6b). Start in a recess and, using a set of undercuts, transfer to the next undercuts above and aim to gain a rounded knob on the slab above. Finish up *Moondance*.

68 **Moondance**	13m	E1	★	1986

(5b). Climb the short thin right-curving break until the slab above can be gained. Move up the slab and climb the left-slanting crack-line above to a ledge.

Final Section

This is a long section which commences with the steep wall of *Free'n' Easy* and a number of other fine routes. Towards the right-hand side it becomes less attractive before petering out.

Descent can be made at either end.

| The Mantelshelf | | V2 | ★ | |

Start below a big tree growing just right of a short ramp.

Gain the ramp directly, from where a long reach to small ledges leads to a hard mantelshelf. Finish right of the tree.

Right: Michael Kenyon on **The Mantelshelf** (V2), Armathwaite. **Photo:** Ron Kenyon

| 69 **Moving Pictures** | | | ★ | Not Led |

(6a/b). Follow *One Hand Clapping* to the mantelshelf and climb the scoop with a long reach for a poor hold.

| 70 **One Hand Clapping** | 13m | E6 | ★★ | 1987 |

A bold climb taking on the challenge of the left-hand side of this wall. Start at a short corner.

(6a). Climb up the corner and pull onto the slab above. Traverse the sloping ledge leftwards for about 3 metres and mantelshelf to below a very shallow scoop. Step right until it is possible to climb straight up to a very hard finishing move.

| 71 **Free 'n' Easy** | 12m | E5 | ★★★ | 1974 |

An outstanding, absorbing and serious climb requiring technical competence and a cool approach.

(6a). Climb the short wall onto a little ledge and reach good holds in the first break. A hard pull up to the next break leads to a rest. Move slightly right onto the sloping holds in the break (wires) and step up leftwards, using the best of a cluster of pockets to establish yourself on sloping footholds below the top crack. Climb the final crack with rising hopes that are soon shattered as the top is approached. Now finish!

| 72 **Plain Sailing** | | | ★★ | Not Led |

A fine pitch of some character and much difficulty

(6b). Climb the left-facing corner to a ledge. The vague arête above is climbed, first slightly left, then right, to two prominent small pockets. Move up and rightwards to finish.

Right: Davina Mouat reaching the crack on **Free 'n' Easy** (E5), Armathwaite. **Photo:** Nick Halbert

Armathwaite Codpiece Area

76	Jelly Terror	E1 **
77	Rise and Shine	NL *
78	Crescent Arête	E6 **
79	Y-Front	E2 *
80	Barnacle Bill	E1 **

v1	Limpet Lil	NL
81	Smear or Die	NL *
82	Andy's Slab	E4 **
v2	Variation Finish	NL
83	Codpiece Left-Hand	E1 **
84	Codpiece	E2 **
85	Pick Pocket	E3 **

Photo: Ron Kenyon

73 **Sailing Shoes**			★ ★	Not Led

(6a). Start as for *Plain Sailing* and climb to the ledge. Ascend the wall above bearing right to an obvious horizontal overlap. Undercling this and make a desperate move right onto a sloping ledge. Finish up the slab and corner above as for *The Crescent*.

A huge boulder forms a narrow passage between itself and the crag. At the top of the passage a jammed block bridges the gap creating a tunnel.

74 **Mr Bundy's Best Friend**			★	Not Led

Start below the steep wall to the left of the huge boulder.

(6b). Climb the wall directly for 3 metres to gain the centre of the curving shelf of the initial traverse of *The Crescent*. Climb the wall above, just right of the obvious jug which marks the crux of *Crescent*, and gain a line of pockets above and on the right. Move right from these to a very strenuous finish.

| 75 **The Crescent** | 13m | E3 | ★ ★ | 1974 |

A climb with an intimidating and unprotected crux. Easier for the tall. Start just left of the tunnel.

(5b). Climb onto the obvious curving shelf and follow it leftwards for 4 metres to where the shelf curves up. Sharp but small edges on the wall above provide the means of gaining a good jug. From this, pull up, stand up and move left, then finish easily up the slab and corner above.

| 76 **Jelly Terror** | 9m | E1 | ★ ★ | 1974 |

A strenuous but protectable climb. Start on top of the jammed block below the obvious crack.

(5b). Gain the ledge and climb the slim crack to pass a bulge. The wider cracks above are easier but maintain interest.

| 77 **Rise and Shine** | | | ★ | Not Led |

(5c). Climb a flake just right of *Jelly Terror* then traverse right to climb the upper wall just left of *Crescent Arête*.

Five metres right of the tunnel the crag bends into a prominent deep corner capped by a triangular overhang.

| 78 **Crescent Arête** | 10m | E6 | ★ ★ | 1987 |

A serious climb. Start below a narrow wall just left of the prominent corner.

(6a). Climb the centre of the widening wall, with use of the left arête, to gain a cluster of finger pockets. Use these to pull up and swing over the edge of the arête to gain a standing position. Climb the yellow friable wall above by the line of least resistance.

| 79 **Y-Front** | 11m | E2 | ★ | 1974 |

A bold climb but on generally positive holds.

(5b). Climb *Barnacle Bill* until stopped by the triangular roof. Pull out left to gain side holds and step onto the rib below the hanging cleft. Climb the cleft, transferring onto the left wall, to finish at the top of the arête.

| 80 **Barnacle Bill** | 13m | E1 | ★ ★ | 1973 |

A superb classic corner with a delicate and fairly bold crux.

(5b). Climb the layback corner to the roof. A very fine sequence of moves right under the roof gains the continuation crack which is thin though protectable, or do you just go for the top?!

v1 *Limpet Lil* Not Led

(5c). Climb *Barnacle Bill* to the roof then pull over this to the next horizontal break. Move slightly right and up to gain a good right handhold, then make a long reach to the top.

| **The High Girdle** | 60m | E6 | ★ ★ | 1975 |

A fantastic expedition which crosses the most imposing part of *The Final Section* at a high-level. Start at the left-hand end of the *Final Section* just right of *The Mantelshelf*.

(6a/b). Gain the obvious sloping ledge and foot-traverse this rightwards passing below the thin final crack of *Free 'n' Easy*. Continue rightwards with great difficulty, round the blunt arête, to gain the break across the wall above *The Crescent*. Follow this to *Jelly Terror* and continue rightwards on suspicious rock to gain *Barnacle Bill* by descending slightly. Finish up the final corner of *Barnacle Bill*.

| 81 **Smear or Die** | | | ★ | Not Led |

(6b). Start as for *Andy's Slab* and follow this until, instead of moving right from the sloping ledge, move up and slightly left to a layaway for the right hand at the left-hand end of the obvious curving feature in the centre of the slab. Use this hold to gain a shallow left-facing scoop just right of *Barnacle Bill* and finish up *Barnacle Bill*.

| 82 **Andy's Slab** | 13m | E4 | ★ ★ | 1974 |

A much tried test-piece. Remarkable for its time, before 'sticky rubber'! Start at the vertical break in the smooth lower slab.

(6a). Climb the break and stand on a very sloping ledge. The next moves follow a tenuous series of scrapes diagonally rightwards to gain the right-trending gangway (crux). Follow this, swing right onto the left-trending ramp of *Codpiece Left-Hand* and follow this to the top, or use the ramp as a handrail.

Right: Alice Woodhouse padding up **Andy's Slab** (E4), Armathwaite. **Photo:** Ron Kenyon

v2 *Variation Finish to Andy's Slab* Not Led

(6a). Follow *Andy's Slab* to gain and use the left-trending ramp of *Codpiece Left-Hand* as a handrail, then continue diagonally leftwards to finish just right of *Barnacle Bill*.

Left: Alan Greig demonstrating the moves on **The Crescent** (E3). **Photo:** Anne Greig

Armathwaite

Codpiece and Pickpocket Area

Photo: Rob Kenyon

83 **Codpiece Left-Hand**	12m	E1	★★	1973

An easier and more attractive finish to *Codpiece*.

(5b). Climb the crack and gain the ramp by a difficult step up (crux). The ramp above leads to easier climbing, leftwards up ledges to the top.

84 **Codpiece**	12m	E2	★★	1973

The prominent flaring crack-line. A test piece of poor jams and layaways with awkward protection from small wires.

(5c). Climb the crack and gain the ramp by a difficult step, then step back right and continue up the crack with continued difficulty. Climbing the crack directly without resorting to the ramp is 6a.

85 **Pickpocket**	11m	E3	★★	1974

A very fine climb of sustained difficulty and interest. Start as for *Codpiece*.

Right: Sam Greig finding the finger locks on **Codpiece** (E2), Armathwaite. **Photo:** Anne Greig

(5c). Climb the crack until a line of foot pockets can be traversed rightwards assisted by a difficult hand change and a long reach right. Better pockets lead rightwards to a hand-ledge in a horizontal slot. Use this to gain the wall above and climb it via a prominent protuberance.

86 Pickpocket Superdirect	9m	E3	★ ★	1975

Start below and just right of a left-facing layaway hold at 3 metres.

(6a). Gain the layaway by a very hard move on low finger pockets and finish as for *Pickpocket*.

87 The Black Russian			★	Not Led

A very hard finish to *Pickpocket Superdirect*.

(6b). From the layaway hold on *Pickpocket Superdirect*, use pockets on the right to gain a series of horizontal creases which enable the upper wall to be climbed direct, just left of the normal finish.

88 Pickpocket Direct	9m	E2	★	

Start at a ledge at waist height which runs rightwards into a small bulge-capped recess.

(5b). Traverse right along the ledge into the recess. Move onto the slab above below a steep wall and move left to gain a horizontal slot. Use this to gain the wall above and finish via the obvious protuberance (as for *Pickpocket*).

89 Solitaire	13m	E2	★	1974

This route finds a way rightwards up the steep slab capped by the red bulge. Start as for *Pickpocket Direct*.

(5b). Traverse the ledge as for *Pickpocket Direct* but move out of the small bulge-capped recess rightwards. Traverse diagonally right to finish at the obvious silver birch at the top.

Diamond Lil	10m	E3		1997

Start below and one metre left of a silver birch.

(5c). Climb the wall direct into a small recess at 5 metres. Step left and gain the ledge above on slopers then finish up the short wall to the birch.

Cluedo	11m	E2		1974

Start at the foot of the buttress at the lowest point directly beneath a huge pine tree.

(5b). Climb to a ledge with help from a small beech on the right. The flakes above lead up to a very dirty finish (prior inspection recommended) ending at the pine.

John's and Frog's Route		9m	E2		1986

Start 2 metres right of *Cluedo* below a right-facing small flake just right of the small beech.

(5b). Climb the wall to the flake, then the face above to finish at a silver birch.

The Field of Dreams					Not Led

Start 4 metres right of *John's and Frog's Route* below a left-slanting ramp at 5 metres.

(5c). Climb the bulging wall via poor layaway holds to gain the ramp then move leftwards up this to the top.

Tramlines		6m	E2		1975

Start at a short wall below a birch growing right on the edge at the top.

(5b). Climb the wall using the thin line of intrusions.

The Green Knight		6m	HVS		1986

Start at the far right end of the wall below two small roofs and 2 metres left of a tree growing close to the crag. A pleasant climb when clean.

(5a). Surmount the first bulge to reach the ledge. Step one metre left and, using poor handholds on the slab above, surmount the overlap and continue to the top direct.

Lazonby

Grid Reference: **NY 526 425**   Altitude: **60m**
Faces: **East**   Approach: **15 mins**

These important crags form a major feature of the Eden Gorge, lying on the west bank of the River Eden between the villages of Lazonby and Armathwaite. They comprise a number of separate walls and buttresses strung out along two miles of river bank. There are three main groups of outcrops with the central (and largest) group being one of the most impressive sandstone crags in England and having the best climbing.

The crags face away from the prevailing weather and this combined with their sheltered position in the gorge means that climbing is possible throughout the year and the rock dries quickly after rain.

The rock varies from a soft red type to a form which is almost gritstone-like in hardness: sometimes all variations can be experienced in the course of just one climb. A peculiar feature of these crags are the presence of veins of harder rock which, due to differential weathering, stand out as small ribs or sometimes as large protruding fins. Several climbs make use of these. A warning must be sounded with regard to protection on these climbs. As with all sandstone, great care must be exercised when placing runners and trusting them to hold long falls is not sensible. In addition, when damp, the rock tends to break much more readily than when dry.

Lazonby has a unique and powerful atmosphere which can easily intimidate the first-time visitor. For the competent and experienced climber, coming to terms with the climbing here will give a taste of the best that the Eden Valley has to offer.

Approach:

Unfortunately access has long been banned at Lazonby and, despite the fact that climbing had taken place for many years without problem, repeated attempts to negotiate with the landowners have got nowhere. The descriptions are given to maintain the historical record only and in case a change of ownership allows climbing to take place once again. No right or encouragement to climb is implied.

In case access is allowed again, the original access route is described **(NB There is currently no right of access via this route)**. Approach from the road running north-west from Lazonby to Baronwood and park at NY 522 425, half a mile before a cattle grid, on the wide verge on the west side of the road opposite to the gated track of "Lazonby Estate Route 3". The track which leads downhill brings one to another gate. Pass through this and cross the Carlisle-Settle railway line. Turn right and follow a track past a circular stand of conifers on the right. This track leads to the top of *Cave Buttress*, identifiable by the many magnificent scots pines growing there. A gate in a wooden fence is passed and the wide track curves steeply down below *Cave Buttress* to meet the riverside path.

As one faces the river immediately below *Cave Buttress*, the *Far Upstream Buttress* is reached by turning right and following the muddy path alongside the river in an upstream direction. *Wirewalk Buttress* is immediately on one's left and the rest of the crags are downstream of this.

Far Upstream Buttress

The easiest approach is to stay close to the river bank when walking upstream from the *Cave Buttress* area. The first rocks are met just before a large oak tree. Some lines have been climbed here, but the rock is composed of large detached blocks and cannot be regarded as safe. Some 50 metres further upstream, the crags gain height and are very vegetated and broken to begin with. The first recorded climbs are located just beyond an elder tree growing from the foot of the crag where a huge rectangular recess splits the upper part of the buttress.

The climbs are described from **right** to **left**, moving upstream, in contrast to the climbs on the other buttresses.

Stained Class	15m	VS	★	1987

Follows the rib right of the rectangular recess.

(4c). Climb a short groove to below a large roof. Move left to bypass this then climb the crack and rib above to finish at a tree.

Gothic Horror	15m	VS		1987

Start below and left of the rectangular recess.

(4b). Climb the gardened wall to gain the base of the recess. Follow the crack system up the left retaining wall moving left near the top to an exposed finish.

Moving upstream, the rock retreats once more beneath a cloak of vegetation. About 20 metres beyond *Gothic Horror* is:

Nemesis Towers	25m	HS		1987

Start below a large roof to the right of a shallow gully.

(4b). Climb a groove to the roof then traverse left into the gully. A tricky move above here gains easier ground which leads to the final overhang. Avoid this by finishing to the left.

The remaining routes are located on another buttress further left which is set up the bank at a higher level facing upstream.

Far Above the Splat Mat	13m	E1	★	1987

Start near the right edge of the buttress at a shallow square niche.

(5b). Climb the wall directly above the niche. Pull onto the undercut upper slab to finish awkwardly at a small pine tree.

Herbal Abuse	12m	VS		1987

Further left the wall is pierced by a prominent cave.

(5a). Gain the cave from below and slightly left. Finish up the interesting jamming crack above.

Snowball	12m	VS		1987

Start left of *Herbal Abuse* and 3 metres left of a vegetated groove.

(4c). Climb the wall direct to a prominent projecting block. Finish by moving rightwards towards a tree.

Cave Buttress (or Samson's Cave Buttress)

The Cave in this buttress is a comfortable hide-out and is named after its one-time occupant, a fugitive Irish navvy employed on the building of the Settle–Carlisle railway, who was eventually hunted down by police for his part in the murder of another navvy during a drunken brawl at Armathwaite. The event forms the basis of a novel by the Lakeland writer Graham Sutton.

The *Cave* can be reached quite easily from the foot of the left-hand side of the buttress. Start below an obvious big left-facing corner, and follow a short scramble and a couple of tunnels.

The rock on this buttress can be rather soft in places – take care!

The first climb is located on a small roofed buttress to the left of the the *Cave* scramble.

I Can't Breakdance!	8m	E1	★	1987

Start below the roof.

(5c). Climb into a niche then undercling the crack which splits the roof. A gymnastic pull round this leads to an earthy scramble off.

Demolition Dancing	12m	HVS		1988

Start just left of the *Cave* scramble.

(5a). Climb the short corner above and move right to a ledge. From here follow the hanging rib to a landing on steep soil.

The next four routes are gained by scrambling up to the ledge below the big corner, as for the *Cave* scramble.

The Crack	12m	S		1970

The crack on the left wall of the open-book corner is climbed to a good ledge. Move right to an earthy finish.

Cave Corner	12m	MVS		1971

(4b). Climb the obvious steep corner.

Technical Ecstasy	12m	E4	★ ★ ★	1986

A brilliant sustained route with good protection. The wall to the right of *Cave Corner* is split by a thin crack which runs the full height of the face.

(6a). Climb the crack to finish over a small roof.

To find the next route it is necessary to crawl through the tunnel into *Samson's Cave*.

The Fearful Void	12m	E3	★ ★ ★	1987

An intimidating pitch with a wild finish! Start in the mouth of the *Cave* and belay here (big thread).

(5c). Climb the pillar on the right of the entrance (facing into the *Cave*) for a few metres. Step left above the *Cave* and traverse below the overhang to gain a crouching position on the jutting neb of rock. Finish directly above here at a small tree.

The remainder of the routes on *Cave Buttress* are described moving right from the scramble to the *Cave*. The ground slopes down and a number of small trees just in front of the crag are useful for locating climbs.

Dirty Old Pillar	9m	S		1972

Start just right of the scramble to the *Cave* and follow a crack which widens to a chimney, past a thin birch, to belay on the ledge above.

Sahara Crossing	20m	HVS		1986

Start 2 metres left of the first small tree at a winding flake-crack.

(5a). Follow the crack until it peters out (thread out to the left) then move up and left over a bulge. Climb up a few metres then traverse right over soft rock to reach the *Cave*.

Cave Route	30m	S		1970

Start immediately right of the first tree.
1 15m. Climb up to and ascend the steep difficult chimney to the *Cave*.
2 15m. Traverse right and ascend the loose chute, trending left to a tree belay.

Neanderthal Man	15m	VS		1972

Start midway between the second and third trees.

(5a). Climb the wall to a ledge then ascend another wall to a ledge on the right. Enter the V-groove and follow this moving leftwards to the *Cave*.

Pneumoconiosis	30m	E3	★	1971

A commiting and serious route. Start at a shallow groove in the centre of the buttress.

(5b). Climb the lower wall with ease. The overhang above is awkward and a pull-out left onto a wall can be made. Climb the wall, trending left, until better rock can be followed rightwards to a chimney, up which the climb finishes.

| **Phred** | 30m | VS (Aid) | | 1972 |

Right of *Pneumoconiosis* is a large arch-shaped recess. Directly above this is a V-groove high up. Start right of this in another bramble-choked recess.

    (4c). Move leftwards below the corner/groove of *Barney*, but continue to traverse horizontally leftwards to reach the V-groove (2 pegs for aid). Follow the groove then move right to a tree at the top.

| **Barney** | 25m | VS | | 1972 |

Start in the bramble-choked recess as for *Phred*.

    (4b). Move leftwards to a corner/groove and climb it. To finish, either move out leftwards, or head right for a tree and climb a vegetated groove to the top.

| **Mandrax** | 18m | S | | 1973 |

Not a very pleasant experience! Start further up the slope where a large bulge has a short groove to its left.

    Climb the loose groove.

| **Rattle and Hum** | 12m | HS | | 1988 |

Start directly below the large bulge.

    (4b). Climb up to this and pull out right to a ledge above. Ascend the front of the pillar above direct.

The easy gully on the right divides *Cave Buttress* from *Wirewalk Buttress* and provides a useful means of descent.

Wirewalk Buttress

Known locally as *Chain Rock*, *Wirewalk Buttress* is the biggest of the *Lazonby Outcrops*. The majority of routes are steep, hard and most have a very serious feel to them – this is certainly no place for the faint of heart! In general, the rock is better on the upper sections than those near the river. However some climbs have good rock throughout (for sandstone!). For ease of description, *Wirewalk Buttress* is divided into three sections: *Upstream Face*, *River Face* and *Downstream Face*.

    The *Upstream Face* has a tree-lined ledge at half-height and is in full view from the approach path below *Cave Buttress*. The *River Face* rises directly out of the river and thus cannot be easily viewed, although in dry summer conditions a pleasant "plodge" will allow a cursory inspection of lines on the right side of the face. It is possible to traverse the foot of the face via a ledge and iron stanchions in all but flood levels. The *Downstream Face* is dank and uninspiring.

Upstream Face

Red Barchetta	12m	HVS		1988

Opposite *Rattle and Hum*, across the gully, is a short rib. Start on the wall right of this and below a tiny overhang.

(5c). Move up and left to a jug on top of the rib. Go up this to a ledge then climb the awkward chimney on the left.

Fear Is The Key	12m	HVS	★	1986

Start between the rib and the prominent corner at a shallow left-facing groove.

(5a). Climb the rib past an overlap to a ledge then finish up the short wall above.

Adam	12m	S		1970

Climb the obvious corner, exiting up a short chimney on the left.

Virtually Part One	12m	S		1972

Start in the corner of *Adam* but climb the wall just right of it and finish up a short groove.

Mystery Achievement	15m	E1	★ ★	1986

The bewildering crux can be well protected using runners on the tree. Start at the foot of the arête next to a tree.

(6a). Gain the top of the detached block then make tricky moves up and left round the arête. Easier climbing follows, moving right near the top for maximum exposure.

Pavane	13m	E2		1989

A bold route. Start below the obvious gully right of the arête.

(5b). Scramble up to reach the dog-leg crack on the left wall (good runners). From the top of this launch up and left over a slight nose to finish straight up.

Eve	12m	VD		1970

Climb the loose gully in its entirety.

Moving right from *Eve* the ground drops away and a ledge holding two birches can be gained. The nearer of the two trees provides a useful belay for the next three routes whilst the further one overhangs the void.

Footfall	9m	E2	★	1988

Start below the wide groove next to the birch belay.

(5c). Climb the groove past an awkward bulging section to finish on good jugs.

Lazonby Wirewalk Buttress

1	Fingers	E1 **
2	Silicosis	E1 **
3	Perilous Journey	E3 **
4	Inside a Cosmic Orgasm	E2
5	Machoman	E4 *
6	Gadzowt	HVS **
7	Tigerfeet	E2
8	Red Chipper	E3 *
9	Ace of Wands	E4 **
10	Hernia	E2 *
11	Merry Monk	VS *
12	Merry Monk Direct	HVS ***
13	Cobweb	E3 **
14	Why Flymo When You Can Napalm	E5 ***
15	Variations on a Swinger	E3 *
v1	King of the Swingers	HVS *
16	The Swinger	HVS

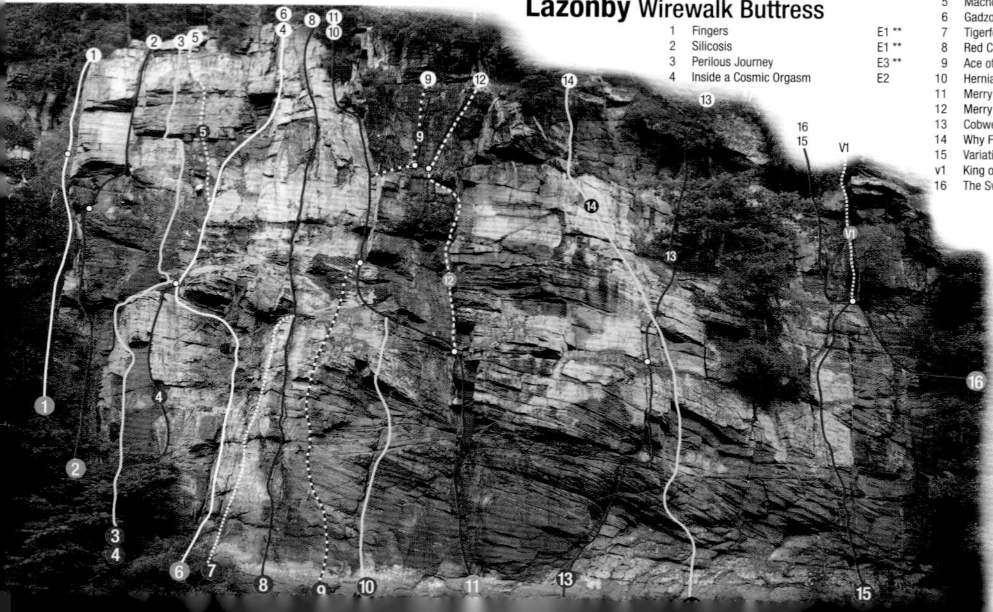

Photo: Ron Kenyon

1 **Fingers**	26m	E1	★★	1975

A steep and fascinating climb, in turn both bold and exposed. Start below the birch tree ledge 3 metres right of a burned stump.

1   13m (5a). Climb the wall direct on small holds to reach the birch tree ledge and belay. A bit short on protection!
2   12m (5a). Climb the impressive wall above the right-hand tree past a horizontal break to reach a crescent-shaped overlap. Step right from here to finish. A superb pitch.

Eye in the Sky	12m	HVS	★★	1987

Enjoyable climbing in a stunning position. Start at the birch tree belay used by the previous routes.

(5b). A gently rising traverse leads rightwards onto the exposed blunt rib. Excellent protection can be arranged here which makes the awkward moves up the rib more palatable. Finish on good jugs.

The Toe	6m	VS		1988

The isolated pinnacle on the slope below *Fingers*.

(5b). Climb the arête facing the river. Hard to start.

River Face

An impressive piece of rock whose true proportions can only be fully appreciated from further upstream or from across the river. The left-hand side is merely vertical whilst to the right of the incredible central groove of *Merry Monk*, the rock gently overhangs.

2 **Silicosis**	30m	E1	★★	1971

A fine climb marred slightly by the worrying nature of the first pitch. Start on a large sloping shelf in a recess at the left-hand side of the face.

1   15m (5b). Climb the awkward shallow groove, then the crack, to a ledge on the left. Take care with the rock.
2   15m (4c). Traverse right and ascend the gangway and corner to the top. A fine pitch.

3 **Perilous Journey**	30m	E3	★★	1986

A tremendous route which saves its hardest moves until the end. A large Friend will help those in peril on the crux! Start to the right of the recess of *Silicosis* where a steep vein slants up the left-hand side of the red wall. **NB** The flakes on the first pitch have fallen off (1990) and the pitch has not been climbed in its present state. However Pitch 2 is superb on its own.

1   15m (5b). Climb the vein then move left to a creaky flake (runners). From the top of the flake move left onto another flake. Enter a shallow scoop above this then move up and right to a belay on a large ledge. Serious.

2   15m (5c). Climb the groove directly behind the belay to reach a large jammed block. Pull through the overlap just left of this then sprint up the leaning headwall passing, amongst other things, some horizontal breaks (Friends).

4 **Inside A Cosmic Orgasm**	15m	E2		1974

Contrived and hard to protect. On the first ascent a peg runner was used to protect the moves on and beyond the traverse. Start at the vein in the red wall.

(5b). Climb the vein for a short distance until a finger-traverse leads rightwards across the steep wall. Move onto the rounded arête and beyond. Climb the wall until one can move back left into a narrow but prominent groove. Climb this to a ledge and belay. Finish as for *Gadzowt*.

5 **Machoman**	15m	E4	★	1988

The free version of the old aid route *Microman* gives a sensationally positioned pitch. Protection is good only where it is most needed. Start from the belay ledge shared by the previous two routes. An alternative start is provided by the first pitch of *Gadzowt*.

(6a). Climb a short rib on the right (as for *Gadzowt*) to arrive at the impending headwall below two parallel cracks. Climb the left-hand crack with increasing difficulty to the top.

6 **Gadzowt**	33m	HVS	★ ★	1970

One of the easier climbs on the river face but nevertheless an exposed climb which can prove thought-provoking. Start to the right of *Perilous Journey* below a short but very steep crack which opens out into a big recessed bowl at 6 metres.

1   15m (5a). Climb the awkward crack then ascend an open groove to the overhang above (good runners - at last!). Traverse left under the overhang to a good ledge.

2   18m (4c). Climb the rib on the right to a ledge then move right and follow a short awkward crack to the top.

7 **Tigerfeet**	30m	E2		1974

A serious route up an impressive wall. Unfortunately its finish, which it shares with *Red Chipper*, is a bit of a disappointment. Start below the wall to the right of *Gadzowt*.

(5a). Climb the wall via a crack and continue up to a ledge below an overhang. Move right to enter a short groove which leads up to the middle ledges. Climb the grooves above (as for *Red Chipper*).

| 8 **Red Chipper** | 30m | E3 | ★ | 1975 |

A good, steep and technical initial section gives way to easier climbing above. Start 4 metres right of the cracked corner of *Gadzowt* below the fine wide rounded crack which terminates tantalisingly out of reach.

(5c). Gain the foot of the crack passing the eradicated chipped hold which gave the climb its name. The crack is not easy but better jams soon lead to good handholds. Continue up the steep wall to the area of ledges. The grooves directly above lead logically to the top.

| 9 **Ace of Wands** | 40m | E4 | ★ ★ | 1978 |

A very fine and impressive climb with a technical and bold first pitch and an exciting finale. Start below the steep wall right of **Red Chipper** just right of the 'H. Simmons' inscription.

1   20m (5c). Climb the steep wall to a flat hold and peg runner below the overhang. Climb the overhang and move right to gain a ledge below a square roofed corner (as for *Hernia*).

2   12m (4c). Climb past the overhang (as for *Hernia*) and continue up the steep groove above until a long step can be made rightwards to a good foothold on the arête. Pull around to the right to a good ledge below and to the left of the final pitch of *Merry Monk*.

3   8m (5b). Climb the impending crack above to a resting place in a corner. Surmount the overhang above to finish.

| 10 **Hernia** | 30m | E2 | ★ | 1972 |

Strenuous and bold on the lower section. Start below a steep crack-line, to the right of the 'H. Simmons' inscription.

(5b). Climb the wall then follow the crack to a ledge beneath the overhang. Move left into an overhanging corner where the overhang can be tackled strenuously on large dubious flakes. Easier climbing now leads to a ledge (possible belay), followed by an open corner to the top, finishing at two conifers.

| 11 **Merry Monk** | 33m | VS | ★ | 1969 |

The original climb on the crag provides the easiest way up the *River Face*. Start as for *Merry Monk Direct* below the huge corner/groove.

1   18m (4a). Climb the corner on good holds for about 15 metres then move up and left across the wall to belay beneath a prominent overhang.

2   15m (4c). Move up to the overhang and pass this awkwardly to gain the corner above. This leads to the top passing a number of unstable blocks en route.

12 **Merry Monk Direct**	33m	HVS	★ ★ ★	1970

One of the finest natural lines in the Eden Valley offering continuous interest and exposure. Start below the obvious huge corner which dominates the centre of the buttress.

1   15m (4a). Climb the fine corner on large holds to a small stance by a crack which sometimes 'squeaks'.

2   12m (5a). Climb up the groove above to its top moving right to gain a good ledge below a short steep wall.

3   6m (4c). The wall is awkward. Trend right to a tree.

Neptune	30m	E4		1988

An exciting climb with a steep and strenuous start. Start as for *Cobweb*.

(6a). Climb the overhanging wall as for *Cobweb* but swing left at 5 metres on flat holds. Continue up the steep face above with poor runners until a grassy ledge is reached (junction with *Cobweb*). Climb the green flaky face above until a red section is reached then go leftwards across this to a shallow groove and follow this to a small pine at the top.

13 **Cobweb**	34m	E3	★ ★	1972

Powerful climbing at the start has resulted in many attempts and fewer successes. Start 5 metres right of *Merry Monk* below an optimistic break; a right-facing groove breaching the grossly overhanging wall, but out of reach.

1   16m (5c). Climb the wall to gain the right-facing groove. Exit rightwards to gain a crack which is followed on good jams. Climb past a loose block to a good ledge. Peg belay (not in situ).

2   18m (5a). Pull onto the wall above and move rightwards to gain and climb a short but awkward chimney/groove. Exit on the right.

14 **Why Flymo When You Can Napalm?**	30m	E5	★ ★ ★	1989

A steep and exhilarating route with a wild finale. Start four metres right of *Cobweb Wall* at an iron stanchion.

(6b). Pull up to a peg runner at 3 metres then swing left and climb straight through the roof (crux), past peg runners, onto a short wall. Move up into a right-facing corner capped by an overhang (peg runner) and pull straight over this and up to a grassy ledge. Move left 4 metres and climb the wall above trending slightly leftwards until below the final overhang. Climb this past two peg runners, using brittle holds and finish via a large protruding spike.

Right: Paul Shorrock on **Merry Monk** (VS), Lazonby Crag, back in the days when you were allowed to climb it. **Photo:** Stephen Reid

15 **Variations on a Swinger**	35m	E3	★	1978

A good climb once the indifferent rock on the crux has been negotiated. Start at the third iron stanchion of the old wirewalk (counting from the downstream end).

1   26m (5c). Climb strenuously up a bulging crack into a niche (Friend 3.5 above could prevent a splash landing!). Traverse left with difficulty on soft rock to reach a small sloping ledge. Pull onto the ledge and reach a doubtful block. Climb the small overhang and crack above on better rock. From the top, move right and belay at a tree below a chimney.

2   9m (5a). As for pitch 2 of *The Swinger*, climb the chimney to the overhang, then gain the slab on the left. Ascend this, moving right to finish.

v1   ***King of the Swingers*** 9m HVS ★ 1987

This provides a more direct finish to *Variations on a Swinger*. Start from the belay ledge of that route.

(5b). Climb the chimney to the overhang and continue bridging and jamming up the crack to good finishing jugs.

16 **The Swinger**	30m	HVS		1971

An interesting route with good situations. Start at the tree at the right-hand end of the *River Face*.

1   21m (5a). Climb the tree to a point some 5 metres up and level with a ledge above the river. Gain this by a swing on good handholds. Traverse the ledge and climb the wall above, moving left slightly, to a tree below the wide chimney.

2   9m (5a). Climb the chimney to the overhang then gain the slab on the left. Ascend this moving right to finish.

Suspended Animation	30m	E2	★ ★	1986

A fine route with an impressive finale. Start just up the slope from the large tree at the downstream end of the *River Face*.

1   18m (5b). Climb up and left to reach the base of a wide crack on the arête of the buttress. Climb the crack almost to its top then step left onto the face. Climb straight up to belay on a ledge.

2   12m (5c). Move up and left to reach a short thin crack which leads with difficulty to a jammed block below the overhang. Traverse left to a large pocket below the widest part of the roof. Pull over this moving rightwards on excellent holds to the top.

The Mole	25m	HS		1970

Start below the broken crack several metres up the slope from the large tree of *The Swinger*.

(4b). Climb the wall to a sloping ledge. Crawl through a chimney and ascend the groove and crack to a tree belay at the top.

Moving downstream from here for about 100 metres one comes to a steep face with a barrier of overhangs at head-height. This is *Wend Buttress*.

Above and left of *Wend Buttress* is a fairly scrappy wall - **Overgrown Buttress** which provided two routes, **Bucket and Spade Job** (VD, 1972), the groove system on the left, and **Compost Wall** (S, 1972), the corner on the right - feel inspired!!

Wend Buttress

This face is fairly attractive and is recognisable by a barrier of overhangs at head-height on the left-hand side and by a large chimney at the other end.

The Horror	15m	E3	★	1989

A couple of brutish bulges provide all the fun. Reasonable protection can be arranged with a selection of camming devices. Start below the prominent bulges at the left-hand end of the buttress.

(5c). Climb the wall to a ledge below and left of the lower bulge. Launch out rightwards over this and finally tackle the overhanging wall above.

Savage Rib	15m	HVS	★	1986

Enjoyable gymnastics without the ferocity of *The Horror*. Start just right of *The Horror* under the lowest bulge.

(5b). Climb up to and straight over this bulge. Move right to gain the rib and follow this to a tree belay at the top.

One of the World's Many Problems	15m	HVS	★	1972

An enjoyable pitch whose main problem lies in getting off the ground! Start below and right of the corner-crack at 5 metres.

(5b). A hard pull over the bulge gains the corner which is followed to a tree belay at the top.

Cream Cracker Wall	20m	HVS		1970

A worrying climb which weaves its way up the wall to the right. Start 3 metres right of *One of the World's Many Problems*, at the next jagged protruding vein of rock.

(5a). Use the vein to gain a slab above then move left and climb the steep wall on flaky holds. A rightwards traverse on suspect rock gains a long ledge. Climb the steepening wall above to a heathery landing just left of the twin-stemmed birch tree.

Trundle Wall		18m	VS		1971

(4c). Climb the wide crack immediately left of a steep mossy slab to reach a sloping ledge. The steep upper wall leads to an awkward heathery landing between the two trees at the top of the buttress.

Pseudonym		13m	S		1971

Start at a wide groove at the right end of a smooth mossy wall.
Climb the wide groove then make a rising traverse right above bulges. Finish up the wall above.

Swing Off		12m	E3		1978

A bold and commiting lead. Start below and right of the obvious large bulges.
(5c). Climb the short cracks then cut loose up and left over the bulge to gain easier territory above.

Al's Chimney		10m	HS		1970

(4b). Climb the obvious dirty chimney at the right-hand end of the buttress.

Some 200 metres downstream of *Wend Buttress*, a steep path drops down the hillside to meet the riverside path. This path comes down from the approach path leading to *Cave* and *Wirewalk Buttresses* in the vicinity of a copse of conifers and provides the quickest approach to the next two buttresses, *HFL Buttress* and *Evening Buttress*, which are located on either side of this path at its junction with the path running along the west bank of the River Eden.

HFL Buttress

Located on the upstream side of the junction of the paths, this is a small compact buttress whose main feature is a prominent right-facing corner. A vegetated ledge extends along the lower part of the crag some 3 metres above ground level.

Scorpion		9m	HVS		1986

Start at the left end of the vegetated ledge at a short wide crack.
(5b). Climb the crack to a shelf and pull right onto the face. Follow the left edge of the face to an awkward bulging sting in the tail.

Mij		9m	S		1972

Start on the ledge below a groove which contains a tree low down.
Climb the groove.

| **Electric Avenue** | 15m | HVS | ★ ★ | 1986 |

A sustained and well-protected outing. Start on the ledge below the impending front face of the buttress.

(5b). Climb straight up past a square-cut nick and over several overlaps.

| **Cellnet** | 15m | E1 | | 1987 |

Start below the big right-facing corner of *Teragram*.

(5b). Climb the corner until it is possible to move left onto the hanging rib. Follow this with a hard move to reach the birch tree at the top.

| **Teragram** | 15m | S | | 1972 |

Gain and follow the big right-facing corner to a loose finish.

| **Lip Service** | 15m | VS | ★ | 1986 |

Start below the right edge of the slab which extends out rightwards from *Teragram*.

(4c). Climb the edge of the slab then a short flake-crack gaining the left end of an overlap. Traverse right on the lip to a sapling and finish straight up.

| **The Neighbourhood Bully** | 12m | E1 | ★ | 1987 |

A gymnastic little pitch – a bit of a toughie. Start directly below the sapling on the traverse of *Lip Service*.

(5b). Climb easily to the big roof and thug over this - good holds lead to the sapling. Finish direct.

Evening Buttress

This is a small overgrown buttress on the downstream side of the junction of the paths.

| **Jamboree** | 6m | S | | 1972 |

Climb the jamming crack on the left side of the buttress.

| **Moonlight Sonata** | 7m | HS | | 1972 |

Climb the groove right of *Jamboree* to a niche and a vegetated finish.

| **Sunflower** | 6m | VS | | 1988 |

(4c). Climb the clean rib to the right of *Moonlight Sonata* to a tricky finish.

Aviator's Buttress

This is the small buttress that lies a short distance downstream from *Evening Buttress* and is set well back from the path. In appearance it consists of a flat vertical wall split by several horizontal breaks. Towards the left-hand side of the buttress is a vertical vein of rock which runs the full height of the crag.

The Right Stuff		8m	E1			1987

Start 2 metres right of a large detached block at the left-hand side of the buttress.

(5b). Climb a flake-crack to a bulge. Pass this using the tree above to finish.

The Cockpit		8m	VS			1987

(4c). Climb the prominent crack 5 metres right of the detached block.

Red Square Dare		11m	E1			1987

Start further right, below a crack in the overhang.

(5a). Climb the crack in the overhang to gain a niche. From here, step left onto a bulge, then climb the wall above direct.

Gumbo Buttress

This is the next buttress encountered downstream in about 5-10 minutes walk from *Aviator's Buttress*. It is reached by a short steep scramble up the hillside. The main feature is an unclimbed right-slanting corner bounded on the right by a steep and attractive slab. A superb dry cave is located under the crag, to the left of the corner.

Look to the Future; It's Only Just Begun		24m	HVS			1973

This climb finds a way up the steep but relatively broken wall, 6 metres left of the obvious corner. Start below a small tree.

(5a). Climb the rib and move right to the tree. The wall above is climbed with a mantelshelf onto a ledge providing the crux. Move rightwards up ledges to a short wall and circumnavigate it by devious moves left, then right, along ledges. Climb a short groove above to finish at a tree.

Gumbo Variations		18m	HVS			1972

Start at the foot of the obvious corner.

(5a). Climb the corner until it is possible to hand-traverse leftwards across the left wall and onto the front of the buttress. Traverse left and climb up to a tree belay. Climb the corner above to finish.

Sisyphus	21m	VS		1972

Start to the right of the obvious corner and beyond the smooth slabs, below a cleaned corner.

(4c). Climb the wall to a ledge. Move right to pass a tree and move back left to stand on a jammed block. Gain the ledge above and move right to another ledge. A ramp on the left is gained with difficulty. Follow this to an escape on the right and a tree belay.

Isolated Buttress

This is a tall impressive buttress which rises directly above the good riverside footpath less than 100 metres downstream of *Gumbo Buttress*. The rock is very soft millet grain sandstone which does improve the higher one climbs. However the blocky nature of the upper face is also potentially hazardous. The main feature of the buttress is a long corner-crack which is the line of *Catastrophe Corner*.

J.J.	18m	VS		1972

(4b). Climb the corner to the left of *Catastrophe Corner*.

Catastrophe Corner	24m	HVS		1972

Scramble up to the foot of the buttress below the corner-crack.

(4c). Climb loose rock to a ledge below the steep crack. Climb the crack to a sloping ledge and continue up a narrow chimney which leads to a small ledge on the right. Move right to the top.

Rat Salad	30m	HVS		1972

The upper face is seamed by a central groove which has two branches. This climb gains the right-hand groove from the left. Start 6 metres left of a small cave.

1   15m (4c). Climb up and right to a large ledge. Traverse right (peg runner advised) and mantelshelf onto a ledge. Climb the wall above to another ledge and move right to a belay.

2   15m (4c). The groove above is quit in favour of the loose right-slanting wall.

Bolted Variation Start 1972

Included for historical interest – this was made using ring bolts and wooden dowels – never repeated and probably never will be.

Insanity Groove		24m	VS		1972

Start below the corner at the right-hand side of the buttress.

(4c). Climb an awkward wall to gain the foot of the corner. Climb the corner with care, negotiating a small overhang to reach a ledge. Continue up the loose corner to the top.

The Walls

These are a series of small faces extending downstream from *Isolated Buttress* as far as the big meander in the river which is dominated by the huge face of *Red Rock* on the opposite bank. Below the face, just before the meander, is a low cave which has metal boat-mooring ring embedded in the rock nearby.

Gone		12m	S		1974

Start to the right of a V-groove which cuts through the roof above the cave. Climb directly towards a large oak at 6 metres but, before reaching the tree, traverse horizontally left and make a hard move over an overlap. Move up past a small larch and scramble off.

Two other climbs were made hereabouts, **Mr Woo** (S, 1974) and **The Gripe** (VS, 1974), but a recent earthslip has obliterated them.

Going downstream from here, the large face of **Red Rock** on the far bank is most impressive and has been ascended in one place but no record exists. Further downstream on the west bank, beyond an open meadow, is the tall pillar of **Cat Clint**. Some routes have been climbed here but not recorded.

Scratchmere Scar

Grid Reference: **NY 516 380**   Altitude: **220m**
Faces: **South-West**   Approach: **10 mins**

The southerly aspect of this small crag of immaculate Penrith sandstone and its fine position above a wooded slope looking across the surrounding countryside to the Lake District Fells makes for a delectable venue. The climbing is on several buttresses never more than 11 metres high and is always steep, but good holds tend to be plentiful in the form of pockets and flakes. The routes are varied, mainly in the easy to middle grades but with a few harder test-pieces and some bouldering. The crag is quick to dry and numerous trees provide good belays at the top.

Approach:

Scratchmere Scar is best approached from the A6 at Plumpton about 7km North of Penrith (leave M6 at Junction 41 and follow the A6 northwards). From Plumpton, take the B6413 road towards Lazonby and, after 2km uphill, the crag will be seen in amongst the trees across to the left, above Scratchmere Scar Farm. Follow the farm track down to the farm and park in the car park near the farm.

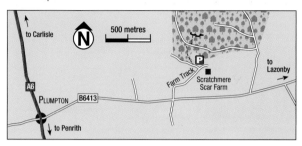

The crag is owned by Marshall's plc and the car park has been built by Messrs Atkinson, the farmers at Scratchmere Scar, as part of a mountain bike downhill centre located in the woods. Climbers owe a debt of gratitude to them for enabling access to the crag – please put some money in the honesty box!

- Marshall's plc and Messrs Atkinson accept no responsibility for anyone entering the land and those entering do so at their own risk.
- It is essential to park in the car park, and not to block any access required by the farmer.
- No dogs should be taken to the crag.
- Fire precautions should be stringently observed.
- Follow posts directing climbers up to the crag.
- There are quarrying activities up and to the right of the crag and climbers should not stray from the area of the crag, ie that stretching from *Sycamore Buttress* to *The Far Rocks*.

To reach the crag, from the left end of the car park follow a path which leads up through the wood to meet a forest road. Turn right along the road and, after 35 metres, follow the path up to the crag. A steep ascent leads to the foot of *Birch Tree Buttress*.

The best **descent** is to the left.

The routes are described from **left** to **right**.

Scratchmere Scar Sycamore Buttress

1	First of Many	VD		5	Side by Side	VD *
2	Life's Problems	E1 **		v4	Over and Under	VD
3	Skeet	VD *		6	The Arête	S *
v1	Skeet Direct	HS		7	Sidelock	D *
v2	Skeeter	HS *		8	Choke	M *
4	Pheasant Groove	D **		9	Boxlock	D
v3	The Famous Grouse	HS		10	Herne	HVS **

Photo: Ron Kenyon

Sycamore Buttress

The buttress at the extreme left-hand end of the crag has a large sycamore tree growing close to its centre.

1	**First of Many**	8m	VD		2005

From the extreme left-hand of the crag, ascend left of the gully to the ledge and move right to climb the front face to finish.

2	**Life's Problems**	8m	E1+	★★	2008

(5c). This accepts the challenge of the wall left of *Skeet*. Athletic moves using holds in the breaks lead up the wall. Lack of friction on the wall gives an added problem.

Left: Michael Kenyon finds one of **Life's Problems** (E1), on the first ascent at Scratchmere Scar. **Photo:** Ron Kenyon

3 **Skeet**	9m	VD	★	

Start at the foot of a tall cave-like recess and gain the sloping shelf on the right. Climb the corner on the right (*Pheasant Groove*) until a swing left on a ledge leads into the upper gully. Finish up the cracked arête on the right taking care with potentially loose blocks.

v1   **Skeet Direct** 8m HS
Climb the crack just right of *Life's Problems*.

v2   **Skeeter** 8m HS ★
Instead of moving right into *Pheasant Groove*, climb the short wall direct.

4 **Pheasant Groove**	8m	D	★★	

A very enjoyable climb. Start below a finger-crack immediately left of the protruding block.

Climb the crack and corner above to a good ledge and finish up the corner on good holds.

v3   **The Famous Grouse** 8m HS 1997
Start up *Pheasant Groove* but climb the face of the pillar between *Skeet* and *Pheasant Groove*.

5 **Side by Side**	8m	VD	★	

Climb the steep wide crack and finish up the short rectangular chimney.

v4   **Over And Under** 8m VD
Start immediately behind the big sycamore.

Climb steeply up cracks to a chimney recess. Move right and climb the short rectangular chimney of *Side by Side*.

6 **The Arête**	8m	S	★	

A delicate climb.

Start just right of the arête and climb its right side using it for the left hand throughout.

7 **Sidelock**	8m	D	★	

Climb the chockstone chimney as for *Choke* until a horizontal crack is reached on the left wall. Swing left on this and pull up to good holds in the next horizontal break. Climb the cracked wall above to the overhang and move left to finish as for *The Arête*.

8 **Choke**	8m	M	★	

Climb the chockstone chimney.

Scratchmere Scar
Leaning Tower and Birch Tree Buttress

8	Choke	M	*
9	Boxlock	D	
10	Herne	HVS	**
11	Schrodinger's Cat	E1	*
12	Blondie	E1	**
13	Leyline	VD	*

14	Extraction	HVS	*
15	Out of the Dark	MS	*
16	Peanuts	E5	**
v1	Into the Light	E2	*
v2	Charlie Brown	E2	**
17	Stormy Petteril	VS	**
18	Overdose	NL	*
19	The Black Streak	E2	**
20	Milligram	E1	**

Photo: Ron Kenyon

Itchmere Nose	8m	VS		2010

(5a). Tackle the overhanging rib between *Choke* and *Boxlock* with help from a foothold out on *The Arête*. Alternatively, from below the rib, move onto the right wall then climb up to move left onto and up the rib to finish.

9 **Boxlock**	8m	D		

Start below the right-hand break of the bay and climb the recessed groove to a ledge and finish to the right of a protruding block.

Leaning Tower

This monolithic block has a fine off-width crack splitting its front face (*Blondie*). The upper part of the face is cut by a wide ledge below the capping overhang.

10 **Herne**	9m	HVS	★ ★	1981

A really good climb worth hunting out – bold with a spectacular finish. A Friend 2 is useful.

(5a). Start in the gully, move right to the arête and climb this on its left side.

Scratchmere Scar Birch Tree Buttress Right

15	Out of the Dark	MS *	20	Milligram	E1 **
16	Peanuts	E5 **	21	Scratch	E4 **
v1	Into the Light	E2 **	22	Greta's Climb	MVS **
v2	Charlie Brown	E2 **	v3	Greta's Climb Direct	MVS **
17	Stormy Petteril	VS **	23	Don't Worry	VS
18	Overdose	NL *	24	Be Happy	MVS
19	The Black Streak	E2 **	25	High Squeeze	VD

Photo: Ron Kenyon

11 **Schrodinger's Cat**	10m	E1+	★	1997

(5c). Start just left of *Blondie* and climb up and left to the arête, which is ascended on its right side. Pull over the roof onto the ledge and finish direct.

12 **Blondie**	10m	E1-	★★	1970s

(5a). Climb the perplexing off-width crack with speed and determination - a Friend 5 (or two) helps one's determination enormously. From the ledge, pull directly over the overhang to finish.

13 **Leyline**	14m	VD	★	

A traditional classic following a totally illogical series of weaknesses up a steep section of rock.

Starting as for *Blondie*, move rightwards up a glacis and ascend a short corner to a sycamore tree. Step delicately left until the good shelf is gained and traverse left along this to the left-hand end of the overhangs. Excellent holds enable the bulge above to be overcome.

Right: Alan Davis on **Blondie** (E1), Scratchmere Scar. **Photo:** Steve Goodwin

Birch Tree Buttress

This is the main central buttresses and projects out of the hillside.

| 14 **Extraction** | 10m | HVS- | ★ | |

(5a). Start from an embedded flake and climb the arête on flat holds to a recess below an overhang. Continue up the rib above via a square hole.

| 15 **Out of the Dark** | 14m | MS | ★ | 1970s |

A climb with a steep start but a sympathetic conclusion.

Starting at the left arête, pull up steeply and struggle onto the top of the flake. Traverse right to a corner by the birch and climb up to gain a ledge (possible stance and belay). Finish up the shallow corner on the left.

| 16 **Peanuts** | 11m | E5 | ★ ★ | 1983 |

This climb accepts the challenge of the awesome roof at the top left of the buttress. Start just right of the left arête.

(6b). Climb onto the top of the flake and gain a small ledge above. The middle of the steep wall is climbed on small holds (harder for the short) to the horizontal break beneath the roof. Overcome the roof in the centre and finish up the wall above.

v1 *Into the Light* 13m E2 ★ 1985

(5c). Follow *Peanuts* to the roof and traverse left under the roof to finish up the top of *Extraction*.

v2 *Charlie Brown* 12m E2- ★ ★

(5c). Gain the top of a block below the shallow left-facing corner.

Above: Sue Kettle heads **Into the Light** (E2), Scratchmere Scar. **Photo:** Euan Turner

Climb the corner and, when below a small overlap, move out right to gain the obvious slanting crack of *Stormy Petteril* to finish.

17 **Stormy Petteril**		12m	VS+	★ ★	1970s

A fine climb with a slippery feel to the rock in the higher section. Start directly below the big birch tree on the face.

(5a). Climb the vertical fist-wide crack to gain the ledge. Easy rock leads right until a swing left on smooth holds gains the fine left-slanting crack above.

To the right of the birch is a smooth wall split by a central groove. The wall is capped by a small roof and provides four short but technical climbs on impeccable rock:

18 **Overdose**			6c	★	Not Led

Climb the wall just left of the central groove to the roof. The wall above the roof is green-streaked and provides a desperate sequence involving long reaches and some pretty nifty footwork.

19 **The Black Streak**		6m	E2	★ ★	1980s

(6a). Climb the central groove to the roof and surmount this to finish up the shallow dimpled black-streaked scoop.

20 **Milligram**		6m	E1	★ ★	

A magic route.

(5b). Start just right of the central groove and climb to the roof. Gain the flake and proceed carefully to the top.

21 **Scratch**		7m	E4	★ ★	1980s

Sustained and devoid of runners – a very high highball boulder problem.

(6b). Climb the right-hand side of the arête to a horizontal pod at half-height. From the pod, move slightly rightwards up the steep wall above.

22 **Greta's Climb**		11m	MVS+	★ ★	1970s

Strenuous and a bit bold with a superb finish.

(4c). Start from the top of the pedestal block and layback boldly up the flake-crack to gain the large ledge. Reach a good horizontal break in the smooth wall above then swing excitingly rightwards along this to reach a groove and good finishing holds. A more direct line to finish can be made to the knob at the top (5a).

Overleaf: Pete Gunn under a blue sky on **Milligram** (E1), Scratchmere Scar.
Photo: Pete Gunn Collection

23 **Don't Worry**	9m	VS		1988

    (4c). Climb a groove to the cave then finish directly or rightwards.

24 **Be Happy**	9m	MVS		1988

Rather contrived but still worthwhile. Start to the left of the large birch tree.
    (4b). Climb the wall behind the tree using a thin crack and the right-hand edge of the cave. The block at the top is of dubious stability.

25 **High Squeeze**	9m	VD		2008

    Climb the chimney-crack just right of *Be Happy*.

The Block

To the right the crag is broken for about 10 metres until a fine isolated pillar-like block lies below and just left of a massive oak.

The left arête with a sitting start gives a good **6b/c** top-rope problem.

Spiral Stairs	7m	S	★ ★	

Easier for the tall! A bold route starting at an embedded block at the foot of the pillar.
    Move up and rightwards on ledges to gain and finish up the steep right arete.

Scratchmere Buttress

This is a fairly extensive buttress which is hard to view as a whole – it can be identified by a barrier of overhangs at the bottom and another at the top of the crag. To the left of the gully is a rib which fades into a steep upper wall immediately left of the big oak tree.

26 **Hesitation**	7m	VS		1988

    (5a). Climb the rib to the left of the open gully until a tricky move on the wall above leads to a swing left and good finishing holds.

27 **John's Climb**	8m	HS	★ ★	1970s

An intriguing climb with an exciting finale on good handholds.
    From a flat rock ledge, make a stiff pull over the overhang and move left onto a slab then up to a ledge. The rib above has a shallow cracked groove on its right - climb it.

Scratchmere Scar Scratchmere Buttress

26	Hesitation	VS		v1	Get Close	VS *
27	John's Climb	HS **		30	Jam Today	HS
28	Fitch	VD *		31	Hob	D
29	No Comebacks	HVS *				

| 28 **Fitch** | 8m | VD | ★ | |

Start just right of the bottom barrier of overhangs and climb right-wards and up a block corner to a big ledge. Pull out and right onto the front of the rib, gain good footholds, then finish with pleasant climbing on good holds.

| 29 **No Comebacks** | 8m | HVS+ | ★ | 1988 |

The fine finger-crack in the upper front wall gives a good challenge.
(5b). Start from a pedestal at chest height and climb the *Problem Wall* to the big ledge. Bridge up the corner above then left to the roof and pull left into the finger-crack which is followed to the top.

v1 *Get Close* 7m VS ★ 1988
(5a). Follow *No Comebacks* to the roof but pull round up to the right and finish up a short jamming crack.

| 30 **Jam Today** | 7m | HS | | 1988 |

(4c). Climb the wide crack and move left over the bulge to finish as for *Fitch*.

| 31 **Hob** | 6m | D | | |

Climb the steep gully taking care with potentially dangerous blocks.

Home Buttress

The wall and arête immediately right of the corner of *Hob* and its more broken continuation rightwards.

| 32 **Home Sweet Home** | 6m | HVS | | 1988 |

(5b). Climb the steep wall to the right of *Hob* (and just left of the arête) to an awkward sloping finish.

| 33 **Bobbery** | 6m | VS | ★ | |

(4c). Climb the arête easily until it steepens, where a short sharp section on small finger holds leads to an easier finish.

Scratchmere Scar Home Buttress

31	Hob	D
32	Home Sweet Home	HVS
33	Bobbery	VS *
34	The Cheesepress	D *
35	Manics of a Different Breed	VS

Photo: Ron Kenyon

34 **The Cheesepress**		7m	D	★	

Start to the right of the arête below a steep flake-crack then finish easily up the enjoyable crack.

35 **Manics of a Different Breed**		7m	VS+		2008

(5a). Climb up broken rock to a wall and climb this just left of its right arête.

The Far Rocks

About 100 metres right of and level with *Home Buttress* are the *Far Rocks*, a bouldering area which is well worth carting your mat along to.

1 **Stew's Eliminate**			V2-	★	

Sitting start. From a low rail, climb the bulging green wall at the left end of the buttress, without using the flake on the right.

2 **Stew's Flake**			V2		

Sitting start. Climb the surprisingly awkward twin flake-cracks to a ledge.

3 **The Aspirant**			V6	★★	2007

A great natural line, baffling start and gripping finish makes this a fine proposition.

Scratchmere Scar The Far Rocks

1	Stew's Eliminate	V2 *	7	Bonsai Pineline	V2 *
2	Stew's Flake	V2	8	The Way of the Pine	V1
3	The Aspirant	V6 **	9	A Leap of Pine	V1
4	Snap Away	V0	10	Quality Street	V3 **
5	Crack Away	V0			
6	Wilson Way	V1			

Photo: Ron Kenyon

Climb the shallow groove direct to the roof, step left and continue up the groove above to finish. Awesome.

4 **Snapaway**		V0-		

Climb the wall on superb holds.

5 **Crackaway**		V0-		

Climb the crack.

6 **Wilson Way**		V1		

Climb the wall left of the prow.

7 **Bonsai Pineline**		V2	★	

Sitting start. Climb the right side of the prow, finishing right of the two bonsai pines.

8 **The Way of the Pine**		V1		

An interesting line just right of *Bonsai Pipeline*.

9 **A Leap of Pine**		V1		

Dyno from the first break to reach the second break and finish up the wall above.

10 **Quality Street**		V3	★ ★	

Start as for *Bonsai Pineline* then hand-traverse the rounded ledge rightwards and top out at the right end of the buttress. Quality!

Cowraik Quarry

Grid Reference: **NY 541 309**   Altitude: **200m**
Faces: **South**   Approach: **5 mins**

This sandstone quarry lies on the eastward spur of Beacon Hill, above the town of Penrith. It is nowhere more than 7 metres high but provides a useful bouldering area, with a rope being useful on some of the longer problems. The quarry is a site of geological interest due to the "duning effect" seen in the rock. Set amidst sandy banks, grassy knolls and towering scots pines, the rocks are a very pleasant place to spend an hour or two – however the rock tends to be snappy, especially in cracks, and care needs to be taken.

Approach:

From the A66/A6 roundabout just south of Penrith, follow the A686 Alston road through the village of Carleton. After about 3 km a road joins

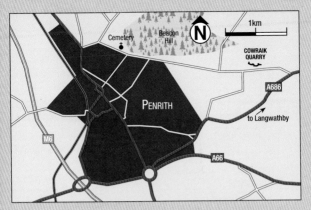

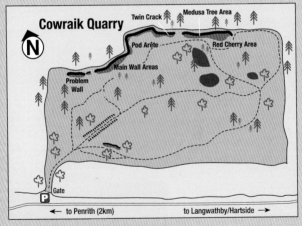

the A686 from the left, signposted to the Golf Course. Turn onto this, with the steep wooded slope of Gibbet Hill on the right. After 400 metres some buildings will be seen on the left-hand side of the road. Just beyond these, at a slight bend, there is a gated lane on the right and a layby to park in. Walk up the lane until it bends right then strike up the left one of three paths. This goes steeply uphill, parallel to the walled field on the left, and brings one to a level area at the left-hand end of the quarry. A path to the right meets a network of paths beneath the quarry walls. The first rock visible through the trees on the left from this path is *California Wall*. The quarry is owned by Eden District Council and no access problems exist.

California Wall

This steep and rather featureless wall has an overlap just above head height. There used to be a climb here called *Yosemite Wall* which has fallen down leaving a loose groove – not quite up to its more famous namesake!

Problem Wall

This lies 10 metres to the right of *California Wall* and is a rectangular wall about 3 metres high. It provides some amusing problems with awkward finishes.

1	**Gratir Pissage**		V0-	

Climb the left end of the wall using a thin crack for the left-hand to pass a pink scar.

2	**White Snake**		V2	

Climb the centre of the wall above the biggest overlap.

3	**Problem Wall**		V0	

Climb the wall in the line of a downward-pointing flake with big layaways to finish.

4	**Pis En Lit**		V0-	

Climb the wall on a vertical sequence of layaways to finish just left of a groove.

A number of traverses have been made – all V1.

Cowraik Quarry
Problem Wall

1	Gratir Pissage	V0
2	White Snake	V2
3	Problem Wall	V0
4	Pis En Lit	V0

Photo: Ron Kenyon

Main Wall and Arêtes Area

Fifteen metres right of *Problem Wall*, the *Main Wall* is steep and seamed by a fine thin crack at its left end and some vaguer lines further right. A steep shallow corner marks the division of *Main Wall* from the *Arêtes Area*. The *Arêtes Area* consists of four corners with intervening walls and arêtes. The second corner has a large pine tree on a ledge at mid-height, above and to the left of it. The rock on *Main Wall* is snappy and requires care but it improves in the *Arêtes Area*.

1	**Udder Crack**		VO-		

Climb the thin cracks 2 metres from the left end of the wall past a niche and up loose rock to finish.

2	**Sacred Cow**	6m	VS	★	

(4c). Climb the continuous thin vertical crack.

3	**Holy Cow**	6m	HVS	★	

Start 2 metres right of the continuous finger-crack.

(4c). Climb the scruffy right-slanting groove and move left up a slanting overlap to a ledge. The wall above is climbed direct via twin cracks.

Cowraik Main Wall and Arêtes Area

1	Udder Crack	VO
2	Sacred Crack	VS *
3	Holy Cow	HVS *
4	What's Coming Up?	HVS
5	Pie in the Sky	HVS
6	Cow Pie	VS
7	The Arête	VS
8	Deadend Groove	VS
9	Jughandle	MVS **
10	Aunt Aggie	VS
11	Scots Pine	MS *
12	Pine Wall	V2 **
13	Dirty Dave	V1 **
14	Desperate Dan	S
15	Tom Thumb	V2 **

Photo: Phil Rigby

| 4 | What's Coming Up? | | 7m | HVS | | |

Should be called "What's Coming Off?"!

(5a). Climb directly up a flaky cracked wall until it is possible to step right onto a small ledge. Move left and climb the thin crack in the wall above.

| 5 | Pie in the Sky | | 7m | HVS | | |

(5b). Climb directly up and over an overlap to gain and climb a groove.

| 6 | Cow Pie | | 6m | VS | | |

(5a). Climb the undercut shallow corner at the right end of *Main Wall*.

To the right of *Main Wall* is a series of corners and arêtes – the *Arêtes Area*.

| 7 | The Arête | | 5m | VS | | |

(4b). Climb the left-hand arête on good holds to an overhang. Finish up a slim groove on the right.

| 8 | Deadend Groove | | 6m | VS | | |

(4c). Climb the loose groove.

| 9 | Jughandle | | 7m | MVS | ★★ | |

(4c). Only one hard move and then only for dwarfs – but it's near the top! Start at a very thin crack in the middle of the fine wall and climb directly on good holds with an interesting move to reach the finishing jug on the left.

Above: Guidebook writer Ron Kenyon finding a **Jughandle** (MVS), Cowraik Quarry.
Photo: Michael Kenyon

A large scots pine grows on a ledge at mid-height and impinges on the next two routes.

10 **Aunt Aggie**		6m	VS	

(4c). Climb the groove just left of the pine to finish up the cracked wall on the left.

11 **Scots Pine**		6m	MS	★

(4a). Climb the big groove to the pine and finish easily above.

12 **Pine Wall**			V2	★★

Climb the right wall of the groove, rather precariously, to gain and climb a high finger-crack.

13 **Dirty Dave**			V1	★★

Climb the fine arête, starting with a technical layaway or a leap to gain a good hold, then finish up the arête above.

14 **Desperate Dan**		5m	S	

Climb the steep corner and ledges on the left, to finish up a loose groove in the left-hand wall.

15 **Tom Thumb**			V2	★★

Climb the arête right of *Desperate Dan* direct. Alternatively, after a few moves, move right to gain and climb a thin crack-line, without use of holds to the right, to gain a good hold back on the arête.

Prunesquallor			V3	★

This low-level girdle of the *Main Wall* and *Arêtes Area* provides an interesting excursion. The move around the arête of *Dirty Dave* is the crux.

Pod Area

The best rock in the quarry is found above a grassy area just to the right of the *Arêtes Area*. A horizontal break (the *Pod*) is a central feature of the upper part of the face.

Right: Michael Kenyon traversing the Pod Area, Cowraik Quarry.
Photo: Ron Kenyon

Cowraik Pod Area

1	Gorse	V0 *
2	Off the Wall	V1 *
3	Broom	V0 **

4	Bedknobs	V3 **
5	Broomsticks	V1 **
6	Off the Handle	V3 *
7	Brambles	V0
8	Brambles Arête	V0 *

Photo: Phil Rigby

| 1 | **Gorse** | | V0 | ★ | |

Climb the diagonal groove-line up left.

| 2 | **Off the Wall** | | V1 | ★ | |

Start as for *Gorse* and take a direct line up the wall.

| 3 | **Broom** | | V0 | ★★ | |

Climb the crack to gain the *Pod* then move slightly left and finish up the fine little crack above on improving holds.

| 4 | **Bedknobs** | | V3 | ★★ | |

Climb directly up to the centre of the *Pod* then climb the wall above rightwards to the top.

| 5 | **Broomsticks** | | V1 | ★★ | |

Climb the crack on the right of the jammed block then gain a crack up to the left and finish up this.

| 6 | **Off the Handle** | | V3 | ★ | |

Climb the initial crack as for *Broomsticks* and finish up the wall to the right of the upper crack.

| 7 | **Brambles** | | V0- | | |

Climb the crack to the right of the jammed block and move up the groove above or finish up *Bramble Arête*.

| 8 | **Bramble Arête** | | V0- | ★ | |

Climb the arête right of *Brambles*.

| | **Prickles** | | V1 | ★ ★ | |

A well used low-level traverse from the left side of the wall to the wedged block on the right of *Brambles*.

To the right the quarry falls back in a big bay.

Twin Cracks Area

Twin Cracks Area is located to the right of the big bay. A very big birch tree grows above a corner. The rock to the left of the birch is loose and unattractive but to the right of the corner is a short slabby wall with, at right-angles to it, a longer steeper wall with a barrier of overhangs low down (almost at ground level on the left). The front of this longer steeper wall has two slim parallel cracks running up the middle of it and gives some good problems (though blinkers may be required). The grades given assume sitting starts.

| 1 | **4.57** | | V1 | | |

Climb the wall left of *Ordinary Route*.

| 2 | **Ordinary Route** | | 4b | | |

Climb the crack to the left of the corner with the birch above it.

| 3 | **Cracked Slab** | | 3b | | |

Start at the arête and climb this via a good slanting crack on the left to a ledge. Finish up the slab on the left moving towards the big birch.

| 4 | **Mungo is Angry** | | V2 | ★ | 2003 |

From a sitting start in the hole under the roof, traverse left using the diagonal break. Move round onto *Cracked Slab* and finish back right. Very satisfying.

5 **Mungo Direct**		V4	★	2003

Start as for *Mungo is Angry* but move directly up the short wall above on crimps. Height dependent.

6 **Fine Tuned**		V0		

Climb the thin crack.

7 **Where the Wild Things Are**		V4	★	

Climb the wall to gain a hold just below the overlap.

8 **Pot Black**		V2	★	2003

Climb the left-hand of the *Twin Cracks*.

9 **Twin Cracks**		V0-	★	

Climb the *Twin Cracks*.

10 **Neanderthal Crack**		V3		2003

The right-hand *Twin Crack*.

Lurch up the thin crack on fingertip jams, without use of *The Vixen* flake on the right.

11 **The Vixen**		V0	★	

Climb the left-facing layback crack, avoiding the use of a convenient ledge on the right below the roof.

Cowraik Twin Cracks Area

1	4.57	V1
2	Ordinary Route	4b
3	Cracked Slab	3b
4	Mungo Is Angry	V2 *

5	Mungo Direct	V4 *
6	Fine Tuned	V0
7	Where the Wild Things Are	V4 *
8	Pot Black	V2 *
9	Twin Cracks	V0 *
10	Neanderthal Crack	V3
11	The Vixen	V0 *
12	The Ferret	V0 *
13	The Polecat	V0 *
14	The Fox	V0

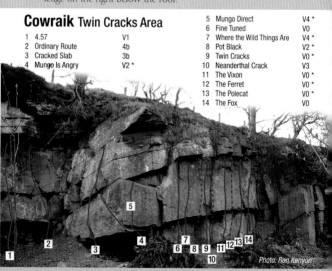

Photo: Ron Kenyon

| 12 **The Ferret** | | V0 | ★ | |

Starting one metre right of *The Vixen*, pull out right onto a good side-pull and surmount the overlap to gain a protruding hold at the top of the wall.

| 13 **The Polecat** | | V0- | ★ | |

Climb the faint break direct to the sawn off tree at the top of the wall.

| 14 **The Fox** | | V0 | | |

Climb the wall 4 metres right of *Twin Cracks*.

| **Upstairs** | | V0 | ★ | |

Traverse from *Cracked Slab* to *The Fox* with hands and feet above the roof.

| **Downstairs** | | V3 | ★ | |

The same as *Upstairs*, but this time with hands and feet below the roof – in either direction.

About 50 metres east of *Twin Cracks Area* is another shallow pit containing an extensive wall.

Above: Michael Kenyon cruising **Mungo Direct** (V4), Cowraik Quarry. **Photo:** Ron Kenyon

Cowraik Medusa Tree-Red Cherry Area

1	Stoneface	HS	8	Who Dares Might Win	HVS
2	Permian Face	E2	9	Pegleg	HVS
3	Medusa	HS	10	Virgin	HVS
4	The Gorgon	HS	11	Nenah Cherry	V5 *
5	Keaton Wall	VS	12	Red Cherry	V1 *
6	The Mirror	VS	13	Black Cherry	V2 **
7	Climb at Your Peril	VS	14	The End	S

Photo: Phil Rigby

Medusa Tree – Red Cherry Area

The rock here is somewhat loose in places and should be treated with care. On the left of the area is a steep wall and a prow of rock pointing leftwards. To the right the face is guarded by a barrier of overhangs at approximately head-height, the most obvious feature hereabouts being the left-facing bottomless layback crack of *Red Cherry*.

1	**Stoneface**		6m	HS		

Start 2 metres right of the extreme left-hand side of the wall.
Climb over the overlap and follow the line of cracks to an overgrown finish.

2	**Permian Face**		6m	E2		

(5c). Climb the wall midway between *Stoneface* and *Medusa*.

3	**Medusa**		7m	HS		

Climb the left-facing flake-crack that runs up the face to the right of the line of overlaps. Finish at the *Medusa Tree*.

Right: Michael Kenyon gets to grips with **Neneh Cherry** (V5), Cowraik Quarry.
Photo: Ron Kenyon

| 4 | **The Gorgon** | 6m | HS | | |

Climb the crack to the right of *Medusa*. An elder adds to the complications.

| 5 | **Keaton Wall** | 6m | VS | | |

(5a). Starting one metre right of *The Gorgon*, climb directly to the bulge and ascend the wall above to the left of the yellow veneer. The holds are good but need careful handling.

| 6 | **The Mirror** | 5m | VS | | |

(4c). Climb up a slim crack to the overlap and ascend the cracked shallow groove above to a loose finish.

| 7 | **Climb at Your Peril** | 6m | VS | | |

(4b). Start at the foot of the corner leading into the cave between the prow of rock and the actual rock face, climb into the cave and exit to the left. Needless to say, take great care with the rock.

| 8 | **Who Dares Might Win** | 6m | HVS | | |

Start at the foot of the arête of the prow of rock.
(4c). Use good but loose layaways to reach and climb the middle of the front of the prow on loose holds - sounds really inviting!

| 9 | **Pegleg** | 6m | HVS | | |

(4c). Starting one metre right of the arête, climb the lower groove and then the horrendous-looking upper groove to finish at a tree.

| 10 | **Virgin** | 6m | HVS | | |

(5b). Climb the thin crack exiting right to finish below a huge scots pine.

| 11 | **Neneh Cherry** | | V5 | ★ | 2003 |

Sustained and fingery. Start 2 metres left of *Red Cherry*.
From the break under the roof pull rightwards onto the wall left of *Red Cherry*. Now traverse left on smears and crimps to finish at the finger crack of *Virgin*.

| 12 | **Red Cherry** | | V1 | ★ | |

Start below the prominent bottomless flake-crack and gain and climb the crack to a recess above which is loose. Either continue or leap off.

| 13 | **Black Cherry** | | V2 | ★★ | 2003 |

Start below a hanging scoop at the extreme right-hand end of the wall.
Pull steeply into the grooved scoop and traverse the hanging slab thinly leftwards to finish at a sandy groove. Jump off or continue left with more difficulty into *Red Cherry*.

14 The End		5m	S		

Start one metre left of the right-hand end of the overlap.

Reach up for a good hold and keep moving right on good holds to finish on a heathery ledge below a bent pine tree.

In Search of the Chinaman			V2	★	

A continuously interesting low-level traverse. Start at *Medusa* and keep moving right to finish, strangely enough, at *The End*.

Climbs have been recorded at **The Otterstones** (NY 554 238), a small limestone crag tucked away in a secluded valley. Some of the routes are on excellent rock but popularity has eluded them.

King's Meaburn

Grid Reference: NY 618 213   Altitude: **150m**
Faces: West   Approach: **3 mins**

More properly known as **Jackdaw Scar**, this outcrop of variable quality carboniferous limestone atop a band of soft sandstone is situated just west of the village of King's Meaburn. It has an idyllic location above the River Lyvennet.

The crag comprises a series of bays forming a continuous wall. It is well sheltered by trees and, with its sunny location, is climbable throughout the year. The rock is generally good though care should be taken with brittle edges and occasional lichenous areas and substantial rock falls over the years testify to the instability of some sections. Ivy is prolific and has overgrown several routes.

Approach:

The village of King's Meaburn lies in the middle of the Penrith, Appleby and Shap triangle. In the village, just to the south of the White Horse Inn, a road drops down westwards to a ford and footbridge over the River Lyvennet. The crag is visible to the right above and left of a cottage. Park on the roadside and follow a path in front of the cottage and up to the crag to arrive at a massive beech tree in the *Third Bay*. The cottage is a holiday cottage - details on: www.lyvennetcottages.co.uk.

The following restrictions apply:
· No educational groups, except army groups, are allowed to climb at the crag.
· Parking is not allowed in front of the cottage or obstructing the road to the cottages.

- Approaches for toilets, water or other facilities to the inhabitants of the cottage should not be made.
- Climbing is not allowed to the right of the drystone wall, above the cottage.
- No excessive noise.
- Care should taken with the fence at the top of the crag and the field behind the crag should not be used.

Descents can be made by descending a path at the left of the crag or by abseiling from one of the trees (please use a sling).

The routes are described from **right** to **left**.

First Bay

A huge rockfall has affected this area which lies to the left of the drystone wall on the right of the crag.

Crippling Crack (S, the corner 10 metres right of *Titus Groan*) and **Flic-Flak Crack** (VS, the wide crack 6 metres right of *Titus Groan*) cannot be recommended.

Titus Again	12m	HVS		2004

The wall right of the cleft of *Titus Groan*.
    (5b). Move up steeply to gain a flake leading right to the arête, just above a large tree. Climb the arête moving left at the top.

Titus Groan	12m	E1		Mid '70s

(5a). The obvious cleft – adventurous due to the presence of several tons of "hanging death". Start in the corner of the bay and climb up the cleft. Using the right wall, bridge the left wall up to the overhang. Overcome the overhang and finish up the groove above.

Second Bay

This is the bay with a large beech tree growing on the path.

Titus Alone	12m	Ungradeable	1981

    (5b). Health warning job – climb the right-hand arête.

The ivy in the corner of the bay was once battled with to produce **Something to Remember** (VS, crack in right wall), **Toolie Corner** (MVS, in the corner) and **Curvy Crack** (VS, curving crack in the left wall). The ivy won.

King's Meaburn Main Wall

1	The Gebbeth	E1 *
2	Windkey	E3
3	Gont	E3 *

4	Leo's Line	E5 **
5	The Windeye	E5 **
6	Marik	HVS **
7	Celadon	E1 ^^
8	Havnor	VS *
9	Main Wall Traverse	E2 *

Photo: Ron Kenyon

Second Bay

Third Bay

| 1 | **The Gebbeth** | 14m | E1- | ★ | 1974 |

(5b). A steep little number just right of the left arête. Climb up to the roof, pass it, and continue up via discontinuous cracks to the top.

Third Bay

This is the main bay and arrival point at the crag. It has a continuous right wall.

| 2 | **Windkey** | 14m | E3 | | 1987 |

The stability of this route has been affected by the collapse of the sandstone base. Strenuous and technical.

(6a). Start at the foot of the right-hand arête. Climb the sandstone base to a ledge. Move up leftwards to a short thin crack and climb this (crux) to better holds and the wall above.

| 3 | **Gont** | 14m | E3 | ★ | 1980s |

This route has also been affected by the collapse of the sandstone base and has been reclimbed with a different start. Technically not too difficult, however the gear (or lack of it) leaves something to be desired.

(5b). Climb up the corner in the sandstone base to gain the upper wall and finish up the crack-line that leads up leftwards.

| 4 | **Leo's Line** | 14m | E5 | ★ ★ | Early '90s |

An audacious line up the centre of the wall.

(6a). Climb up through the overlap to gain the upper wall. Continue up the wall past a peg runner.

| 5 | **The Windeye** | 14m | E5 | ★ ★ | Late '80s |

This superb route tackles the overhang and wall right of *Marik*. Following the collapse of the sandstone base and disappearance of an in situ sling, it has increased in difficulty and seriousness. Start below a finger of rock beneath the main overlap.

(6a). Climb up to the roof, then move left through it, to gain the upper wall with the assistance of a thin crack above. Hard moves trend up and left into a very faint scoop. Finish diagonally rightwards on improving holds.

| 6 | **Marik** | 14m | HVS | ★ ★ | Early '70s |

A superb climb, unfortunately becoming polished due to its popularity. A large block came away from the base of the crack leaving a remaining block of dubious stability.

(5a). Overcome the sandstone base and gain the ledge. Move into the crack from the left and climb this to a ledge. Either finish directly, or move right, then back left again just below the top.

Above: Max Biden on **Marik** (HVS), at King's Meaburn. Photo: Shaw Brown.

King's Meaburn The Flake Area

7	Celadon	E1**
8	Havnor	VS*
9	Main Wall Traverse	E2*
10	Leaning Crack	HS
11	Trundle Crack	HS*
12	Blinkered Vision	HVS
13	Kirsten Wall	HS*
14	Just for Kicks	HVS*
15	Teenage Kicks	HVS*
16	Babel Towers	HS*
v1	Var. Bogey Arête	VS*
v2	Var. Just for Shirl	VS*
17	Scarlet Lyvennet	MVS
18	The Flake	HS**
19	The Flange	VS*
20	Bulging Crack	HS*
21	The Small Assassin	VS*
22	The Bulge	E1
23	Fickle Flake	HVS
24	Fast and Hideous	HVS

Photo: Ron Kenyon

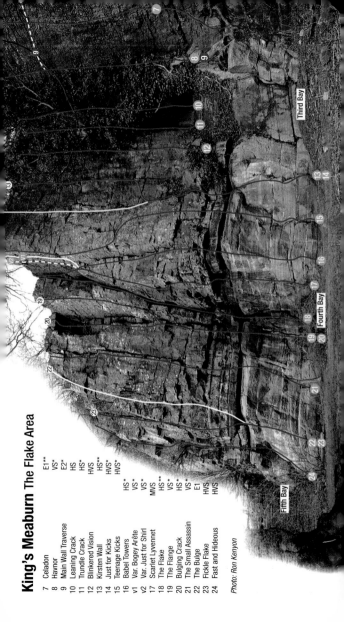

| 7 **Celadon** | 14m | E1+ | ★★ | 1997 |

(5b). Start just left of *Marik* and climb up to the large tree on the ledge. Surmount the bulge and continue in a direct line up the wall just to the left of *Marik*. Sustained but well protected and on good rock.

| 8 **Havnor** | 11m | VS | ★ | |

Often overlooked but well worth doing.

(5a). Start on the ledge at the back of the bay behind the tree, just right of *Leaning Crack*. Climb the wall above, trying not to use the tree.

| 9 **Main Wall Traverse** | 24m | E2 | ★ | 1990s |

(5b). An interesting excursion starting up *Havnor* then moving right across *Celadon* to the ledge on *Marik*. Launch out rightwards across *The Windeye* to pass *Gont* and finish up *Windkey*.

| 10 **Leaning Crack** | 11m | HS | | 1974 |

From the ledge at the back of the bay, climb the corner-crack.

| 11 **Trundle Crack** | 11m | HS | ★ | 1974 |

Climb the crack to the left of *Leaning Crack*.

| 12 **Blinkered Vision** | 11m | HVS | | 1996 |

(5b). An eliminate taking the rock between *Trundle Crack* and *Kirsten Wall* but not using either.

| 13 **Kirsten Wall** | 12m | HS | ★★ | 1974 |

This impressive looking wall is not as hard as it looks, though it has a little sting in its tail.

Climb an awkward corner and ascend the fine crack above then move rightwards to finish directly up the wall.

| 14 **Just for Kicks** | 12m | HVS- | ★ | 2008 |

Start as for *Kirsten Wall*.

(4c). Climb the crack and continue directly up the wall above.

| 15 **Teenage Kicks** | 12m | HVS | ★ | 2003 |

The arête on the left of the bay.

(5a). Overcome the sandstone base and ascend the wall above then the arête to its top.

Right: Peter Simpson gets **Teenage Kicks** (HVS), King's Meaburn. **Photo:** Ron Kenyon

Fourth Bay

This is the small bay with the prominent rightward-slanting flake-crack of *The Flake*.

| 16 **Babel Towers** | 12m | HS | ★ | |

Start at the base of the arête and climb this to gain a cracked groove which is followed to a ledge. Move left to finish as for *The Flake*.

v1   ***Bogey Arête*** 12m VS ★
    (4c). From the ledge, finish up the arête on the right.

v2   ***Just for Shirl*** 12m VS ★ 1993
    (5a). From the ledge, go directly up the slight bulge and the wall above.

| 17 **Scarlet Lyvennet** | 10m | MVS | | |

    (4b). Climb the wall over an arch-shaped overlap to the ledge and finish as for *Babel Towers*.

| 18 **The Flake** | 11m | HS | ★★ | 1974 |

The obvious line of the great flake seen when arriving at the crag.
    Gain the base of the flake and move up rightwards awkwardly, then continue with decreasing difficulty up the groove above.

| 19 **The Flange** | 9m | VS- | ★ | 1988 |

    (4c). Start as for *Bulging Crack* but, at the first bulge, move right and climb the right edge of the large flake to the top.

| 20 **Bulging Crack** | 9m | HS | ★ | |

    Climb the crack at the back of the bay and finish up the corner at the top.

| 21 **The Small Assassin** | 9m | VS+ | ★ | 1988 |

On the left wall of the bay is a prominent crack with a tree at three-quarters height.
    (4c). Overcome the sandstone base to gain the crack, which is followed, either by passing the tree on its left, or by climbing the wall on the right.

Right: Alan Hinkes above the sandy break on **The Small Assassin** (VS), King's Meaburn. **Photo:** Ron Kenyon
Left: Max Biden and Ian Gray catching the evening sunshine on **Bogey Arête** (VS), King's Meaburn. **Photo:** Ron Kenyon

King's Meaburn Tove Wall Area

25	Percy Throwup	S *
26	Headmaster Ritual	E3 *
27	Rune Wall	HS

28	Borderliner	E3 *
29	Tove Wall	MVS *
30	Crabstack	VS
31	Steph	MVS *

Photo: Ron Kenyon

Fifth Bay

This is behind a huge yew tree.

22 **The Bulge**		9m	E1		

Deserves a health warning due to suspect rock and poor protection.
(4c). Start as for *Fickle Flake*, but move rightwards below the bulge and onto the arête and ascend it if you dare.

23 **Fickle Flake**		9m	HVS		

A steep and serious route starting 1.5 metres left of the right arête of the bay.
(4c). Climb the sandstone base and surmount a bulge to gain the thin flake. Layback awkwardly on doubtful holds to the top.

24 **Fast and Hideous**		9m	HVS		

(4c). Start 6 metres right of *Percy Throwup* and climb a steep crack, past a tree, to the bulge. Pull round this awkwardly to the right.

The Ring of Confidence	9m	E1		1989

Once good but now somewhat overgrown with ivy. Start just to the left of *Fast and Hideous*.
> (5b). Move rightwards above the overlap to gain the edge of the wall. Pass a thread trending slightly leftwards to finish up the wall above.

25 **Percy Throwup**	9m	S	★	

A popular and interesting struggle.
> Start at the corner of the bay and climb the steep twin cracks finishing either left or right.

26 **Headmaster Ritual**	9m	E3	★	1988

A bold fingery climb taking the tapering pillar.
> (6a). Start up a very thin crack then climb the pillar to reach better holds near the top.

27 **Rune Wall**	9m	HS		1974

> Pass the small thorn bush at the base of a wide crack and continue up the crack past a wedged block and a tree.

28 **Borderliner**	9m	E3	★	2003

This route takes the pillar without using the cracks on either side.
> (5c). Thin moves above the initial overlap gain a horizontal crack (peg on right). Move up left, then right, to gain a good flake-crack and finish awkwardly past a tree.

29 **Tove Wall**	9m	MVS	★	1975

> (4a). Climb the steep crack to the right of the thorn bush passing a small ledge.

30 **Crabstack**	9m	VS		

> (4b). Follow *Steph* up the crucial groove then move right and finish up the steep crack above.

31 **Steph**	9m	MVS	★	1974

Start on the ledge 2 metres right of the arête.
> (4b). A short undercut groove provides a difficult start then move up easily and follow the crack in the arête.

Sixth Bay

Towards the left end of the crag is a drystone wall; this bay lies to the right of it. A huge three-stemmed sycamore grows from a ledge 2 metres up the right wall.

King's Meaburn Bay Rum Area

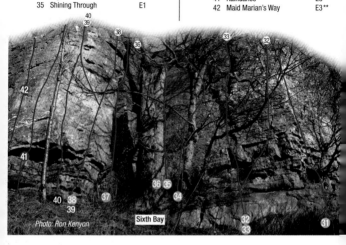

Photo: Ron Kenyon

Sixth Bay

| 32 **Double Jeopardy** | 9m | HVS | | 1988 |

(5a). Start as for *Ged* but then climb carefully up and rightwards over two big jammed blocks. Finish directly up the wall above and groove on the right.

| 33 **Ged** | 9m | MVS | ★ | 1974 |

Start 3 metres right of the three-stemmed sycamore.
(4c). Overcome the sandstone base and continue up the cracked wall above.

| 34 **Nightride** | 9m | VS | | 1974 |

(4c). Climb the wall just right of the corner of *Bay Rum*, then move up rightwards and back leftwards on doubtful flakes to finish.

| 35 **Shining Through** | 11m | E1- | | 2005 |

(5c). This fine fingery exercise directly up the centre of the wall just right of *Bay Rum* has an unprotected crux at 4 metres before the finishing flake is reached.

King's Meaburn Phall Area

36	Bay Rum	VD**	45	Phall Direct	E1*
37	Slipway	HS*	46	Phall	E1**
38	Liang Shan Po	VS*	47	Ten Years After	E1*
39	Trilogy	E3*	48	TD Corner	MS*
40	Barry's Arête	E5	49	Puss In Boots	HVS
41	Raindance	E3**	50	Twist and Shout	MVS
42	Maid Marian's Way	E3**			
43	Ivy Crack	E1**			
44	Phallacy	E2*			

Photo:
Ron Kenyon

Sixth Bay

Seventh Bay

36 **Bay Rum**	9m	VD	★ ★	1974

Gain the ledge behind the three-stemmed sycamore and climb the easy-angled corner leftwards to a steep finish.

37 **Slipway**	9m	HS	★	

Climb the sandstone base and follow the fine steep corner, moving right at the top to finish up a short wall.

38 **Liang Shan Po**	9m	VS+	★	1975

(5a). Overcome bulging rock and follow the rightward-slanting crack.

39 **Trilogy**	9m	E3	★	1975

(5c). Gain the rightward-slanting crack of *Liang Shan Po*, pull onto the wall on the left, and climb directly to an overlap. Move left with difficulty into a short corner just right of the arête and finish up the arête.

Seventh Bay

This consists of two walls at right angles. The right wall, following the demise of a large tree in its centre, gives some clean and interesting routes.

40 **Barry's Arête**	8m	E5		1990s

(6b). The arête right of *Raindance*. The exact line is not known.

41 **Raindance**	8m	E3-	★ ★	2002

The apparently blank wall right of *Maid Marian's Way*, with some surprisingly good gear but still serious and thin.

(5c). Layback the initial overlap to gain the wall, then move up and slightly rightwards to finish.

42 **Maid Marian's Way**	8m	E3	★ ★	1975

(5b). The wall direct gives a very bold route passing just left of the patch of rippled calcite to gain better holds at the top.

43 **Ivy Crack**	8m	E1	★ ★	

Transformed enormously since the demise of the tree which grew at the base of the crack.

(5b). Hard moves gain and overcome the crack. Continue awkwardly, then, either move leftwards to gain and climb the crack on the left, or climb directly up to the top.

Right: Shaw Brown reaches the upper break on **Ivy Crack** (E1), King's Meaburn.
Photo: Ron Kenyon

| 44 Phallacy | 8m | E2 | ★ | 1993 |

A direct line up the crag.

(5c). Climb on to the first ledge and, using a small two finger pull-up, climb round the overhang to gain a ledge, then finish up the wall above.

| 45 **Phall Direct** | 8m | E1 | ★ | 1993 |

(5c). Climb a short-lived crack to gain the ledge of *Phall*. Finish up to the right of the huge tree.

| 46 **Phall** | 9m | E1- | ★ ★ | 1974 |

A delicate wall climb without any protection.

(5b). Start 3 metres right of *TD Corner* and climb gymnastically to a small ledge. Move right, then up and left, under the huge tree and finish up to the left of the tree. It is also possible to climb up directly to below the tree.

| 47 **Ten Years After** | 8m | E1+ | ★ | 1997 |

Start one metre right of *TD Corner*.

(5c). Climb the wall past a horizontal slot (gear!) and continue up to finish just left of the huge tree at the top (as for *Phall*).

| 48 **TD Corner** | 8m | MS | ★ | 1973 |

The corner of the bay is climbed on good holds.

| 49 **Puss in Boots** | 20m | HVS | | 2008 |

A fine rising traverse with two bold and serious sections. Start as for *TD Corner*.

(5a). Climb the corner for 3 metres, then traverse the obvious ledge rightwards across *Phall* to the ledge on *Phallacy*. Continue horizontally rightwards on the rounded but dimply break to within 2 metres of the *Barry's Arête* and finish rightwards up the wall.

| 50 **Twist and Shout** | 6m | MVS | | |

(4b). Start immediately left of the corner and climb the thin left-slanting crack.

| **Owl Crack** | 6m | M | | |

The obvious crack in the centre of the left wall.

| **First Wall Eliminate** | 6m | HVS | | |

Blinkers required. Start below a narrow pillar, just right of *Tree Chimney*.

(5c). Climb the pillar without resorting to holds in the adjoining cracks.

Tree Chimney	6m	D		

Climb the chimney behind the tree on the left wall.

Further short and unmemorable routes have been recorded on **Far Left Wall**, the buttress to the left of the descent path.

In olden times a few climbs were recorded at **Morland Byesteads Old Quarry (NY 604 217)** just south of Morland. It is doubtful that the passing years have improved them. Permission to climb here must be sought at the farm.

The Hoff

Grid Reference: **NY 675 180**   Altitude: **160m**
Faces: **West**   Approach: **3 mins**

The crag in the meadow! *The Hoff* is a strange eruption of lovely vertical conglomerate rising abruptly out of a tranquil pasture above Hoff Beck.

For those operating in the lower grades the situation could hardly be bettered. The rock, brockram, is a conglomerate of lumps of sandstone and limestone in a very strong natural cement. The climbing tends to be steep but the holds are usually good. The rock is clean and dries quickly – however the finishes on the level turf top can be quite bold, especially when damp.

Unfortunately access has recently been banned at The Hoff after a change of ownership. Contact has been made with the owner by the BMC Access Representative and it is hoped that an access arrangement can be reached in due course. The owner wishes only to be contacted through her solicitor. Climbers and/or organisations should not try to contact her directly and any communication should be via the BMC. The descriptions are given to maintain the historical record only and in case access is allowed in the future. No right or encouragement to climb is implied.

Approach:

The Hoff is 2km west of Appleby, adjacent to the B6260 between Appleby and Tebay (Junction 38 on M6). Just to the west of the village of Burrells, the crag is visible in a field to the north of the road. There are parking places just west of the gate and also on the left of the road, over a bridge in the hamlet of Hoff.

The crag is approached through a gate into the meadow. The crag is on private land and access had previously been granted on the under-standing that:

- Livestock should not be disturbed.
- No litter.

- No damage to the property.
- No dogs.

Belay stakes have been placed at the top of the crag. Please note that:
- None of the stakes have been load-tested – climbers should exercise their own judgment in using them.
- Belay slings should be placed at the base of the stakes to avoid leverage.
- At least two stakes should be used when belaying.
- If top-roping, belay systems should extend over the crag edge to limit erosion.
- Climbers should not climb the fence into the field beyond the crag.

The crag is of considerable geological interest and interested individuals and groups may appear with hammers to remove samples. It is suggested that such misguided souls be advised to remove samples already detached rather that doing further damage to the crag.

Descents can be made on either side of the crag – they can be very slippery in damp conditions.

The routes are described from **left** to **right**.

New York Arête

This is the name given to the arête left of the tree left of *Afterthought Wall*.

Apple Sponge	8m	VD		1996

Starting at the base of the arête, move slightly leftwards whilst keeping to the right of a small tree, and climb easily to the top.

Apple Crumble	8m	S		1996

Starting at the base of the arête, climb it direct, via two good ledges, to a thread belay.

Apple Pie	8m	MVS		1996

(4b). Start one metre right of the arête and climb the first 2 metres on good holds, then, avoiding tree branches, finish up loose rock with poor protection. Sounds inviting!

Left: Dom Donnini finds a **Spare Rib** (HS) at The Hoff. **Photo:** Nick Wharton

The Hoff

Photo: Ron Kenyon

Afterthought Wall

The steep wall left of the *Main Wall* has a stepped arête on the right.

Afterthought		8m	MS		

Climb directly up the steep wall.

Little Wall		8m	S		

Climb the right-hand side of the wall to finish over a bulge at a break in the arête.

Main Wall

Afterlife	8m	VS+		1988

(4c). Climb the prominent jutting arête left of the corner on its right-hand side.

1	**The Corner**	8m	MS		

The obvious but not very good corner at the left-hand end of *Main Wall*.

2	**Going Green**	8m	MS		

Climb the wall in the line of a small tree just below the top.

3 **Rainbow**	8m	HS	

(4a). Climb the left side of the rib, just left of a shallow corner.

4 **Dig For Victory**	8m	MVS	

(4c). Climb the wall just right of the shallow corner and move into the corner to finish. Suspect rock at top.

5 **The Shades**	8m	VS	★

(4b). Climb the smooth wall right of the shallow corner and surmount with pleasure an overlap at 3 metres using a pocket. Follow the shallow runnel directly to the top.

6 **The Devon**	8m	HS	

(4a). Climb the wall and overlap just left of the crack of *Mojo*.

7 **Mojo**	8m	MS	★

Climb the crack in its entirety, passing the tree either to the left or right.

8 **Left-Handed Gromerzog**	8m	HVS	★

(5b). Climb the left-hand side of the wall using the pockets just right of the crack, and the wall above.

9 **Gromerzog**	8m	E2	★

Unfortunately more and more polished and thus harder than ever.

(6a). Climb directly up the steep smooth wall eschewing all pockets on the left. Continue over the right-hand end of a tapering overlap at 5 metres. Not knowing what eschewing means is not an excuse to cheat – look it up!

10 **Blonde Ella**	8m	HVS	★

(4b). Climb the rough textured wall right of *Gromerzog* trending leftwards to finish left of the band of small overhangs at the top.

11 **Slap Bang in the Middle**	8m	VS	★★

Exactly as it says. Start at the incipient crack, just right of *Blonde Ella*.

(4c). Climb directly up the steep wall through an area of very compact rock and finish via a layaway flake in the centre of the overhang.

12 **Brant**	8m	S	★

Start at a set of left-pointing flakes on the wall and climb these and the very faint rib above to finish up a shallow scoop.

Right: The fine pocketed wall of **Brant** (S) at the Hoff looks much harder than its grade.
Photo: Stephen Reid

| 13 **Barwise** | 8m | S | ★★ | |

Super holds! Start immediately below a small stump at head height.
Climb past the stump and continue up an obvious runnel to finish directly up the steep wall.

| 14 **Slosh Wall** | 8m | HS | ★ | |

Follow the wall just left of *Havers Crack*, passing a 'hole' near the top.

| 15 **Havers Crack** | 8m | S | ★ | |

The very obvious crack.

| 16 **Spare Rib** | 8m | HS | | |

Climb the rib to the right of *Havers Crack*.

| 17 **Pig Meat** | 8m | HS | ★ | |

Climb the shallow groove, just right of *Spare Rib*.

| 18 **Wormrigg Wall** | 8m | S | ★ | |

Follow the steep wall slightly rightwards on a series of sharp flakes to finish left of a small sapling.

| 19 **Murenger** | 8m | VS | ★ | 2005 |

(4c). A fine route on micro jugs direct up the grey shield just right of *Wormrigg Wall*.

| 20 **Saxon** | 8m | S | | |

Climb the wall directly below the small sapling.

| 21 **Burrells** | 8m | S | ★ | |

Start directly below the small tree sprouting just below the top of the crag and climb direct, via cracks, to and past the tree.

| 22 **The Arête** | 8m | VD | | |

Ascend the right-hand arête of *Main Wall*.

In the valley of the beck one kilometre north of *The Hoff* is **Cuddling Hole** (NY 673187) which consists of outcrops of conglomerate rock. A few climbs have been made but none recorded. It is not known what the access situation is.

Coudy Rocks

Grid Reference: **NY 687 202**   Altitude: **160m**
Faces: **South**   Approach: **3 mins**

This impressive sandstone wall is located in the centre of Appleby, on the east side of the River Eden. As the rock is quite soft and does not lend itself to protection the crag has been bolted – please treat the rock carefully!

The crag is on private land and access has been granted by the land-owner on the understanding that:

- Access is available for bone fide climbers.
- Any livestock should not be disturbed.
- The gate is left closed.
- No litter.
- No damage to property.
- No dogs are allowed in the field below the crag.

Approach:

From near the Royal Oak on Bongate, follow Mill Hill, on the opposite side of the road, down to a car park next to the River Eden. At the far, north, end of the field, next to the car park, the crag will be seen. Walk up the road and go through a gate (notice indicates "Private Land") and cross the field to the crag. *Main Wall*, which is seen on the approach, has a large tree at its base on the left. Fifty metres to the left of the tree is the *Megamoose Area* with the distinctive slanting crack-line of *Megamoose*.

Descents are by lower-offs. Access to the top is available to the right of the crag.

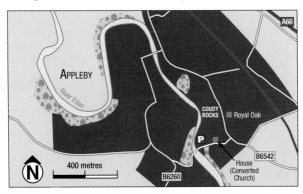

Coudy Rocks Megamoose Area

1	The Wider Sea	F6b +
2	Project	
3	El Presidento Robbo	F6b **
4	Megamoose	F6c +*
5	Project	

Photo: Ron Kenyon

Megamoose Area

1	**The Wider Sea**	7m	F6b+		2010

Climb the slab and rib, using a crucial small vertical edge on the slab to move left to the finishing ledge.

2	**Open Project**	7m			Not Led

Climb a short corner and battle up the continuing crack-line above.

3	**El Presidento Robbo**	8m	F6b	★ ★	2010

Climb the shield of rock and finish up the fine arête above to an awkward clip into the belay bolts.

4	**Megamoose**	10m	F6c+	★	2010

The main interest here is the crack-line slanting up from left to right.
Gain the arête on the left and following the crack-line with sustained interest to gain a short groove and finish at a belay on the right.

5	**Open Project**	7m			Not Led

Climb directly up the thin wall to the same belay as *Megamoose*.

Right: Coudy Rocks – Dom Bush and Mary Grace Brown go **Big in Japan** (F7a), while Chris King and Tony Mawer stretch to **Two Pints and a Packet of Crisps** (F6b+). **Photo:** Ron Kenyon

Coudy Rocks Main Wall

6	Perfect Weather to Fly	F7a **
7	Project	
8	Big in Japan	F7a **

9	Resisting Chiptation	F6c+ **
10	Two Pints and a Packet of Crisps	F6b+ **
11	The Sands of Time	F6a+ **

Photo: Ron Kenyon

Main Wall

6 **Perfect Weather to Fly**	12m	F7a	★★	2010

Start behind the large tree and overcome the overhung base to gain the wall above, then ascend leftwards by the arête.

7 **Open Project**	10m			Not Led

Start below the right side of the overlap and use widely spaced holds to gain the upper wall, continuing with much interest.

8 **Big in Japan**	10m	F7a	★★	2009

Sustained climbing up the wall leads to an obtuse finish.

9 **Resisting Chiptation**	10m	F6c+	★★	2009

Interesting climbing leads to a crucial traverse left on crimps to finish.

10 **Two Pints and a Packet of Crisps**	10m	F6b+	★★	2009

Weave up the wall before or after refreshment in the Royal Oak.

11 **The Sands of Time**	10m	F6a+	★★	2009

Climb the vague arête to finish slightly left of a tree.

12 **Headbutt the Bed**	11m	F6c+	★	2010

Climb rightwards up a groove, then climb up the wall with interest to finish.

13 **Sequence Dance**	9m	F7b+	★ ★	2010

Climb up gymnastically and with difficulty to gain the obvious finishing crack.

14 **Buffalo Bill**	8m	F6a	★	2009

Climb the right arête.

15 **New Fair Invasion**	7m	F6a+	★	2010

Climb a short corner, or wall on the right, and finish up the wall above.

16 **Here's to the Coalition**	7m	F5+		2010

Make awkward moves to reach the large ledge. Gain the slabby wall above and move up leftwards to a bolt belay.

17 **Bongate Boogy**	7m	F5		2010

Gain the large ledge and continue up the steep wall, keeping away from the corner-crack on the left.

18 **Hooray for Harold**		7m	F5	★	2010

Start up carved steps to gain the end of the large ledge. Overcome the steep wall to gain and climb a crack.

19 **Helm Bar**		4m	F4+		2010

The short wall up and right of *Hooray for Harold* gives a pleasant diversion.

20 **Helm Arête**			V1		2010

A boulder problem taking the fine arête just right of *Helm Bar*. At the top either jump off or traverse right and descend.

High Cup Nick

Grid Reference: **NY 745 261**   Altitude: **550m**
Faces: **West**   Approach: **60 mins**

This deep and dramatic U-shaped valley on the Pennine fellside at the top of High Cup Gill has walls of dolorite, part of the well-known Whin Sill. Some areas are composed of unstable stacked blocks whilst other parts are sounder – these have yielded a few climbs. For a mountain crag it is surprisingly unvegetated but it does have a coating of lichen which is very slippery when damp and problematic when dry; a wire brush is recommended. The character of the climbing is similar to other crags on the Whin Sill, such as Crag Lough. Various climbers have visited the crag over the years but only recently has anything been put down in writing – it is likely some of these climbs have had earlier ascents.

NB. *High Cup Nick* is one of only three English locations for alpine saxifrage and "gardening" should not take place!

Approach:

High Cup Nick is on the Pennine Way and can be reached from Dufton in the Eden Valley or Cow Green Reservoir on the border of Cumbria and County Durham. The shortest approach is to park just above Bow Hall Farm, near Dufton (NY 704 251), then follow the bridleway up the hill and along the north side of *High Cup Nick*.

A pinnacle on the north side has been climbed, **Nick's Last** (VD).

The following routes can be found at the left end of the southern escarpment, just right of where High Cup Gill descends from the plateau into the valley. The crag is best approached by following High Cup Gill

High Cup Nick

1 Sound as a Trout		VS
2 Turbot Don't Dyno		HVS

3 Julian Bream		E1
4 Young Turbots Go For It		VS
5 Bonington's Sardine Solution		S
6 A Surfeit of Lampreys		VD

Photo: Ron Kenyon

and scree down to its left. A belay stake or two would be useful as there are none in place.

1	**Sound as a Trout**	18m	VS		1999

(4b). Start 2 metres right of the arête and climb a wide crack to a big ledge. Move right slightly into a corner-crack and follow this to the top.

2	**Turbot Don't Dyno**	19m	HVS		1999

(5a). Follow *Sound as a Trout* to the big ledge, then move right around a narrow undercut rib and into a sentry box. Make a hard pull out of the box to a ledge on the right whence easier climbing leads to the top.

3	**Julian Bream**	20m	E1		2009

Ten metres right of *Sound as a Trout* is a V-groove with three cracks to its right.

(5b). Climb the cracks to a sentry box then climb this and exit via a hard move and a long reach to finish. A selection of cams is useful.

4	**Young Turbots Go For It**	20m	VS		1999

Ten metres right of *Julian Bream* is a right-angled corner. Start at a crack 2.5 metres to its left.

(5a). The crack leads to a ledge on the right. Make a difficult move off the ledge to gain a crack which is followed to the top.

5	**Bonington's Sardine Solution**	20m	S		1999

(4b). Climb the front face of the buttress right of the right-angled corner (mentioned above). Follow the crack until it steepens to gain a ledge on the right. Move up to a loose flake then step left and up to a hollow block to move right to finish.

6	A Surfeit of Lampreys	20m	VD		2009

Ten metres right of *Bonington's Sardine Solution* is a shallow square-cut bay with a steep pillar to its right.

Climb the open square-cut groove above to a grassy bay and scramble off to finish.

Murton Scar

Grid Reference: **NY 737 227**   Altitude: **470m**
Faces: **South-West**   Approach: **15 mins**

Perched high on the southern slopes of Murton Pike, this single steep limestone wall banded by overhangs occupies a prominent position overlooking the Upper Eden Valley. It offers few easy options and, although there are some worthwhile lower-grade climbs, it will appeal most to the lover of technical limestone. The crag is exposed to the prevailing winds but also catches the sun and dries quickly

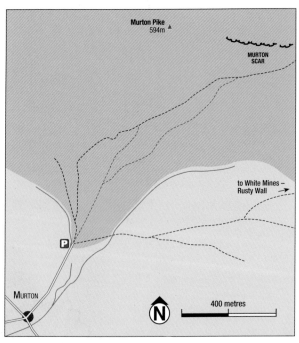

Murton Scar

1	Earl Street	E3 **
2	Earl Street Direct	E3 *
3	All Along the Watch Tower	E3 **
4	The Haunted Smear	E3 *
5	Morgan's Lane	E3 **
6	Mind Over Matter	E1 ***
7	Sunshine Super Sal	E1 *
8	Body Rock	VS
9	Deadend Groove	VS
10	Keach	

11	Bitter Fingers	VS
12	Red Hot Spankers	E3 **
13	Murton Moggy	HVS **
14	Catlike Tread	VS
15	Meal Ticket	HVS **
16	Brown Dirt Cowboy	HS

17	Bigus Dickus	VS *
18	Incontinentia Buttocks	E3 *
19	Wilkes's Wander	HS *

The Egg

Photo: Ron Kenyon

after rain. The rock is sound and compact on the lower part of the crag but caution is necessary near the top where it is more broken. The ground below the crag falls away steeply and this adds to the atmosphere of the routes. Several of the harder climbs are equipped with in situ pegs and threads – the threads were replaced in 2009.

Approach:

Murton village is easily reached from the A66 near Appleby. Follow signs for Hilton and Murton. After passing Hilton, the road enters Murton and crosses a bridge over the beck. Immediately beyond this, turn right and park at the car park at the foot of the fellside. A gate allows access to the open fell and a track can be followed, first left and then right, as it cuts across the flank of Murton Pike. A more pleasant and direct route is to follow the obvious tracks running through the bracken to reach the track below the crag. Steep grass leads to the foot of the buttress.

Descent is to the right.

The routes are described from **left** to **right**.

Main Crag

1	**Earl Street**		15m	E3	★ ★	1983

Start below the second crack from the left, which curves leftwards.
    (6a). Climb the thin crack, passing an in situ ring peg. Continue in this line to the roof. Traverse right for a couple of metres until a break in the overhang containing a wedged block is reached. Surmount the roof and finish up easier grooves above.

2	**Earl Street Direct**		15m	E3	★	1983

Start below a thin crack just right of *Earl Street*.
    (5c). Climb the crack direct to the good foothold on *All Along the Watch Tower*. Climb direct to the roof and surmount it just to the right of the wedged block. Above the roof, step left and finish as for *Earl Street*.

3	**All Along the Watch Tower**		16m	E3+	★ ★	1983

A superb line with continuously interesting climbing. Start 3 metres right of *Earl Street* at the foot of the question mark-shaped curving flake.
    (6a). Climb the flake, passing an in situ thread at 5 metres. Step left to a good foothold. Make a difficult pull up and right, and through the roof 2 metres right of the break containing the wedged block of *Earl Street*. Finish up a deep groove which contains a flake-edged block.

Right: Michael Kenyon on **Morgan's Lane** (E3), Murton Scar. **Photo:** Ron Kenyon

| 4 | **The Haunted Smear** | 15m | E3+ | ★ | 1983 |

(6b). Climb the centre of the smooth wall, passing a peg, and move slightly right to an in situ thread and a junction with *Morgan's Lane*. Move left to enter a groove which leads up to a metre-wide roof above. Climb this at its centre on excellent jugs and finish up easier rock.

| 5 | **Morgan's Lane** | 16m | E3 | ★ ★ | 1983 |

(5c). Start below a 2 metre thin crack and climb this, then step right into a little grassy recess. Climb up and leftwards on underclings, passing a couple of in situ threads, to a junction with *The Haunted Smear* and finish up this.

| 6 | **Mind Over Matter** | 15m | E1 | ★ ★ | 1983 |

(5a). Climb the faint crack-line just right of *Morgan's Lane*. Continue via tricky moves to enter the niche containing a sapling. Climb up and out of the niche, following the groove, to exit rightwards to easier rock and the top.

| 7 | **Sunshine Super Sal** | 15m | E1 | ★ ★ ★ | 1976 |

A magnificent climb starting at a one metre high blunt spike of rock below a thin crack-line.
(5b). Climb the thin crack-line, taking care with a semi-detached finger of rock in the lower part. At a downward pointing spike, step right under the bulge to move up to a good ledge below the *Main Overhang*. A good crack leads diagonally leftwards, following a sensational traverse line through the roof. After a couple of metres, climb directly up the vertical continuation crack in the headwall. Easy ledges lead to the top.

| 8 | **Body Rock** | 15m | E3 | ★ | 1983 |

This route accepts the challenge of the *Main Overhang* and starts below a faint groove in the crozzly wall directly beneath it.
(5c). Climb the slim groove and wall to below the major break in the overhang. Climb the break into a slim groove above, which has a protruding block in it, pass an in situ runner on the left, and finish easily above.

| 9 | **Deadend Groove** | 17m | VS | | 1975 |

(4c). Climb the obvious slim groove on reasonable holds until the roof is reached. Traverse right for about 4 metres, to reach the continuation steep cracked corner above the block-filled chimney of *Keach*, and finish up this.

| 10 **Keach** | 15m | VS | | 1975 |

(4c). Start at the foot of the open block-filled chimney/gully and climb it steeply to a ledge. Finish up the steep cracked corner above (as for *Deadend Groove*). Take care with the rock and protection.

| 11 **Bitter Fingers** | 15m | VS | | 1975 |

(4c). Climb the shallow corner to a grassy ledge above which is a patch of smooth grey rock. Move directly up to another ledge and climb the twin cracks above to the top.

| 12 **Red Hot Spankers** | 16m | E3 | ★★ | 1983 |

A bold climb. Start below the middle of a very steep and narrow white wall which has an in situ thread runner at mid-height.

(5c). Climb the wall direct to finish by pulling leftwards over the prow to the left of the finish of *Murton Moggy*.

| 13 **Murton Moggy** | 16m | HVS- | ★★ | 1975 |

An excellent line starting where a white cone of rock, cracked on either side, leads up to a pronounced groove.

(4c). Climb the left side of the cone to the groove which is followed to a ledge below a bulge. Overcome the bulge by means of a left-trending crack-line then finish up ledges above.

Five metres right of *Murton Moggy* is a left-slanting crack-line at the base of which is a downward-pointing small nose of rock. The next two climbs start at the foot of this crack-line.

| 14 **Catlike Tread** | 15m | VS+ | | 1975 |

(4c). Follow the left-slanting crack-line to some small saplings then continue above and rightwards on loose rock.

| 15 **Meal Ticket** | 15m | HVS- | ★★ | 1976 |

Start below the downward-pointing tongue of rock, as for *Catlike Tread*.

(4b). Move up rightwards to ascend a fine blunt rib leading to a prominent narrow corner-groove. Ascend this with interest to ledges and the top.

The Egg

This is the prominent short steep buttress of excellent rock at the right end of the crag.

| 16 **Brown Dirt Cowboy** | 12m | HS | | 1976 |

Climb the corner on the left side of *The Egg*, either in the corner, or via its left wall.

| 17 **Bigus Dickus** | 12m | VS+ | ★ | 1983 |

(4c). Start below the front face of *The Egg*, to the right of *Brown Dirt Cowboy*, and climb the wall direct, passing an overhang at mid-height. Finishing up the cracked groove above.

| 18 **Incontinentia Buttocks** | 12m | E3 | ★ | 1983 |

(5c). Climb the steep crack in the arête direct on excellent rock.

| 19 **Wilkes's Wander** | 12m | HS | ★ | 2005 |

Start as for *Incontinentia Buttocks* but climb the crack on the right to the top.

Above: Eric Parker strolls up **Wilkes's Wander** (HS), Murton Scar. **Photo:** Ron Kenyon

White Mines – Rusty Wall

Grid Reference: **NY 744 227**   Altitude: **450m**
Faces: **North**   Approach: **25 mins**

This short steep limestone wall is found at a disused mine on the south side of Gasdale, which is the valley just to the south of Murton Pike. Only two routes have been climbed here though there are other possibilities.

Approach:

The crag lies just to the north of the MOD Range on designated Access Land. Park as for the approach to *Murton Scar* (see page 202) at the car park at the head of the village and go through the gate to gain access to the fell, then follow a track rightwards to cross a ford. Ascend the fell on the left to gain and follow an obvious track, below Delfekirk Scar, which leads to a rocky valley containing an abandoned old tractor. On the right side of the valley, looking up, is a series of buttresses – the best being *Rusty Wall* which has an overlap at two-thirds height and lies about 50 metres up from the tractor. On its left is an arête and just right of a steep slabby wall is a diagonal crack, rising from right to left.

Can You Feel It?	8m	E1	2001

(5a). The steep left arête.

Scrogbank Ravers	8m	E7/8	2001

(7a). A very technical and serious outing which climbs the steep wall left of the diagonal crack direct.

Above: A fine view out over the Eden Valley from Murton Scar. **Photo:** Ron Kenyon

Helbeck Wood Crag

Grid Reference: **NY 787 167**   Altitude: **380m**
Faces: **South-West**   Approach: **25 mins**

This limestone crag is situated at the north end of Helbeck Wood, above Brough. The rock is sound and compact with small holds and there are some excellent natural lines.

Unfortunately the crag is on private land and at the time of writing the land owner has refused to allow access. Details of the climbs are included for purpose of historical record and in case there is a change in the access arrangements. Meanwhile, please don't climb on this crag.

Approach:
The crag is approached as for *Brough Scar* (p 213) then by following the fellside westwards along by a wall until just behind the crag, whence the top of the crag can be gained.

The routes are described from **left** to **right**.

A major feature of the left end of the crag is a large roof with two parallel grooves leading up to it.

Sergeant Rock	12m	HVS		1989

(5a). Follow the right-hand groove and at the roof swing right onto a small ledge. Finish up blocks above.

Shoot to Kill	12m	E4	★ ★	1989

To the right of *Sergeant Rock* is a large easy-angled corner.

(6a). Follow the parallel cracks in the left wall, finishing above the left-hand one. Desperate.

Fylingdale Flier	13m	HS		1989

Climb the easy-angled corner.

Variation VS

(4c). At two-thirds height, break out onto the left wall and finish up this.

Judge for Yourself	12m	VS		1989

(5b). Start midway along the right wall and climb this direct. An easier start utilizes the undercut flake-crack just to the right.

| **Rabbit on the Windscreen** | 15m | HS | | | 1989 |

Start just right of one of the stems of a large tree resting against the rock.

(4b). Layback the crack and continue up the groove-line to a ledge.

| **Crossfire** | 17m | VS | ★★★ | 1989 |

(4c). Follow the right-slanting ramp to the overlap. Swing up and right on good holds then continue in the same line to finish.

| **Silkworm** | 15m | E2 | ★★ | 1989 |

(5b). Climb boldly up the wide open groove right of *Crossfire* and, at the overhang, pull up left to join and finish up *Crossfire*.

| **Stealth** | 15m | HVS | ★★ | 1989 |

Start from blocks below the rib right of *Silkworm*.

(5a). Reach up for a good hidden hold to gain the rib which is followed delicately. Finish up a tiny corner and short crack.

| **The Hollow Karst** | 15m | VS | | 1989 |

Start below the groove right of *Stealth*.

(4c). Climb up the groove and over the roof to finish at a large prominent flake.

| **The Professionals** | 15m | E2 | ★★★ | 1989 |

Start 4 metres right of *The Hollow Karst* below a corner capped by some large roofs.

(5b). Climb the corner to the first roof. Pull into a short groove then move right below the second roof to finish up a hanging rib in a fine position.

| **Lethal Weapon** | 13m | E3 | ★★ | 1989 |

Start below the rib to the right of *The Professionals*.

(5c). Climb the rib which is difficult to start but eases near the break. From here, pull up into and finish up the hanging groove just to the right.

The following section of the crag is vegetated. The next route is at the right side of a smooth wall some 25 metres right of *Lethal Weapon*, where a small tree grows out of a crack and there are some large fallen blocks.

| **Trench Warfare** | 15m | E2 | ★★ | 1989 |

Start below a small dog-leg crack at 3 metres.

(5c). Gain the crack and the break above, which has good holds. Move right and pull onto a clean ledge. Climb the wall above to a tricky finish.

| **Rocket to Russia** | 15m | E1 | ★ ★ | 1989 |

Four metres right of **Trench Warfare** is a large roof. Start below the corner.
(5b). Climb the corner then swing right to gain the top of a massive flake. Climb the blunt rib to the break then finish up the wall above.

The next two routes start in the small bay just to the right of **Rocket to Russia**.

| **Fight or Flight** | 15m | E2 | ★ | 1989 |

Start at a crack formed by the massive flake.
(5b). Jam the crack and make gymnastic moves to stand on the top of the flake. Climb the blunt rib to the break then finish up the wall above (as for **Rocket to Russia**).

| **Deterrent** | 15m | E1 | ★ | 1989 |

Start below the obvious crack at the back of the bay. NB A rockfall has removed the lower part of this climb and it is not known to have been climbed since.
(5b). Climb the crack to an overlap then move right to ascend a faint scoop, passing another overlap.

| **Superpower** | 20m | HVS | | 1989 |

Start below the prominent corner, capped by overhangs 10 metres right of **Deterrent**.
(5b). Climb the corner easily, then traverse awkwardly left to a niche in the arête. Difficult moves past a bulging rib gain good finishing holds.

| **Privates on Parade** | 15m | S | | 1989 |

Some massive blocks abut the face near the right end of the crag.
Climb the chimney 4 metres left of the massive blocks then follow the right-hand layback crack to a large ledge. Finish easily.

| **Judgemental Jibe** | 15m | HS | | 1989 |

Start 2 metres right of **Privates on Parade**.
(4c). Mantelshelf onto a ledge and take one of various possible finishes above.

Brough Scar

Grid Reference: **NY 795 165**   Altitude: **380m**
Faces: **South**   Approach: **15 mins**

Brough Scar is the name given to the area of limestone escarpments
high up on Musgrave Fell to the north of the A66 near Brough.
These escarpments look attractive and are often remarked upon
by climbers driving past. However, on closer inspection, the crags,
although reasonably continuous, lack any height in all but a few
places. These few areas have been developed and provide enjoyable
climbing on mostly excellent rock.

Main Buttress offers the best climbing on the *Scar* and presents a
very compact face guarded at its base by a belt of bulges and overhangs.
The rock is good and in many places provides natural thread runners.
Although only short, it gives steep fingery and usually strenuous climbing.
Route appearances are often deceptive, looking easier and shorter than
they are. A stake above the crag provides an anchor for belaying.

Approach:

See map on page 215. From the village of Brough, adjacent to the A66:
at the west end of Brough Main Street, a road is signposted to Helbeck
Quarry. Follow this road uphill for about 2km until a large quarry is
reached on the left and park here. A track leads past the quarry entrance
and uphill. After passing through a gate, a small quarry marks the junction
of another track. Leave the main track and follow the left-hand track along
the fellside. The compact face of *Main Buttress* will be seen on the hillside
above; follow the slope steeply to its base. The crag is on Access Land.

The left-hand end of the buttress is scrappy above 5 or 6 metres, whilst
below this it is uniformly overhanging. The main challenges here are
represented by two cracked breaks the first of which has an undercut edge.

1	**Boogey Down**		12m	E1	★	1984

(6a). Starting below the first break, gain undercuts and pull over the
bulge via a thin vertical crack.

2	**Dynamo Hum**		12m	E4	★ ★	1984

(6b). Where the bulge eases, extend up and right (thread runner)
across the bulge to a good hold. Climb direct to the top.

Brough Scar

1	Boogey Down	E1 *
2	Dynamo Hum	E4 **
3	Arty Farty	E2 *

4	Magic's Wand	E3 *
5	Necromancer	E1 **
6	Roxanne Shante	E3 **
v1	Chicken Variation	E3 *
7	Style of the Street	E4 **
8	Cuttin' Herbie	E1 **

Photo: Ron Kenyon

3	**Arty Farty**	12m	E2	★	1984

Start below the fine slim left-trending groove, one metre right of an embedded block. The groove is guarded by a bulge at head height.

(5c). Climb the groove until it meets a bulging headwall, then move right and up the corner.

4	**Magic's Wand**	12m	E3	★	1984

(6a). Start as for *Necromancer* by climbing into the groove. Quit this almost immediately in favour of a very shallow left-trending gangway in the thin wall on the left. Finish leftwards through bulges.

5	**Necromancer**	12m	E1+	★ ★	1984

(5b). Start below the most obvious groove-line and climb this to a thread runner. Finish up the square-cut hanging corner.

Three metres right of *Necromancer*, the face has a shallow but large diamond-shaped feature at mid-height. The left-hand side of the feature is unclimbed but the right-hand side provides the next route.

6	**Roxanne Shante**	12m	E3	★ ★	1984

(6a). Climb to the first thread; well-protected but thought-provoking. Continue past another thread runner and finish directly over a roof (taking care with the holds).

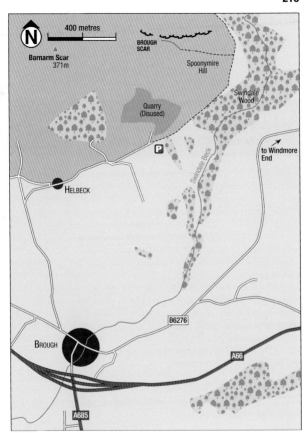

v1   *Chicken Variation* E3 ★ 1984

    (6a). From the second thread, escape rightwards to a tiny rowan tree. Moving rightwards, the bulges guarding the base of the crag become bigger.

7 **Style of the Street**	12m	E4	★★	1984

A very fine route that requires strength in reserve once the initial bulge is overcome. Start at a white pillar just right of a little clean-cut corner.

    (6b). Climb up to and across the roof, past a thread (or maybe a place that a thread was), to a good hold. Reach through for a jug and finish at a tiny rowan tree.

| 8 | **Cuttin' Herbie** | | 9m | E1 | ★ ★ | 1984 |

Sensational roof climbing at a more modest grade. Start an obvious slanting handrail which cuts through the roof from left to right.

(5b). Gain a bracket-type hold (thread runner) and make a long reach for jugs above the lip. Rock over into a small groove to the left of the rib and finish left at a thread. Abseil off.

Windmore End

Grid Reference: NY 822 167   Altitude: 410m
Faces: South-West   Approach: 5-10 mins

Windmore End is a long escarpment of quarried limestone situated close to the Brough to Middleton-in-Teesdale road. Quarrying finished many years ago and the rock has weathered sufficiently to provide a rough, almost natural surface. Loose rock can be a problem on some climbs, especially on finishes; in general the rock is sounder towards the right-hand end of the crag. The crag is exposed to the elements and is quite capable of living up to its name – against this, on a fine sunny day, the views of the Upper Eden valley are breathtaking, the rock is very quick drying, and climbing may be possible throughout the year. There are good climbs at most grades with the bulk of routes featuring thin crack or technical wall climbing; a rack of micro wires is useful. The routes are at most 13 metres high, with many being shorter. On some, protection is non-existent and for these a bouldering mat is recommended. There are a number of belay stakes along the top of the crag. The wall along the top of the crag should not be climbed on or damaged.

With regards the belay stakes - please note:-
• None of these have been load tested – climbers should use their own judgement when using them.
• Belay slings should be placed at the base of the stakes to avoid leverage.
• At least two stakes should be used when belaying.
• If top-roping, belay systems should be extended over the edge of the crag to limit erosion.

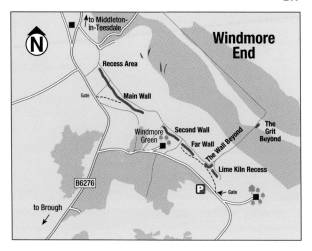

Approach:

From Brough, follow the B6276 towards Middleton in Teesdale. Continuing uphill, the long smooth faces of *Windmore End* will be seen on the right-hand side of the road. After 3km a minor road branches off to the right. To reach the left-hand section of the crag, ignore this turn off and park beyond the next bend at a gate on the right. The crag can be reached by going through this gate and walking up the field. To reach the right-hand section (*Far Wall*) turn right on the aforementioned minor road. There is room for several vehicles in a small layby 100 metres beyond the cottage of Windmore Green. Further along the road a gate allows access to the field and the crag is quickly reached by slanting leftwards up the hill below an old lime kiln. Please do not climb over any walls. The left-hand section belongs to the Parish Council, the middle section to the owners of Windmore Green and the right-hand section to the farmer at Windmore End Farm.

Unfortunately at the time of writing, access to the left-hand side of the crag, the area left of the second wall (comprising Recess Area and Main Wall), has been banned by the landowners (the Parish Council) despite there having been no problems in the previous 30 years of people climbing here. It is hoped that some access agreement can be reached in the future and so details of this excellent section of crag have been included, though this does not imply any right to climb there.

The climbs are described from **left** to **right**.

Windmore End Recess Area

1	Scarface	MVS
2	Wiselocks	VS
3	Cow Howe	MVS
4	Pollaxed	HS

5	Jingle Wall	VS
6	Jingle Crack	MS
7	Fingers Wall	HVS
8	Continuous Crack	VS *

Photo: Ron Kenyon

Recess Area

This is the left-most section, to the left of the stone wall where one reaches the crag. It comprises an area with a wall set back (*Recessed Wall*) and a *Right-Hand Wall*. The first route is on the left of *Recessed Wall*.

NB At the time of writing, climbing is banned on this section (see above).

| 1 | **Scarface** | 4m | MVS | | |

(4b). Climb the wall just left of the rock scar.

| 2 | **Wiselocks** | 5m | VS | | |

(5a). Climb the faint crack-line, finishing just right of the rock scar.

| 3 | **Cow Howe** | 5m | MVS | | |

(4c). Climb the wall.

| 4 | **Pollaxed** | 5m | HS | | |

Climb the twin cracks.

| 5 | **Jingle Wall** | 5m | VS | | |

(4b). Climb the wall just right of the twin cracks.

| 6 | **Jingle Crack** | 5m | MS | | |

Climb the crack left of the grassy crack, with use of the pillar or crack at the bottom.

7	**Fingers Wall**		5m	HVS		2004

(5b). Two metres left of *Continuous Crack* is an unprotected wall which is climbed on fingery holds; not as loose as it looks.

8	**Continuous Crack**		5m	VS	★	2004

(4b). Four metres left of *Phreatic Crack* is a continuous crack. Follow it, with reasonable protection, to a niche and loose finish.

9	**Blank Wall**		5m	HVS	★	2004

(5b). Climb the wall 2 metres left of *Phreatic Crack*. There is some protection in the horizontal crack at half-height.

10	**Corner and Wall**		5m	VS		2004

(4b). Follow the corner feature, just to left of *Phreatic Crack*, to half-height and then climb the wall above.

11	**Phreatic Crack**		5m	VS	★	2004

(4c). Climb a thin fairly well-protected crack, 4 metres left of the corner adjacent to *Twin Cracks*.

12	**Phreatic Twin**		5m	HVS	★	2004

(5a). Climb the wall 3 metres left of the corner adjacent to *Twin Cracks*, via small ledge at two-thirds height.

13	**Twin Cracks**		5m	HS	★	

Climb the twin cracks up the left-hand side of the right-hand end of the *Recess Area*.

| 14 **The Mantelshelf** | 5m | HS | | |

Climb the crack to the right of *Twin Cracks* to gain a ledge (care!) and the top.

| 15 **Coral Arête** | 5m | HS | ★ | 2004 |

Climb the arête to right of *The Mantelshelf*.

| 16 **Coral Sea** | 5m | VS | | |

(4c). Climb the faint crack-line, moving left at the top.

| 17 **Barnarm** | 5m | VS | | |

(4b). Climb the obvious crack-line.

| 18 **View to Mount Ida** | 5m | VS | ★ | |

(4c). Start below a slight bulge at the top of the wall and climb the wall moving left at the top.

| 19 **Seavy Rigg** | 5m | HS | | |

Climb the shallow corner.

Main Wall Left

This is the expanse of rock stretching rightwards from the left-hand stone wall to end in a steep square-cut arête. The left end is set forwards some 5 metres right of the stone wall.

NB At the time of writing, climbing is banned on this section (see above).

| 1 **Filter Tip** | 4m | VD | | |

Climb the arête just left of *Tabend*.

| 2 **Tabend** | 4m | S | | |

Climb the centre of the wall via a thin crack.

To the right of this the crag forms a long flat wall whose main features are two stepped overlaps, a left-slanting one near the left-hand end and a right-slanting one near the centre.

| 3 **The Hum** | 6m | HS | | |

Climb the hand-width crack, which ends in a grass-choked slot.

| 4 **The Buzz** | 8m | HVS | | 2005 |

(5a). Start left of the left-slanting corner and climb the wall passing the square-cut corner and the wall above.

Windmore End Main Wall Left

1	Filter Tip	VD
2	Tab End	S
3	The Hum	HS
4	The Buzz	HVS
5	Verteris Outlook	VS *
6	Agrippa	MVS **
7	Cassandra	VS *
8	Romulus	MVS *

9	Remus	S *
10	Longman	S **
11	Augustus	MS *
12	Gumbarley	MVS
13	HTZ	HS
14	Colin's Dilemma	VS *
15	Mike's Overlap	VS
16	Fingers	VS *
17	Wild Thyme	HVS **
18	Aeolian	E1 **

19	The Baggins Effect	HVS *
20	Harebells	MVS
21	Kel Floff	S
22	Well Head	VS *
23	Head Stone	HS
24	The Tomb	VD *
25	Snowflake	S *
26	Mike's Arête	VS

Photo: Ron Kenyon

| 5 | **Verteris Outlook** | | 8m | VS | ★ | 2005 |

(4c). Climb up and over the left-slanting overlap and finish up the wall above.

| 6 | **Agrippa** | | 8m | MVS | ★ ★ | |

Start immediately right of the left-slanting overlap.
   (4b). Climb the pleasant finger-crack to a ledge.

| 7 | **Cassandra** | | 8m | VS | ★ | 2005 |

(4c). Awkward moves gain a ledge above an overlap. Finish up the wall above.

| 8 | **Romulus** | | 8m | MVS | ★ | |

(4b). Climb the thinner left-hand diverging crack.

| 9 | **Remus** | | 8m | S | ★ | |

Climb the twin right-hand crack which gives a good jamming exercise.

| 10 | **Longman** | | 8m | S | ★ ★ | |

Climb the crack-line with a tiny pod just below half-height.

| 11 | **Augustus** | | 8m | MS | ★ | |

Climb the rightward-slanting crack.

| 12 | **Gumbarley** | | 8m | MVS | | |

(4b). Climb directly up the wall between *Augustus* and *H.T.Z.*

| 13 | **H.T.Z.** | | 8m | HS | | |

Start one metre left of the overlap by two boreholes at the foot of the crag.
   Climb the crack which leads interestingly past a ledge near the top.

| 14 | **Colin's Dilemma** | | 8m | VS | ★ | |

(4c). Climb the wall direct immediately left of the overlap. A tricky move gains the ledge.

| 15 | **Mike's Overlap** | | 8m | VS | | 2005 |

(4c). Climb the obvious corner, over the overlap, to gain a ledge and wall to finish.

| 16 | **Fingers** | | 8m | VS | ★ | |

(5a). Climb the thin crack, 2 metres right of the overlap, with difficulty to a ledge and tiny corner.

17 **Wild Thyme**	8m	HVS	★★	2005

(5b). Start just right of *Fingers*, where hard moves (or a dyno) lead to a horizontal break and a good hold. Small holds above enable better holds to be gained with easier climbing above.

18 **Aeolian**	8m	E1	★★	1990s

Start 5 metres right of the right-slanting overlap below a faint crack.
(5b). Gain the crack and make interesting moves to the top without resorting to holds on *The Baggins Effect*. Excellent.

19 **The Baggins Effect**	8m	HVS	★	2005

Start between the cracks of *Aeolian* and *Harebells*.
(5b). Awkward moves gain a horizontal break with a good hold just above it. Continue up with interest.

20 **Harebells**	8m	MVS		2005

(4b). Climb the triple cracks left of *Kel Floff*.

21 **Kel Floff**	8m	S		

Seven metres left of the right-hand arête is a prominent straight crack. Climb it.

22 **Well Head**	8m	VS	★	2005

(4c). Starting left of a right-slanting overlap, gain the crack above and, with use of a ledge on the right, follow it to top.

23 **Headstone**	8m	HS		

Climb the wall and crack left of *The Tomb*.

24 **The Tomb**	9m	VD	★	

Climb the V-crack 3 metres left of the right-hand arête then move right along ledges almost to the arête.

25 **Snowflake**	7m	S	★	

The thin crack-line just left of the arête gives an interestingly delicate problem.

26 **Mike's Arête**	7m	VS		2005

(4c). Climb the left side of the arête all the way to the top.

Andy's Arête	7m	HVS+	★	1987

(5a). Climb the right side of the arête, pulling onto the left side near the top.

Rain Stopped Play	7m	HVS+	★	1987

(5a). Climb the bulging right wall of the corner by using a crack up to the right.

Spider's Dinner	7m	VS		2006

(4c). Climb the arête just right of *Rain Stopped Play*.

Main Wall

This is a long section of crag which starts with an impressive high wall. **Descent** is possible down the ledge complex to the left of this, or via the unusual chimney at the start of the *Main Wall-Far Right* section. Pegs give additional security on some climbs.

NB At the time of writing, climbing is banned on this section (see above).

27 **Bowline**	13m	VS		

Near the left-hand side of the flat wall is a prominent right-facing corner. (4b). Climb the corner to a bulge at 4 metres, then gain a ledge and finish up the cracked wall above.

28 **Nightlight**	13m	E2	★	2006

(5c). Climb the wall and thin crack left of *Plumbline* to finish up the loose headwall with care.

29 **Plumbline**	13m	HVS		

(4c). Climb the straight crack that widens near the top.

30 **The Tasp**	13m	HVS	★	

(5a). Climb the wall 2 metres right of *Plumbline* to reach a sloping ledge. Finish carefully up the wall above.

31 **Nightshift**	13m	E1	★ ★	2006

(5b). Starting 2 metres right of *The Tasp*, gain a thin crack with difficulty and follow this to a ledge. Finish carefully up the loose headwall.

32 **Supremo**	13m	HVS	★	

(4c). Climb the very thin crack, 7 metres right of *Plumbline*, which goes straight up the wall past a ledge at 6 metres. Finish carefully up the loose headwall.

33 **Serendipity**	13m	VS	★	

(4b). Climb the prominent rightward-slanting crack which leads to a loose square-shaped sentry-box at the top.

Windmore End Main Wall

27	Bowline	VS
28	Night Light	E2 *
29	Plumbline	HVS
30	The Tasp	HVS *
31	Nightshift	E1 **
32	Supremo	HVS *

33	Serendipity	VS *
34	Hobbit	VS
35	Staircase	HS
36	First Choice	VD *
37	Pork Chop	HVS
38	Second Best	S *
39	Mealybugs	HVS *
40	Purk	S *

41	Flying Rabbits	HVS *
42	Little Pinkie	VS *
43	Cool Runnings	E2 **
44	Comeback	VS
45	Wandering Everywhere	HS
46	Little Piggies	MVS
47	Brass Monkey Job	HS *
48	Pressure Crack	HVS *

Photo: Ron Kenyon

34 **Hobbit**	13m	VS	

Three metres right of *Serendipity* is a short right-facing corner.
(4c). Climb the corner to a small ledge, step right and follow thin converging cracks to a ledge and then the top.

35 **Staircase**	13m	HS	

Two metres right of *Hobbit* is a short hand-crack which leads to a comfortable ledge. A tricky move leads up to broken ledges and the top.

36 **First Choice**	11m	VD	★

Climb the obvious wide crack that contains a large jammed block at 5 metres.

The crag now continues as a series of corners. The first one has an overhang at 3 metres.

37 **Pork Chop**	11m	HVS	

(4c). Ascend the overhung corner to an overlap, then cross the wall diagonally rightwards to finish above a short wide crack. Bold.

38 **Second Best**	11m	S	★

Three metres right of the overhung corner is an obvious wide right-slanting crack.
Climb this to a ledge and then to the top.

39 **Mealybugs**	10m	HVS	★

Just right of *Second Best* is a slanting overlap.
(5a). Climb directly up a thin crack. Pull over onto the wall above, avoiding the loose block, and trend slightly rightwards to finish.

40 **Purk**	10m	S	★

Gain a small grass ledge at one metre and climb the crack system above to meet the end of the rightward-trending overlap.

41 **Flying Rabbits**	10m	HVS	★	2006

(5a). Climb the wall between *Purk* and *Little Pinkie*.

42 **Little Pinkie**	10m	VS	★

(4b). Climb the thin crack-line, just right of a short corner, with a slight deviation to the left near the top.

43 **Cool Runnings**	10m	E2	★★	2006

(5b). Climb the wall between *Little Pinkie* and *Comeback* – keep your cool!

Windmore End Main Wall Right

47	Brass Monkey Job	HS *
48	Pressure Crack	HVS *
49	Imbalanced Pressure	E2 *
50	Hughie's Route	VD *
51	Most Sincerely	HS

52	Arty	S
53	Andon	VD *
54	Farty	S *
55	Chocky	VS
56	Strangler	E1 *

57	Confidence Trickster	VD
58	Moss Trooper	VS *
59	A Week Before the Beast	E1 **
60	Short and Sweet	HS *
61	Steppin' Up	HVS *
62	Steppin' Out	HVS *
63	Steppin' Away	VO *

Photo: Ron Kenyon

| 44 **Comeback** | 10m | VS | | |

(4c). Climb the wall with a hairline crack in it just right of *Little Pinkie*.

| 45 **Wandering Everywhere** | 9m | HS | | |

Climb the short corner then the crack above to a loose finish.

| 46 **Little Piggies** | 8m | MVS | | |

(4b). Climb the short overlapping arête left of the corner, or corner itself, then the crack above.

The crag now cuts back.

| 47 **Brass Monkey Job** | 7m | HS | ★ | |

Climb gymnastically up the left side of the arête.

| 48 **Pressure Crack** | 7m | HVS | ★ | 1990s |

(5a). Climb the crack just right of the arête.

| 49 **Imbalanced Pressure** | 7m | E2 | ★ | 1990s |

(6a). Climb directly up leaning wall below the slab of *Hughie's Route* and follow the tapering pillar up to the left.

| 50 **Hughie's Route** | 9m | VD | ★ | |

Climb the corner where the crag cuts back then move up and left across a slab to the arête.

| 51 **Most Sincerely** | 8m | HS | | 1987 |

Start 3 metres right of the corner of *Hughie's Route* and climb directly up the wall using a thin crack.

| 52 **Arty** | 8m | S | | |

Start at a shallow square-cut groove and climb the thin left-hand crack.

| 53 **Andon** | 8m | VD | ★ | |

Climb the wide right-hand crack.

| 54 **Farty** | 8m | S | ★ | |

Climb the left side of the arête right of *Andon*.

| 55 **Chocky** | 8m | VS | | |

(4c). Climb the thin jagged crack-line 3 metres right of the corner to a steep awkward finish.

Right: Catherine Kenyon on **Strangler** (E1), Windmore End. **Photo:** Ron Kenyon

| 56 **Strangler** | | 7m | E1+ | ★ | |

(5a). The crag now cuts back to form a steep arête - climb this boldly on its right side.

| 57 **Confidence Trickster** | | 7m | VD | | |

Climb the corner to the right of the arête of *Strangler*.

| 58 **Moss Trooper** | | 7m | VS | ★ | 1987 |

(5a). Climb the wall 2 metres right of *Confidence Trickster*. A hard start leads to a faint scoop.

| 59 **A Week Before The Beast** | | 7m | E1 | ★★ | 1987 |

(5b). Climb the hairline crack in the bulging wall just right of *Moss Trooper*.

| 60 **Short And Sweet** | | 7m | HS | ★ | |

Climb the slanting crack-line to a loose finish.

| 61 **Steppin' Up** | | 7m | HVS+ | ★ | 2006 |

(5c). A direct start to *Steppin' Out*, starting directly up the pillar.

| 62 **Steppin' Out** | | 8m | HVS | ★ | 1987 |

(5a). Climb the right-facing groove to a bulge then move left and ascend the wall direct.

| 63 **Steppin' Away** | | | VO | ★ | |

Start to the right of *Steppin' Out* and make interesting moves up the wall, just left of the arête, to a ledge.

Left: Alan Dougherty and Ron Kenyon
Steppin' Up (HVS), Windmore End.
Photo: Michael Kenyon

Main Wall – Far Right

This is the sector extending towards the next drystone wall, which is some distance away. The rock gradually diminishes in height and many more problems have been worked out beyond what is recorded.

NB At the time of writing, climbing is banned on this section (see above).

An unusual chimney/gully with a grassy cone at its foot marks the left-hand boundary of this area and is a useful means of **descent**.

Room 101	6m	HS		1987

The crack-line just left of *Workout*.

Workout	6m	S	★	

Climb the wide weatherworn crack 7 metres right of the *Descent Gully*.

Pump It Up	6m	VS	★	1987

(4c). Climb the smooth wall marked by hairline cracks just right of *Workout*.

Postman's Knock	6m	HS		

Three metres right of *Workout* is a thin crack.
 Climb this moving right to an insecure finish.

Second Time Around	6m	HS		

Climb the cracked face one metre right of a short right-facing corner to the right of *Postman's Knock*.

Teatime Special	6m	S		

Climb the wide crack 3 metres right of the corner.

Second Wall

Behind *Windmore Green* cottage is the *Second Wall* area which lies between two drystone walls. The area consists of two sections divided by a wide grassy bank which provides a useful means of **descent**.
 The face to the left of the grassy descent bank has a low grassy ridge a short distance in front of the crag. The main feature of this left-hand side of *Second Wall* is the straight corner of *Fern Crack*, which runs the full-height of the face. To the left again is an area of short corners and ledges.

Windmore End
Second Wall Far Left

1	Rottweiler	V3 *
2	Winalot	V1 *
3	Distemper	V1
4	Dogleg	V1 **
5	H.T.J.	S *
6	Consolation	S
7	Zoot Route	VD *
8	Fern Wall	E1
9	Fern Crack	VS **
10	Lastra Wall	E3 **
11	Lost on 66	E4 **
12	Right on 66	E3 *
13	Sauron	S *
14	Chinook	V2 *
15	Archtype	S *
16	Epitaph	VS **
17	Scoop and Wall	E2 *
18	Ardrox	HVS *
19	Yellow Peril	HVS *
20	Gulliver's Traverse	HVS
21	Nature Trail	S

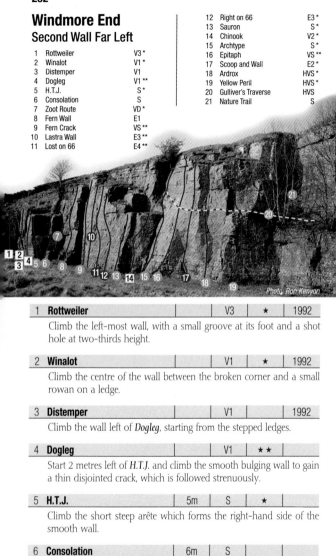

Photo: Ron Kenyon

1	**Rottweiler**		V3	★	1992

Climb the left-most wall, with a small groove at its foot and a shot hole at two-thirds height.

2	**Winalot**		V1	★	1992

Climb the centre of the wall between the broken corner and a small rowan on a ledge.

3	**Distemper**		V1		1992

Climb the wall left of *Dogleg*, starting from the stepped ledges.

4	**Dogleg**		V1	★★	

Start 2 metres left of *H.T.J.* and climb the smooth bulging wall to gain a thin disjointed crack, which is followed strenuously.

5	**H.T.J.**	5m	S	★	

Climb the short steep arête which forms the right-hand side of the smooth wall.

6	**Consolation**	6m	S		

Gain the large ledge just right of the arête then climb a short corner.

| 7 | **Zoot Route** | | 10m | VD | ★ | |

Gain the ledge of *Consolation* from the right and climb the wall to another ledge. Continue to the top past a small tree.

| 8 | **Fern Wall** | | 10m | E1 | | 1990s |

(5b). Climb the wall just to left of *Fern Crack*.

| 9 | **Fern Crack** | | 10m | VS | ★★ | |

(4c). Climb the obvious fern-bedecked corner which runs the full height of the crag. Quite sustained.

| 10 | **Lastra Wall** | | 11m | E3 | ★★ | 1998 |

A serious but superb route starting just to right of *Fern Crack*.

(5c). Follow the unprotected rightward-slanting shallow groove on sometimes wobbly small flakes.

| | **La'al Wall** | | 11m | E4+ | ★★ | 2011 |

A superb (very) highball boulder problem (V4) starting 3 metres right of *Fern Crack* at the right-hand end of the head-height overlap.

(6b). Climb the fine steep wall direct – the crux is gaining the obvious square-cut undercut pinch at 5 metres.

| 11 | **Lost on 66** | | 11m | E4 | ★★ | 2006 |

(6a). A tremendous route which follows the faint crack-line up the centre of the wall.

| 12 | **Right on 66** | | 12m | E3 | ★ | 2006 |

(5c). Climb the crack-line up the wall left of *Sauron* to just below an overlap, then move left and follow a groove to the top.

| 13 | **Sauron** | | 6m | S | ★ | |

Climb the vague rib on good holds to a large ledge.

| 14 | **Chinook** | | | V2 | ★ | 1999 |

Start from a projecting triangular ledge at the foot of an open shallow groove just right of *Sauron*.

Move up and right around the rib to finish up the slim wall.

| 15 | **Archtype** | | 12m | S | ★ | |

The smooth slab is bounded on its left by a slanting corner.

Climb the slab to gain a large ledge then follow the corner above past a tiny hawthorn.

| 16 Epitaph | 12m | VS | ★ ★ | |

(4c). Climb the slab, just right of *Archtype*, directly to a short headwall and ascend this to the top.

| 17 **Scoop and Wall** | 12m | E2+ | ★ | |

Start just right of the slab below an open bulging scoop.

(5c). Climb up the right side of the scoop with difficulty to gain the arête above. Move left onto the slab without using the triangular ledge on the arête, then ascend the slab and headwall above. Very bold.

| 18 **Ardrox** | 12m | HVS | ★ | |

(5a). Climb the shallow left-trending groove to a triangular ledge, then finish up the short corner above.

| 19 **Yellow Peril** | 12m | HVS- | ★ | |

(4c). Climb the blunt rib just right of *Ardrox* which leads steeply to a small ledge and a finish up the wall above.

The centre of the bay contains a large ledge on which grow several small trees.

Windmore End Second Wall
Centre Left

| 19 | Yellow Peril | HVS * |
| 20 | Gulliver's Traverse | HVS |

21	Nature Trail	S
22	Simulator	HVS **
23	The Helm	E3 **
24	The Motivator	HVS *
25	66 The Highway Speaks	E2 *
26	The Greave Speaks	E2 *
27	Coffastroni	E2 *
28	Trime	VD

Photo: Ron Kenyon

| 20 Gulliver's Traverse | 18m | HVS- | | |

This is a traverse of the left side of *Second Wall*, starting at the left-hand end of the large tree-covered ledge of *Nature Trail*.
   (4c). Move left onto the ledge of *Yellow Peril* then continue leftwards onto the slab of *Epitaph* to finish up the corner of *Archtype*.

| 21 **Nature Trail** | 18m | S | | |

Well-named! Start below the right end of the tree-covered ledge.
   Jungle-bash up to the ledge and hack your way through to the corner on the left, which provides a means of escape.

| 22 **Simulator** | 12m | HVS | ★★ | |

Start just to the right of the tree-covered ledge.
   (5a). Climb the crack/groove which runs the full height of the crag.

| 23 **The Helm** | 12m | E3 | ★★ | 1980s |

Excellent technical climbing up the face between *Simulator* and *The Motivator*. Desperate start!
   (6a). Gain the thin crack and follow this to the break at half-height. Climb the wall above, just left of the blunt arête.

| 24 **The Motivator** | 12m | HVS- | ★ | |

   (4c). Climb the large left-facing corner with an overhang at the top.

| 25 **66 The Highway Speaks** | 12m | E2 | ★ | 1995 |

This takes the hanging arête which bounds the right corner of *The Motivator* and has an excellent finishing position! Starting as for *The Motivator*.
   (5c). Swing rightwards to gain a ledge at left side of the face. Ascend using the arête for the left-hand as necessary and taking care with loose rock and limited protection.

| 26 **The Greave Speaks** | 12m | E2 | ★ | 2006 |

   (5c). Either start as for *Coffastroni* or climb a thin crack on the left to gain the small ledge. Follow the thin crack in the wall on the left and the wall above.

Right: Jim Greave on the first ascent of **The Greave Speaks** (E2), Windmore End. **Photo:** Ron Kenyon

| 27 **Coffastroni** | | 13m | E2 | ★ | |

(5b). Start just left of *Trime* and climb up leftwards to a small ledge. Finish straight up the wall above. A serious route and now complicated by the growth of the tree.

| 28 **Trime** | | 11m | VD | | |

Climb the short loose corner to a fight with the large tree on the ledge above. Escape rightwards here or climb the wall behind the tree.

To the right of the grassy descent bank lies the more open, right-hand section of *Second Wall*.

| 29 **Sneakthief** | | 8m | HS | ★ | |

Start near the left-hand side of the wall below a small grass ledge at head height.

Climb the short left-facing corner, then the continuation crack above.

| 30 **Bloodbath** | | 9m | HS | | |

Climb the small square-cut corner to a series of ledges and finish up the wall above.

| 31 **Centurion** | | 9m | HS | ★ | |

Climb a short jagged crack to a ledge on the left and finish up the wall above.

| 32 **Legion** | | 9m | HS | ★ | |

Climb the slab just right of *Centurion* and a shallow cracked groove leading to a ledge. Finish up the wall above.

| 33 **Legion Slab** | | 9m | VS+ | ★ | 2006 |

(4c). Climb the slab between *Legion* and *Zephyr*, gaining a "thank God" hold and then a ledge, to finish up the wall above.

| 34 **Zephyr** | | 9m | E1 | ★ | 1999 |

(5b). Climb the arête and finish up *Palace Guard*.

| 35 **Palace Guard** | | 9m | E1 | ★ | |

(5b). Climb from the sentry-box up a steep crack to the ledge of *Legion*. Finish up the right-hand side of the wall above.

Left: Not difficult to feel motivated on a glorious evening like this: Stephen Reid and Chris King on **The Motivator** (HVS), Windmore End. **Photo:** Ron Kenyon

Windmore End Second Wall
Centre Right

29	Sneakthief	HS *
30	Bloodbath	HS
31	Centurion	HS *
32	Legion	HS *

33	Legion Slab	VS *
34	Zephyr	E1 *
35	Palace Guard	E1 *
36	Zero Route	HS **
37	Mistral	E3 **
38	White Wall	E3 **
39	A Fistful of Garnetts	E3 **
40	A Scent of Orchids	E3 **

Photo: Ron Kenyon

36 **Zero Route**	9m	HS	★ ★	

The pleasant corner to the left of the white-flecked wall.

The white-flecked wall holds four superb hard climbs on excellent rock, all bold with limited or no protection.

37 **Mistral**	8m	E3	★ ★	1994

(6a). The wall between *Zero Route* and *White Wall* - escape to the right below the top wall.

38 **White Wall**	8m	E3	★ ★	

(5c). Ascend the centre of the wall below the square-cut bay at the top of the crag.

39 **A Fistful of Garnetts**	8m	E3	★ ★	2006

(5c). Gain and climb the faint crack below the left-hand side of the prominent block overhang.

40 **A Scent of Orchids**	8m	E3	★ ★	

(5c). Climb the faint sustained crack up to the right of the prominent block overhang.

Windmore End Second Wall Far Right

41	Serutan	VD	45	Jizzle	VS *	49	Differential	VD
42	Rubstic Direct	E3**	46	Sun Trip	S *	50	Parson's Nose	VD
43	Rubstic	E2 *	47	Cranch	VD *			
44	Scirocco	E2 *	48	Ribble	HS *			

Photo: Ron Kenyon

The crag is now interrupted by a series of broken ledges.

41 **Serutan**	6m	VD		

Start part way up the broken ledges and climb the wall direct.

42 **Rubstic Direct**	8m	E3-	★★	1980s

(5c). Climb the corner as for *Rubstic* then move up and left onto the face and climb this boldly to the top.

43 **Rubstic**	8m	E2	★	1980s

Start just right of the broken ledges at a slim right-facing corner. A bold route.
(5b). Climb the corner then move right into a shallow groove to gain a ledge. Finish up the short wall above.

44 **Scirocco**	8m	E2+	★	1999

(5c). Start as for *Jizzle* but climb a vague groove direct to the right side of the ledge on *Rubstic*.

To the right is a sweep of slab with a curved overlap near its centre.

45 **Jizzle**	8m	VS	★	

(5a). Start at the left side of the slab and ascend diagonally rightwards to finish at a small grass ledge.

| 46 **Suntrip** | 8m | S | ★ | |

Climb the centre of the slab to the curved overlap and follow this leftwards onto the ledge of *Rubstic*. Finish up the short wall.

| **Go Carefully as You Go** | 7m | VS+ | | |

(4c). Climb the steep and interesting slab between *Suntrip* and *Cranch* – no protection.

| 47 **Cranch** | 7m | VD | ★ | |

Climb the crack which bounds the slab on the right.

| 48 **Ribble** | 7m | HS | ★ | |

Climb the steep and interesting rib to the right of *Cranch*.

| 49 **Differential** | 7m | VD | | |

Start below the open corner and climb the corner and the short prow above.

| 50 **Parson's Nose** | 7m | VD | | |

Climb the arête to the right of the open corner.

Far Right Wall

This section of the crag lies to the right of the drystone wall right of the cottage of *Windmore Green* and is approached from the gate between *Windmore Green* and *Windmore End Farm*. It is probably the best section of the crag, with good compact rock, though there is some loose rock at the top of some lines. It hosts a good selection of harder climbs and micro-wires are de rigeur, as well as a bouldering mat, for whether led or soloed, many of the climbs are really very high highball boulder problems.

| 1 **Light Bulb** | 6m | VS+ | ★ | |

(5a). Start one metre right of the drystone wall and climb the face by a faint crack-line.

| 2 **Samoon** | 6m | HVS | ★ | 1999 |

(5a). Start 3 metres right of the drystone wall and follow a hairline crack past a small bulge at half-height.

| 3 **Smoke Ring** | 6m | S | ★ | |

Start 4 metres right of the drystone wall and climb to a sloping ledge, then trend right to the top.

Windmore End Far Right Wall Windy Nook

1	Light Bulb	VS *
2	Samoon	HVS *
3	Smoke Ring	S *
4	Far Groove	VD *

5	Windy Nook	D
6	Flake Crack	VD
7	The Wind Cries Mary	E2

Photo: Ron Kenyon

4	**Far Groove**	6m	VD	★	

Climb the groove just right of a blunt rib.

5	**Windy Nook**	6m	D		

Climb the corner-crack.

6	**Flake Crack**	6m	VD		

Climb the short layback crack right of *Windy Nook* to a ledge.

The crag now forms a long steep wall, overhanging at its left-hand end and offering climbing on the best rock at *Windmore*.

7	**The Wind Cries Mary**	6m	E2		1990s

(6a). Climb the thin crack to the left of *Anticlimbax*.

8	**Anticlimbax**	7m	VS	★ ★	

(4c). Climb the overhanging crack left of the bulging wall.

Windmore End
Far Right Wall Rebel Area

8	Anticlimax	VS **
9	Trouble Without a Cause	E4 **
v1	Right Trouble Without a Cause	E4 **
10	Rebel Without a Pause	E3 ***
11	Alverton	E2 *

v2	Viva Garibaldi!	E3 **
12	Strangeways	E3 **
13	Rock and a Hard Place	E4 **
14	Touching the Void	E3 **
15	Chill Factor	E3 *
16	Blowin' in the Wind	E4
17	Becher's Brook	E1 **
18	Squeeze My Lemon	HVS *
19	Lime Street	S *
20	Wall Street	VS
21	Grassy Crack	VD *
22	Beanz Meanz	E3 *

Photo: Ron Kenyon

9	**Trouble Without a Cause**	7m	E4	★★	1996

(6b). Start from the small corner at ground level and make a very long reach leftwards from the seam to an obvious vertical slot. Make another hard move to reach a jug just up to the right, then climb more easily to the top.

v1 **Right Trouble Without a Cause** 7m E4 ★★ 2005

(6a). Start between *Trouble* and *Rebel* and climb up to gain a short corner, then the jug on *Trouble* high on the left. Finish more easily.

10	**Rebel Without a Pause**	7m	E3	★★★	1989

(5c). Climb the excellent line taking the thin crack to the right of the bulging wall.

Right: Steve Crowe finds **Trouble Without a Cause** (E4), Windmore End. **Photo:** Bob Bennett

| 11 **Alverton** | 9m | E2+ | ★ | 1980s |

Start just right of the arched overlap at an indefinite groove-line.
(5c). Climb the groove for a few metres then pull out left onto the wall and finish leftwards to the top.

v2 **_Viva Garibaldi!_** 8m E3 ★ ★ 1989

(6a). A direct start. Start 3 metres right of _Rebel Without a Pause_, below a small arched overlap at 2 metres and climb straight through the overlap to good holds, then move up and finish as for _Alverton_.

| 12 **Strangeways** | 7m | E3 | ★ ★ | 1990 |

(5c). Climb the indefinite groove, as for _Alverton_ then continue directly up the wall above.

A good low level traverse can be made from _Alverton_ leftwards to _Windy Nook_ (V3).

| 13 **Rock and a Hard Place** | 7m | E4 | ★ ★ | 1989 |

(6a). Start 3 metres right of _Alverton_ and climb directly to a tiny arched overlap in the centre of the wall, then continue boldly up the steep wall above.

| 14 **Touching The Void** | 7m | E3 | ★ ★ | 1989 |

(5b). Climb boldly up the wall following a hairline crack to a steep finish.

| 15 **Chill Factor** | 7m | E3 | ★ | 1990 |

(5c). Climb the shallow groove 3 metres left of _Becher's Brook_ then the steep upper wall rightwards on fragile holds.

| 16 **Blowin' in the Wind** | 7m | E4 | | 1990s |

(6a). Start one metre left of _Becher's Brook_ and climb directly to and through an overlap via a faint groove.

| 17 **Becher's Brook** | 7m | E1 | ★ ★ | 1980s |

(5a). Climb the obvious thin crack and either pull left through the overlap to finish or move right to a ledge.

| 18 **Squeeze My Lemon** | 7m | HVS | ★ | 1989 |

(5a). Climb the wall 2 metres right of _Becher's Brook_ trending slightly right to a ledge near the top.

Left: Michael Kenyon ready to commit on **Viva Garibaldi!** (E3), Windmore End.
Photo: Ron Kenyon

Windmore End Far Right Wall Beanz Area

21	Grassy Crack	VD **	26	Windy Moss	S *
22	Beanz Meanz	E3 *	27	Windy Miller	HVS *
23	Heinz	E2	28	Wind Breaker	VS
24	Wind Power	E1 **	29	Wall of Wind	HVS *
25	Cool Man	HVS *	30	Fresh Breeze	VS

Photo: Ron Kenyon

Squeezed Citrus		7m	HVS+	★	

(5c). Just right of *Squeeze My Lemon*, choose one of a number of possible starts to gain better holds which lead up to the finish of *Lime Street*.

19 **Lime Street**		8m	S	★	

Follow a left-trending weakness starting 2 metres left of *Grassy Crack*.

20 **Wall Street**		7m	VS		1989

(4b). Climb the slab just left of *Grassy Crack*.

21 **Grassy Crack**		7m	VD	★	

A pleasant climb following the corner.

22 **Beanz Meanz...**		7m	E3	★	1989

(5c). Climb directly up the pillar which is split by a hairline crack.

23 **Heinz**		7m	E2		1990s

(5b). Climb the wall between *Beanz Meanz* and *Wind Power*.

| 24 **Wind Power** | 7m | E1- | ★★ | 1989 |

(5b). Start 3 metres right of *Grassy Crack* and follow a thin right-trending crack-line.

| 25 **Cool Man** | 7m | HVS | ★ | 2006 |

(5a). Climb the wall between *Wind Power* and *Windy Moss*.

| 26 **Windy Moss** | 7m | S | ★ | |

Gain a small ledge at head height then finish up the wall above.

| 27 **Windy Miller** | 7m | HVS | ★ | 1989 |

(5a). Start 2 metres right of the small ledge of *Windy Moss* and climb the wall direct.

| 28 **Wind Breaker** | 7m | VS | | 1989 |

(4c). Start below a thin crack system and climb the wall.

| 29 **Wall Of Wind** | 7m | HVS | ★ | 1989 |

(5b). Start at the smooth wall and climb it on small incut holds.

| 30 **Fresh Breeze** | 7m | VS | | 2003 |

(4b). Climb the obvious slightly leftward-trending open groove which has some loose rock and poor protection. A more direct line following the face just left of *Sue's Route* is 5a.

| 31 **Sue's Route** | 8m | VS | ★★ | 1980s |

(4c). Climb the prominent crack which slants up rightwards. A loose block at the top needs care.

| 32 **Hurricane Force** | 8m | E2+ | ★ | 1989 |

(5c). Climb the tiny groove to a sloping ledge then enter a scoop below the roof. Step left to finish.

v1 *Hurricane Force Direct* 7m E3 2004

(5c). Start left of the original route and climb up directly.

| 33 **C.90** | 8m | E1+ | ★★ | |

(5b). Climb the thin crack which runs straight up the wall 5 metres right of *Sue's Route*.

| 34 **Crozzly Wall** | 8m | E3 | ★ | 1989 |

Start just right of *C.90* at some small stepped overhangs.

(6a). A desperate start gains the base of a thin crack, then climb the wall direct on mosaic rock.

Windmore End Far Right Wall C.90 Area

30	Fresh Breeze	VS
31	Sue's Route	VS **
32	Hurricane Force	E2 *
v1	Hurricane Force Direct	E3
33	C.90	E1 **

34	Crozzly Wall	E3 *
35	Tamalin	E2 **
36	Speeding Like a Jet	E3 **
37	April Fool	HS

Photo: Ron Kenyon

35 **Tamalin**	8m	E2	★ ★	1980s

(5c). Climb the wall 2 metres right of the stepped overhangs, using thin discontinuous cracks.

36 **Speeding Like a Jet**	8m	E3	★ ★	1989

(6a). Climb the wall, which is split by a vertical hairline crack, with great interest.

37 **April Fool**	7m	HS		

Start below a downward-pointing flake.
   (4c). Climb the wall above the flake, moving right to a tiny ledge, then finish directly.

At the very right-hand end of *Far Right Wall* is the *Arches Area*.

38 **Round the Bend**	6m	VS		

(4b). Climb the crack on the left of the wall.

Left: Michael Kenyon reaching for the thin crack on **Crozzly Wall** (E3), Windmore End.
Photo: Ron Kenyon

| 39 **That Slanting Feeling** | 7m | VS | ★ | |

(4c). Ascend the layback crack then the buttress on the left.

| 40 **Worker for the Wind** | 7m | E1- | ★ | 2006 |

(5b). Climb the crack 1.5m right of *That Slanting Feeling*. Initial fingery laybacking leads to better holds.

| 41 **Months of Rage** | 7m | E2 | ★ | 2008 |

(6a). The unprotected and technical wall in the middle.

| 42 **Underneath the Arches** | 7m | E1- | ★ | 2006 |

(5b). Start to the left of the *Beside the Arches* and climb directly to the top.

| 43 **Beside the Arches** | 8m | HVS | | 2006 |

(5a). Start left of the short corner and climb up to the arch, then directly to the top.

| 44 **Endless Storm** | 7m | HVS- | | 2006 |

(5a). Climb the short corner rightwards and follow a wall on the left to finish.

Windmore End Far Right Wall Arches Area

38	Round the Bend	VS	42	Underneath the Arches	E1 *
39	That Slanting Feeling	VS *	43	Beside the Arches	HVS
40	Worker for the Wind	E1 *	44	Endless Storm	HVS
41	Months of Rage	E2 *	45	What Care the Wind	E1

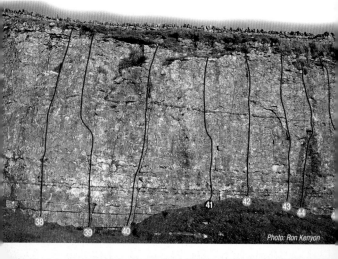

Photo: Ron Kenyon

45 **What Care the Wind**	7m	E1+		2008

Sustained fingery climbing to a loose finish.

(5c). Follow a very thin crack in wall to the right of *Endless Storm* without resource to holds in the wider cracks to either side.

Force 7 Coming In Strong	7m	HVS-		2006

(5a). Climb the narrow wall just right of *What Care the Wind* avoiding use of the vegetated cracks on either side.

The Wall Beyond

To the left of the track leading to *The Grit Beyond* and to the right of *The Far Right Wall* is a 4 metre high buttress providing a few boulder problems.

46 **Wind of Change**		S		2006

Climb the left wall of the square-cut corner on good jugs to a loose finish.

47 **Pissing in the Wind**		VD		2006

Climb the square-cut corner.

48 **Written on the Wind**		V0+		2006

Climb the right wall of the corner, starting with an undercling and stepping right to avoid a loose finish.

Windmore End The Wall Beyond

46	Wind of Change	S
47	Pissing in the Wind	VD
48	Written on the Wind	V0

49	Shadow of the Wind	V0
50	Portent of the Wind	V0
51	Veering	V0
52	Backing	V0

Photo: Ron Kenyon

49	**Shadow of the Wind**		V0+		2006

Climb the leaning scoop to gain a ledge at two-thirds height.

50	**Portent of Wind**		V0+		2006

Climb the wall between the scoop and crack, using a crack to start. Starting left of the crack is V1.

51	**Veering**		V0		2006

Climb the obvious crack.

52	**Backing**		V0+		2006

Climb the wall above the stepped ledges.

Limekiln Recess

This is the 5 to 6 metre high wall up and left of the limekiln and to the right of the track leading to *The Grit Beyond*.

1	**Wind Began to Howl**		V0+		2006

Sustained climbing up the centre of the wall.

2	**Stormbringer**		V0		2006

Climb up by a small arch, taking care with a loose block.

3	**Tempest**		V0		2006

Climb the crack with cherty holds.

Windmore End The Limekiln Recess

1	Wind Began to Howl	V0	3	Tempest	V0
2	Stormbringer	V0	4	Perfect Storm	V0

Photo: Carol Dougherty

| 4 | **Perfect Storm** | | V0+ | | 2006 |

Climb the cracked wall with a mini peapod.

Limekiln Recess – Right

This is the area of rock directly behind and to the right of the lime-kiln, just above the entrance gate. The fact that it is so close to the gate makes it worth the slight detour.

| 1 | **Swing Left** | | V0 | | 2010 |

Climb the left side of the wall directly behind the limekiln, just right of a wide crack.

| 2 | **Swing Right** | | V0 | | 2010 |

Climb the right side of the wall, right of *Swing Left*.

| 3 | **Swinging Gate** | | V0- | | 2010 |

Climb the obvious arête.

| 4 | **Two Step** | | V1 | | 2010 |

Gain a crack and move up with an awkward step.

| 5 | **Tewfitt's Struggle** | | V0+ | | 2010 |

The crack increases in interest towards the top.

Windmore End The Limekiln Recess Right

1	Swing Left	V0	7	Hayturner	V0
2	Swing Right	V0	8	Todd's	V0
3	Swinging Gate	V0	9	Upmanhowe	V1
4	Two Step	V1			
5	Tewfitt's Struggle	V0			
6	Spurrigg Pillar	V0			

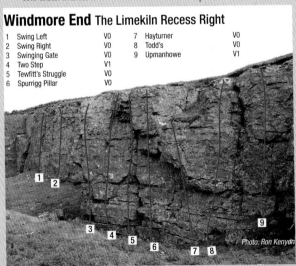

Photo: Ron Kenyon

6 **Spurrigg Pillar**		V0+		2010

Gain and overcome the overlaps and continue up the pillar.

7 **Hayturner**		V0		2010

Climb the incipient corner through the roof.

8 **Todd's**		V0		2010

Delightful climbing up the wall.

9 **Upmanhowe**		V1+		2010

Sustained climbing up the wall just left of the corner.

The Grit Beyond

Some 350 metres north-east of *Windmore End* is a small outcrop of reasonably sound gritstone which offers a number of fair quality problems. It is located just to the right of the stone wall that runs up the fellside to the right of the *Far Right area* and adjacent to a cart-track which passes the old lime kiln.

Leaning Wall		V1/V2		2006

On the left of the stone wall is a short wall. Sit down start. Dynamic – V1. Using intermediate holds – V2.

The following routes are to the right of the wall.

1 **Arenaceous**		V1	★	2006

Just right of the stone wall is a reachy stepped prow with some loose rock.

2 **Refuge of the Dislimed**		V1		2006

The jutting stepped wall just left of the obvious arête contains some loose rock and is easer if finished trending right-wards.

3 **Pining for the Grit**		V0-	★★	2006

Although an improbable looking line at the grade, the obvious prow is straightforward.

4 **Lithological Deviance**		V2	★	2006

Climb the wall just to right of the prow, gain a hold in the notch at 4 metres, then rock-over and reach for the top.

5 **The Eschews**		V4		2006

An interesting problem eschewing all large holds and taking finger-tip

Windmore End The Grit Beyond

1	Arnaceous	V1 *	4	Lithological Deviance	V2*
2	Refuge of the Dislimed	V1	5	The Eschews	V4
3	Pining for the Grit	V0 **	6	Namurian	V0

Photo: Ron Kenyon

pockets up the faint arête to the right – a final slap enables the top to be reached.

6	**Namurian**		V0		2006

The wall to right is broken by a grassy ledge with some loose rock. Reaching for the top from the ledge is easier for the tall.

Augill (NY 818 152) is a delightful limestone gorge worth a visit in its own right. The obvious 30 metre white arête on the north side of the gorge has been top-roped. **Argill Beck (NY 858 133)** is an impressive buttress of rock tucked away in a valley near to the top of Stainmore. **Middle Busk Scar (NY 682 093)** is extensive and easily reached limestone scar in a magnificent position and gives a series of easy boulder problems with average height of 4 metres.

Right: A bouldering mat heads off to Windmore End! **Photo:** Ron Kenyon

Aisgill

Grid Reference: SE 773 975
Faces: **South**

Altitude: **370m**
Approach: **8 mins**

Located on the lower south–eastern flank of Wild Boar Fell in Maller-stang, which is the upper valley of the River Eden, *Aisgill* is a most impressive ravine containing many crags. The best lie relatively low down, only a couple of hundred metres west of Aisgill Farm, on the B6259 road from Kirkby Stephen, through Mallerstang, to Hawes.

Approach:
From the farm, follow the track on the north side of the beck onto the fell and under the railway viaduct of the Settle-Carlisle Railway. Continue along a track towards the ravine, then via slopes to below the crag. The crag is on Access Land designated under the 2000 CROW Act.

The *Main Face* is obvious and up to 20 metres high. To its right is a short steep wall (*Right-hand Buttress*) and further up, where the ravine narrows, is a buttress (*Left-hand Buttress*) with a prominent nose of rock, just before a bend right in the gorge.

Some dodgy stakes have been left in situ – it might be better to bring your own, or make use of the trees at the top of the crag.

Descent can be made at either end of the crag.

The routes are described from **right** to **left** as one enters the ravine.

Aisgill

1	Time Being	E3 *
2	Shark's Fin Soup	VS *
3	Colonel Biffo	VS
4	Grand Designs	E3 **
5	Soft Target	VS
6	On The Footplate	VS
7	Angel in the Centrefold	E1 **
8	Raising Steam	HVS
9	The Navvy	VS
10	Aisgill Experience	E2

Photo: Ron Kenyon

Left-Hand Buttress

Main Buttress

Right-Hand Buttress

Right-Hand Buttress

| 1 | **Time Being** | 13m | E3 | ★ | 1992 |

(5c). The crack in the face right of *Shark's Fin Soup* leads with increasing difficulty to a roof; swing over this to finish. Bridging out onto a branch reduces the grade.

| 2 | **Shark's Fin Soup** | 13m | VS | ★ | 1987 |

Start right of a prominent fin of rock, just right of a crack-line.

(4c). Ascend to a ledge, follow the fin and surmount the final wall.

| 3 | **Colonel Biffo** | 12m | VS | | 1982 |

(4a). The steep chimney/crack-line on the right of the buttress.

| 4 | **Grand Designs** | 17m | E3 | ★ ★ | 1992 |

(5c). Follow a rising ramp in the left side of the wall rightwards to a shallow groove. Traverse left a few metres to better holds, then pull up to a short crack at the top. Move right to a small tree and lower off this.

| 5 | **Soft Target** | 13m | VS | | 1992 |

(4c). Climb the left edge of the wall using a hollow-sounding pillar, then continue past a tree belay at the top of the gully on the left.

Main Buttress

A convenient ledge runs along its base.

| 6 | **On The Footplate** | 20m | VS | | 1982 |

(4b). The more broken face on the right flank of the *Main Face*.

| 7 | **Angel in the Centrefold** | 20m | E1 | ★ ★ | 1980s |

A superb route. Start below a wide chimney/crack at the left end of the gangway.

(5b). Climb the chimney/crack then exit left past a tree stump to below an overlap. Move right and surmount the overlap to gain a ledge. Continue up a wide crack and a crack in the wall above, gaining the top by use of slightly dubious flakes.

Above: Chris King on **Angel in the Centrefold** (E1). **Photo:** Ron Kenyon

8 **Raising Steam**	20m	HVS	

The obvious central crack-line, with a peg for protection.

(5a). An interesting layback leads to a ledge. The final crack has a potentially lethal block below an overlap.

9 **The Navvy**	8m	VS		1982

Even the first ascentionists are not sure where this goes. It could be the obvious prominent corner on the *Left-Hand Buttress* or the corner crack-line left of *Raising Steam* or it could have fallen down!

Left-Hand Buttress

10 **The Aisgill Experience**	13m	E2		2006

Start to the left of a broken rib, left of a prominent corner.

(5b). Climb the crack-line to a ledge below an overlap. Traverse left, with a long step to a foothold, to gain the hanging corner right of the prominent nose. Finish up the corner.

Above: Sign of the times – things are slow to change in the Eden Valley! **Photo:** Ron Kenyon

South Cumbria & South Lakes Limestone

To the south and east of the Lake District fells, lying at a low altitude – in fact in most cases at or just above sea level, arc a series of outcrops of varying size and nature. They are nearly all limestone, though there are a few exceptions, and they provide a very different style of climbing to that found elsewhere within the Lakes. They also offer pleasant climbing on days when conditions prevent access to the more traditional Lakeland crags. Many of the climbs on these crags have been developed as, or have mutated into, sport routes with bolts for protection and it should come as no surprise that many of these are at the harder end of the grade spectrum, though not in all cases. Some opportunities for easier routes and for traditional climbing still exist, as will be discovered in the crag descriptions.

Above: Sun, sea and bouldering – Cherrie Whiteley enjoying the delights of South Lakes limestone at Humphrey Head. **Photo:** Tim Whiteley.

South-East Cumbria Limestone

This area is that part of Cumbria lying east of the River Kent and Kendal and south of the Eden Valley. It has one crag of note in this guide: though Farleton Crag and nearby Hutton Roof are worthwhile, by mutual agreement with the Lancashire Guidebook Committee, they are not described here.

Hebblethwaite Hall Gill

Grid Reference: **SD 698 932** Altitude: **220m**
Faces: **South-East and North** Approach: **20 mins**

Way off to the east, on the other side of the Howgills and in the Yorkshire Dales National Park, is *Hebblethwaite Hall Gill* also known as **Penny Farm Gill**. This delightful crag, which lies a few kilometres outside Sedbergh, provides a handful of short routes (most of which are in the E1 – E2 range) in a small limestone gorge situated at the eastern end of an idyllic wooded valley, which ultimately runs into the River Rawthey a couple of kilometres outside Sedbergh. The crag is in a lovely setting, with a beck running through the gorge. The gorge is sheltered and, as the south–east–facing *First Wall* catches the

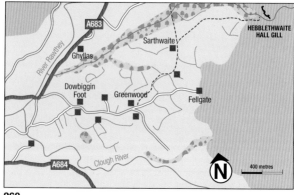

sun, it can be climbed on all year. The routes on the *Pinnacle Face* do not get much sun but are quite steep – these routes are currently a little dirty.

Approach:

Leave Sedbergh on the A683 heading towards Kirkby Stephen (see map on inside rear cover [South Eden Valley Map]). Immediately after the bridge over the River Rawthey is a minor road on the right signposted

Above: Flora Wharton on *Mite* (E1), Hebblethwaite Hall Gill, watched by Tim Whiteley and Bella. **Photo:** Nick Wharton

to Dowbiggin. Follow this for a kilometre to Greenwood, where the road widens at a right-hand bend. There is limited parking here. Follow the signposted footpath past Greenwood Hall and through a gate on the right. Walk diagonally across the first field then follow the right edge of the next to a small footbridge and gate. Cross the field towards the large stone barn. Go through the gate, then follow the wall on the left, through the, now derelict, Sarthwaite. The track through the gate on the right is followed until a left-hand bend. At this point, walk straight on up the rise, following an indistinct bridleway across open fields with the river gorge down to your left. Go through one wall to eventually reach a gate in a second wall. Turn left after the gate and head down into the gorge. About 1800 metres – 20 mins.

A significant cave is located on the east bank of the river by the fence a few metres downstream from the first routes – take a torch!

First Wall

The first routes are on the left side of the gorge as you look up, on a short flat wall that rises almost out of the beck, the left-hand end being brown in colour.

The routes are described from **left** to **right**.

Hebblethwaite Hall Gill First Wall

1	Mite	E1
2	Midget	E1
3	Morsel	E1

| 4 | The Mighty Micro | E1 |
| 5 | Strange Times | E1 |

Photo: Nick Wharton

| 1 | **Mite** | | 5m | E1 | | | 1990 |

(5b). Climb the brown wall direct, starting just right of the curving crack. Bolt belays lie back and left.

| 2 | **Midget** | | 6m | E1 | | | 1990 |

To the right is an arch-shaped overlap.

(5b). Climb the left-slanting crack rising from the left edge of the overlap. Bolt belays as for *Mite*.

| 3 | **Morsel** | | 7m | E1 | | | 1990 |

(5b). Climb through the arch-shaped overlap via a prominent hand-jam slot, then climb the wall direct to a small tree, stepping left to finish. Bolt belays as for *Mite*.

| 4 | **The Mighty Micro** | | 10m | E1 | | | 1990 |

(5b). Climb through the apex of the arch and continue up the fingery wall passing two breaks. Stake belays are available back from the edge.

| 5 | **Strange Times** | | 24m | E1 | | | 1987 |

About 20 metres beyond *First Wall* the beck cascades over boulders in the bed of the gorge. The next route climbs above these, heading for the grooved rib on the right of a series of grassy terraces. Start by the first big boulders in the stream bed.

(5b). From the stream bed pull up to a rightward-rising diagonal break. Traverse right across the slab then up to an overlap below the grooved rib. Climb over this then up, using the groove and the face on the right to reach a large holly. Scramble off rightwards.

| | **Respect Your Elders** | | 14m | VS | | | 1990 |

On the opposite side of the gorge from the previous route, on the inside of the bend, is an undercut buttress with a smooth slab on its right-hand side. Start to the left of a square-cut niche at the left side of the buttress.

(4c). Move up a few metres then step right onto the slab. From the top of this pull into the small niche on the left containing a small tree and finish direct.

Pinnacle Face

Twenty metres further upstream is another steep buttress on the right, this time north-facing. The front of the buttress is formed by a large detached pinnacle, separated from the main crag by an easy rake. The first two routes take the front face of the pinnacle.

The climbs are described from **right** to **left**.

Hebblethwaite Hall Gill
Pinnacle Face

6	Out on a Limb	E1
7	Bitter Creek	E2
8	Like an Arrow	E2

Photo: Nick Wharton

6	**Out on a Limb**		22m	E1			1987

Start at the bottom right-hand corner of the pinnacle.
1   14m (5b). Make hard moves to gain the obvious groove. Follow this more easily to a tree belay.
2   8m (5b). From a split block, step onto a slab and follow the overlap leftwards onto the rib. Finish direct by a small rowan.

7	**Bitter Creek**		21m	E2			1987

Start midway along the front of the pinnacle, right of a small alcove.
1   15m (5c). Climb the bulging crack up and right into a slim groove. Ascend this, using the rib on the right, to reach the top of the pinnacle
2   6m (5b). From behind the pinnacle, gain a sloping shelf then use a short overhanging crack and the rib on the right to finish at a small rowan.

8	**Like an Arrow**		15m	E2	★	1987

Start directly below the obvious right-facing groove in the upper wall.
(6a). Climb directly to the groove, with awkward moves to get established in its base. Follow the groove, past an old peg, to the top.

Farleton Crag (SD 539 796), easily seen just to the east of the M6 and not far south of Junction 36, **Farleton Quarry** (SD 539 809), the nearby bouldering venue of **Hutton Roof Crags** (SD 565 782) and **Fairy Steps** - also known as **Whin Scar** (SD 486 789), although in Cumbria, are covered in full in the Lancashire climbing guide so are not described here.

South Lakes
Limestone & the
Cartmel Peninsula

The Cartmel Peninsula extends southwards into Morecambe Bay between the Rivers Kent and Leven. In the northern part of this area, just west and south of Kendal lies Whitbarrow Scar, a significant limestone escarpment that separates the Lyth Valley from the Wither-slack Valley. The edge of the escarpment provides the impressive White Scar on its south-eastern edge, its less inspiring neighbour, Mill Side Scar on its southern corner and the magnificent Chapel Head Scar on its western flank. Tucked away in the centre of the woods on top of the escarpment is the family friendly Slape Scar.

Away from Whitbarrow, there are a couple of other very worthwhile venues. On the other side of the Lyth Valley, on a corresponding escarpment, lies Scout Scar. This small, compact crag provides a good selection of short bolt-protected routes that catch the afternoon and evening sun, with very easy access. South and west of the other crags is a unique land feature called Humphrey Head, a limestone headland that juts south into Morecambe Bay, its steep westen flank providing short steep cliffs. Whilst strictly speaking these are not sea cliffs, they are the most significant crags on the coast between Llandudno in North Wales and St Bees in West Cumbria!

NB It should be noted that the crags at Whitbarrow, Scout Scar and Humphrey Head are particularly important in conservation terms because they are the only place in the world for Lancastrian whitebeam, a tree with pale–backed leaves, which favours crag edges. Please take extra care not to damage these trees.

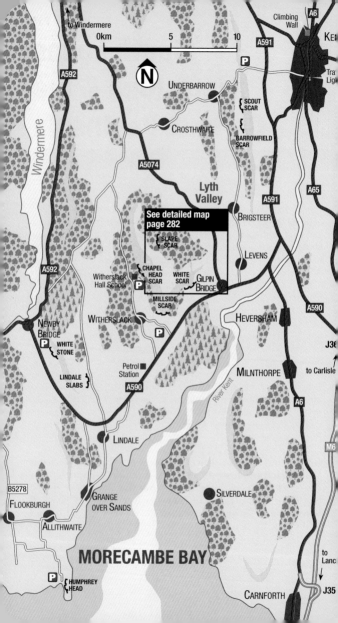

Scout Scar

Grid Reference: **SD 486 915**   Altitude: **200m**
Faces: **West**   Approach: **10 mins**

Scout Scar is the limestone escarpment running north–south and overlooking the delightful Lyth Valley to the west of Kendal. The crag of the same name (though shown on the map as **Hodgson's Leap**) is the highest and most substantial part of the escarpment. The rock on the crag is fairly sound and provides good, easily accessible, though fairly short routes, which, due to the compact nature of the rock, lend themselves to bolt protection. There are a couple of traditional routes that rely on natural gear, but these are not the main reason for a visit.

The crag, and indeed the entire escarpment, are private property owned by the Levens Hall Estate. There is no problem with access however, though climbing is restricted for a few days in midwinter to allow for shooting. These dates, which are updated annually, are listed on the BMC Regional Access Database and the FRCC website. Please respect this limited restriction to help maintain the good relationship and otherwise open access.

The crag is easily reached from Kendal by turning left at the town centre traffic lights, and up Beast Banks on the road to Underbarrow and Crosthwaite. After one mile, this crosses over the bypass and climbs steadily up the next hill. At the top of this, on the right-hand side, there is a car park in a small old quarry. Park here, cross the road and pass through a gate. Follow the path for 500 metres, first up hill and then along the edge of the scar to the "mushroom" (worth a stop on a clear day to identify all the Lakeland fells painted on the inside of the shelter). Another 300 metres beyond the shelter the ground rises up on the left. Just past here it is possible to drop down a level to the right, over a fence and onto an obvious path, which leads through the trees below the scar. Follow the path to the foot of the crag, climbing up at one point. The first proper routes to be reached are on *Undercut Buttress*.

Descent:

All routes that are worth doing are equipped with lower-offs. One or two remain that might result in you topping-out. Descent in this case is best achieved using the approach route.

The routes are described from **left** to **right**.

Descent Route	12m	M	pre-history

About 8 metres left of *Undercut Buttress* is an easy scramble past a large tree - maybe worthwhile if you want to introduce your dog to climbing, otherwise keep walking.

Scout Scar Undercut Buttress

1	9½ Weeks	F7a	*
2	First Blood	F7a +	*
3	Sylvester Strange	F7c	**
4	Meet the Wife	F7b+	*
5	Telegraph Road	F6c +	**

Photo: Al Phizacklea

Undercut Buttress

The first substantial section of crag with a large overhang at the left side and a series of overlaps. The climbing here is short but fierce.

| **Scarfoot Chimney** | 15m | D | | pre-1975 |

The obvious chimney to the left of *Undercut Buttress*. A chockstone sits at the top.

| 1 **9½ Weeks** | 12m | F7a | ★ | 1987 |

Start just left of a flake in the ground and climb past two overlaps to enter and climb the groove/flake above. It is possible to climb either left or right at the second overlap. There is a separate bolt for each direction.

| 2 **First Blood** | 14m | F7a+ | ★ | 1985 |

From the right side of the flake in the ground, climb the roof at its widest point using good undercuts and head for a good hold. Continue up the wall. Excellent powerful climbing.

| 3 **Sylvester Strange** | 12m | F7c | ★★ | 1986 |

Another good powerful climb up the front of the steep buttress. Start at the right end of the roof where the overlap starts to arch upwards to the right.

Battle your way up the wall with both strength and delicacy.

| 4 **Meet the Wife** | 12m | F7b+ | ★ | 1991 |

Start directly below the extreme right end of the roof, just left of the wide steep white depression.

Follow bolts past a downward-pointing spike to eventually join *Telegraph Road*.

| 5 **Telegraph Road** | 15m | F6c+ | ★★ | 1986 |

The easiest route on the wall and probably the best. Start on the right below the steep depression.

Climb up to a small overlap, then step left into the groove/depression and follow this to the top.

To the right of this buttress is a deep vegetated gully with a large yew tree at 10 metres. There are some old traditional routes lurking in here for those with either a spirit of adventure or an unhealthy interest in botany.

| **Gilmin Groove** | 14m | M | | pre-1975 |

The very overgrown left-slanting break above the tree.

| **Arête Finish** | 12m | VD | | pre-1975 |

The rib above the tree.

| **Red Rock Gully** | 18m | S | | pre-1975 |

The even more overgrown main gully, with several bulges somewhere beneath the vegetation.

| **Cliff's Route** | 20m | VS | | 1975 |

A much cleaner option on the right of the gully.

(4c). Ascend the gully for a few metres to a clean layback crack on the right just below the first large yew tree. Climb the crack to reach a steep groove then climb the right arête to gain a slab. Cross this to the right and so up to the top.

| **Brain Salad Surgery** | 18m | VS | | 1977 |

Start just right of the gully and grovel your way up a broken overgrown groove.

Scout Scar Central Area

6	Bornville	F5 +
v1	Grass Roots	E1
7	Born Again	F6a **

8	Born Free	HVS	**
9	Born To Run	F6b	***
10	Fistful of Steroids	F6b+	***
11	Ropearse	F6a	

Photo: Al Phizacklea

Central Area

To the right of *Red Rock Gully* a tree arches over the path. Behind it, next to the crag, is a ledge from where several routes start.

6	**Bornville**	12m	F5+	1993

From the ledge follow the line of bolts rising leftwards across the clean area of rock to a lower-off below the prow and dodgy-looking groove.

v1   *Grass Roots*   21m   E1   1985

(5b). Follow *Bornville* to the lower-off, but rather than doing the obvious, sensible thing – continue up the aforementioned dodgy-looking groove to the top.

Right: Max Biden balances his way up the delicate upper section of **A Fistful of Steroids** (F6b+), Scout Scar. **Photo:** Nick Wharton

7 **Born Again**	26m	F6a	★ ★	1991

A really good longer route that provides a relatively easy sport climb up the largest part of the crag. Start further right on the ledge, beneath the centre of the overlap.

Climb directly through the overlap then head rightwards, climbing ultimately up the centre of the wall 2 metres left of the tower.

8 **Born Free**	26m	HVS	★ ★	1960

The most worthwhile traditional route on the crag – take some gear!

(5b). Start beneath the right end of the overlap and climb up to a flake (thread runner just above), then trend left up a vague groove before a traverse right can be made to the base of the obvious crack bounding the left side of the tower. Follow this to the top.

9 **Born to Run**	24m	F6b	★ ★ ★	1985

A great delicate route, with climbing on small pockets and fingery holds. Start at the blunt rib at the left side of the bay.

Climb the rib and wall above on small pockets then finish up the top wall as for *Born Again*.

10 **A Fistful of Steroids**	24m	F6b+	★ ★ ★	1986

Whilst drug-induced rippling muscles may help power you through the initial bulge, the rest of this excellent route requires style and finesse.

Start below the centre of the arch and climb steeply though the bulge to a ledge and a breather. The climbing now turns more technical. Climb leftwards off the ledge, up the wall and centre of the outer face of the tower to the top. Fantastic.

11 **Ropearse**	16m	F6a		1992

Right of *A Fistful of Steroids* the bulge ends in a flake. Start below this.

Climb the wall and flake to the right of the bulge to a ledge. Continue up the wall above trending slightly rightwards.

The next four routes climb the steep clean wall to the right.

12 **Beers for Fears**	16m	F7a	★	1986

Start just right of the straggly hawthorn tree.

Climb the lower wall trending leftwards towards, then through, the bulges. Finish up the wall above.

Left: In contrast to the previous photo, Neil Cooper muscles his way up the powerful start to the same route, **A Fistful of Steroids** (F6b+), Scout Scar. **Photo:** Nick Wharton

Scout Scar Central Area Right

Photo: Al Phizacklea

| 13 **Crimes of Passion** | 15m | F7a | ★★ | 1986 |

A good route up the centre of the wall.
 Start just right of the previous route below a vague thin crack and
 follow the line of bolts up the centre of the wall.

| 14 **Grave New World** | 13m | F7a | ★★ | 1986 |

Start just right of the short corner at the right side of the wall.
 Climb the wall to the bulge, pull over this and up to the chain.

| 15 **Kathleen's Nightmare** | 13m | F6c+ | ★ | 1986 |

 Follow the arête, with a hard move at half-height, then past a blocky
 flake on the left at the top and so up to the lower-off.

Right: Stuart Wood at the downward pointing spike of **Ivy League** (F7a+), Scout Scar.
Photo: Nick Wharton

Scout Scar Ivy League Buttress

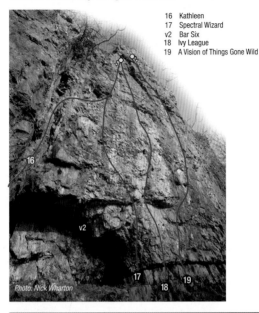

16	Kathleen	E3
17	Spectral Wizard	F7a + **
v2	Bar Six	F7b
18	Ivy League	F7a + ***
19	A Vision of Things Gone Wild	F7b **

Photo: Nick Wharton

Ivy League Buttress

Round the arête are a corner and a deep cave at ground level.

| 16 Kathleen | 16m | E3- | | 1984 |

A worthwhile route up the hanging corner and wall on the right. Start below the corner at the left side of the cave.

(5c). Climb the corner, making awkward moves on the left wall to reach the tree stump. Go up the groove then move out right to the large *Porthole*. Continue up the wall to the lower-off on the next route. A wire in the lower wall and a few slings for the tree stumps protect the route until the move out right allows bolts to be utilised.

| 17 Spectral Wizard | 16m | F7a+ | ★ ★ | 1986 |

Start at the right end of the cave.

Pull left over the roof to an obvious large hold, then left and up, passing to the right of the *Porthole*, over the small bulge and so to the lower-off. Magic!

Scout Scar
Ivy League Buttress Right

20	Idle Times	F7a	*
21	Leather Pets	F6c + *
22	Steppin' Out	E2
23	Broken Zipper	HS

v2 *Bar Six* F7b 1987

A powerful variation start.

Start at the back of the cave and climb direct through the roof to the obvious large hold on *Spectral Wizard*.

| 18 **Ivy League** | 16m | F7a+ | ★ ★ ★ | 1975 |

Probably the best route at the crag - on perfect rock. Start at the right side of the cave.

Climb up the obvious line of pockets and continue up to a small overlap. Overcome this using a small downward-pointing spike and climb the wall above.

| 19 **A Vision of Things Gone Wild** | 16m | F7b | ★ ★ | 1986 |

Another good powerful route. Start one metre right of the cave.

Climb up and right over two overlaps then straight up to the small overhang. Break left through this and then climb straight up.

| 20 **Idle Times** | 15m | F7a | ★ | 1986 |

Start at the right end of the wall, where the ground starts to rise.

Climb a vague groove to a square-cut overlap; go over this and up the wall and short corner.

| 21 **Leather Pets** | 16m | F6c+ | ★ | 1991 |

Start at a slightly higher level and climb the right-hand edge of the wall to reach a bulge. Climb over this then trend slightly left and continue to the same lower-off as *Idle Times*.

22 **Steppin' Out**	16m	E2		1975

Somewhat superseded by the previous two routes, with limited gear and poorer rock – but don't let that put you off! Start just right of *Leather Pets*.

(5c). Climb the shallow groove just right of *Leather Pets*, through a higher bulge, then pull out left and across to finish up *Idle Times*.

23 **Broken Zipper**	26m	HS		1977

The rather loose and vegetated right-facing corner.

Far Right Buttress

24 **Cross of Lorraine**	25m	VS		1975

A wandering line that takes in some surprisingly good rock. Start right of the large corner and left of the left-facing hanging groove.

(4c). Follow the hanging groove until it is possible to step left and stand on a flake. Climb the slab above until about one metre below a dodgy-looking hanging block. Traverse right to the twin bolts on *Poetry in Motion*. From here either finish direct or continue traversing right to the small tree on *Icicle* and finish up this.

Scout Scar Far Right

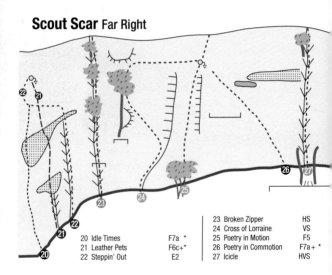

				23 Broken Zipper	HS
				24 Cross of Lorraine	VS
	20 Idle Times	F7a *		25 Poetry in Motion	F5
	21 Leather Pets	F6c+*		26 Poetry in Commotion	F7a+ *
	22 Steppin' Out	E2		27 Icicle	HVS

Right: Dave Toon high on **Poetry in Commotion** (F7a+), Scout Scar. **Photo:** Al Phizacklea

25 Poetry in Motion	12m	F5		1991

Just to the right, the lower wall is good solid rock. Up and right is an obvious overlap at half-height. Start at the bottom left of the wall, behind a clump of hazel bushes.

Climb straight up the wall past the left side of the overlap. Either lower off the twin bolts or, if feeling adventurous, finish as for *Cross of Lorraine*.

26 Poetry in Commotion	12m	F7a+	★	1986

This route takes a rising leftwards traverse on good rock to join *Poetry in Motion* at the lower-off.

Start just left of the corner and, using some fingery holds, head up and left to the left-end of the overlap.

27 Icicle	16m	HVS		1975

(5b). Climb the obvious corner/groove behind the large tree. A smaller tree is passed a few metres from the top.

Pits Stop	9m	VD		1986

This route is located about 35 metres further right, just left of the second yew.

Climb up a wide, open groove and exit left past a holly at the top.

Barrowfield Buttress (SD 487 908)

This completely separate buttress lies further along the scar to the south, directly above the farm. It is reached by a few minutes walk along the top of the scar. Descend the steep ground where the scar fades into the hillside then bushwhack back underneath the scar until you find the most solid-looking bit of rock. The bolts give it away.

Crumblefoot	18m	F6a+		1986

Climb the right-hand side of the wall to an area of broken rock and up steeply past three bolts.

Blue Screw	18m	F6c+		1986

A more solid route.

Climb the centre of the wall past four bolts.

Toirdealbach	18m	E3		1986

(5c). The obvious large overhung corner on the left, direct. Beware of loose rock!

Slape Scar

Grid Reference: **SD 448 865**   Altitude: **180m**
Faces: **West**   Approach: **40 mins**

Slape Scar is quite different to anything else on Whitbarrow, in fact it is more akin to the small outcrops further south around Silverdale and Warton. The rock is excellent and the location idyllic, being lost in the heart of the woodland on top of the Whitbarrow plateau. Perhaps because of its location and the perceived challenge of finding the crag, it is very quiet and any party will nearly always find they have the crag to themselves. The routes are only short and will undoubtedly be most attractive to those climbing at the lower grades, although there is more than enough to provide fun for all the family. The rock is generally quite featured, with cracks and flakes providing plenty of opportunities for a wide range of nuts and slings and the routes are almost exclusively protected by traditional means. An abundance of trees at top and bottom of the crag provide plenty of belays.

Approach:

Travelling west along the A590, take the first right after the A5074, Gilpin Bridge turning. After a few hundred metres turn right again down a narrow road that leads to Raven Lodge Farm. Follow the track round the bend at the farm and park on the left or, if no space here, about 100 metres further up the track. Walk along the track below **Raven Close Scar** (routes exist here but climbing is currently banned) past a barn on the right until the farm is reached. Turn left past the front of the house and into the wood. The path goes through a gate then zig-zags up the hill, eventually reaching a forestry track. Turn left here and stay on this track, passing another track joining from the left. Pass through a gate in a stone wall, soon entering into more open country where the former forest cover has been cleared. The track veers north to meet a track junction close to a delightful alpine chalet-like wooden cowshed and pens. Take the less obvious right branch, which re-enters woodland. After passing through another gate the track descends slightly for 300 metres in a valley to reach an indistinct junction. Turn left uphill, passing over some bare slabs, for about 400 metres to where the track levels out close to a couple of square-cut blocks on the left. The crag starts up on the right. Just beyond here a large boulder on the right (the *Fallen Block*) lies beneath the *Main Overhang Area*. About 50 metres further on, an even larger boulder lies on the right; the *Roof Area* is immediately above here, through the trees. This approach takes around 40 minutes. The crag can also be reached from Witherslack Hall in a similar time, passing over the summit of Lord's Seat en route.

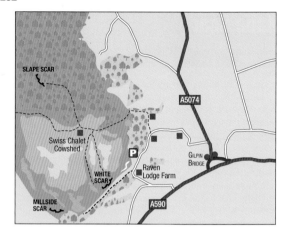

Descent is by short easy scrambles at either end of the crag.

The climbs are described from **left** to **right**.

Square Cut Chimney Area

About 60 metres left of the *Main Overhang Area*, above the even larger boulder by the path, is a buttress with a characteristic large roof at mid-height split by a thin crack (the *Roof Area*). The first routes are found a further 10 metres left of here on a short wall split by a shallow, square-cut chimney.

Slape Scar Square Cut Chimney Area

1	Halloween Outing	HVS		4	Square Cut Chimney	MS
2	Undercut	E2		5	Pagan Ritual	VS
3	Critical Friend	E2				

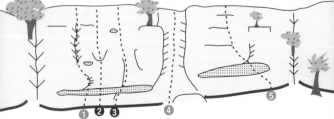

1	**Halloween Outing**	6m	HVS			1999

Start 3 metres left of the shallow chimney.

(5b). A difficult start using flake side holds leads to easier ground above.

2	**Undercut**	6m	E2			2000

Squeezed in between the routes on either side.

(5b). Climb the wall below the undercut (the crack on the right was used as a sidepull). Gain the undercut and a large pocket above then make a long reach to the top or use intermediate crinkles.

3	**Critical Friend**	6m	E2			1999

Just left of the shallow chimney a short crack finishes in the middle of the wall.

(5b). Follow the crack and continue to the top (Friend 0).

	Soft Option	6m	HS			2008

The wall immediately left of *Square Cut Chimney*, passing a tree.

4	**Square Cut Chimney**	6m	MS			1999

Climb straight up the obvious feature.

5	**Pagan Ritual**	7m	VS			1999

Start 6 metres left of the yew stump marking the start of *Uclid*.

(4a). Climb steeply on good holds until a move left leads to a finish up the centre of the wall.

	Idolatry	6m	HS			2008

The narrow wall one metre right of *Pagan Ritual* that forms the left side of a tree-choked corner.

Roof Area

A few metres left of the large roof the stump of a yew tree grows from the rock near the base of the scar.

6	**Uclid**	8m	VS	★	1992

Start just to the left of the yew stump.

(5a). Climb the wall leftwards to a crack, then move right and finish direct.

7	**Slapester**	7m	S			1999

Start immediately behind the yew stump and follow the crack over a small bulge.

| 8 | **Rose Tinted** | | 9m | HVS | ★ | 2008 |

Start directly below the left end of the large roof.

(5b). Climb bulging rock and pull over the roof on big holds, finishing up the wall above. A varied route on good rock.

| 9 | **The Slickrock Trail** | | 9m | E1 | | 1992 |

(5b). Climb the bulging lower wall, just left of *Big Job*, moving left to finish up the hanging corner. Alternatively, step right to finish up the face.

| 10 | **Big Job** | | 9m | E3 | ★ ★ | 1992 |

(5c). Ascend the broken groove to the obvious roof crack. Hopefully, with a lot of effort and some appropriate grunting, the hard bit will be passed and relief gained, as the remainder is quite soft!

| 11 | **First Past the Post** | | 9m | VS | | 1992 |

(4b). The wall and groove which bound the roof on its right.

| 12 | **Party Politics** | | 9m | HVS | | 1992 |

Two metres to the right is another groove with a small tree near the top.

(5a). Use flake-cracks on the right to enter the groove and climb it.

| 13 | **White Groove** | | 8m | HS | | 1996 |

The deep groove on the right.

| 14 | **Crusher Run** | | 8m | VS | | 1992 |

(4c). Start just to the right of *White Groove* and climb to a small overlap, then finish up the cracked wall above.

| 15 | **Slim Groove** | | 8m | HS | ★ | 1996 |

Climb the slim groove on the right and finish up the wall above.

Slape Scar Roof Area

6	Uclid	VS *	10	Big Job	E3 **
7	Slapester	S	11	First Past the Post	VS
8	Rose Tinted	HVS *	12	Party Politics	HVS
9	The Slickrock Trail	E1	13	White Groove	HS
			14	Crusher Run	VS
			15	Slim Groove	HS *

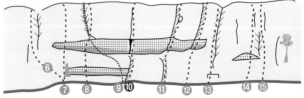

Overlap Wall

Further right the rock is more vegetated and there is a large square block lying at the foot of the crag. About 10 metres past this there is a wall with a small square-cut overlap near its top.

Type One	8m	VS	★	1992

(4c). At the left side of the wall, climb a shallow groove rising from a small block then finish up the continuation crack.

Poll Position	8m	HVS	★	1992

(5b). Gain and follow a thin crack which leads to the right-hand end of the overlap. Pull out right to finish.

Two short and rather unpleasant routes start near a yew at the foot of the crag. **Late Scoop** (6m, VD, 1998) takes a scoop 2 metres left of the yew, finishing up a crack on the left, and **Loose Pinnacle** (6m, VD, 1998) follows the V-groove and arête directly behind the yew.

Cat 955	6m	VS		1992

(4c). Climb a shallow groove to a long overhang then finish up a crack above and right.

K9	6m	HVS		2000

(5a). Climb the wall between *Cat 955* and *Easy Groove* to the roof then pull over this using holds on the left.

The V-groove on the right is **Easy Groove** (7m, VD, 1997).

Slape Scar Main Overhang Area

16	D6	VS
17	Slape Victim	HS
18	Traffic Light	S
19	Green Light	VS
20	ZZZZ!	VS
21	Geryon	E1
22	Pingora	HVS **
23	Icarus	HVS **
24	Spike	HS
25	The Ostrakon	VS *
26	Amazon	E2 **
27	Axiom	F8a+ **
28	Jump for Joy	E3 *
29	It's My Party	E1
30	RB22	VS
31	Stone Rose	HS
32	Little Yosemite Rib	VS

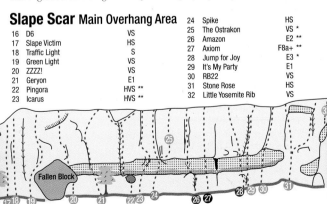

Two metres left of the *Fallen Block* another yew grows from the crag foot.

16 **D6**		6m	VS		1992

(4c). Start left of the yew and climb into the depression behind it, finishing up the rib on the left.

Recount VS 2000

(5a). Gain the rib finish of *D6* direct.

17 **Slape Victim**		7m	HS		1992

Enter the depression of *D6* from the right, then follow the hanging rib above.

18 **Traffic Light**		7m	S		1999

Just right of the depression on *D6* is a jagged crack - follow this. Almost indistinguishable from *Slape Victim*.

19 **Green Light**		7m	VS		1999

(4c). Climb the undercut left arête of the *Fallen Block* then step across leftwards to climb the crinkly wall left of *Zzzz!*

20 **Zzzz!**		9m	VS		1991

(4c). Bridge up the gap between the scar and the right edge of the *Fallen Block*. Pull onto the face and finish directly. No snoozing en route!

21 **Geryon**		10m	E1		1991

Start behind a straight yew tree three metres right of the *Fallen Block*.
(5b). Climb the wall, move left, then pull over the bulge (crux) to reach a good crack. Finish on the right.

Main Overhang Area

This area starts at the large roof right of the *Fallen Block* and continues to the end of the scar.

22 **Pingora**		10m	HVS	★ ★	1991

This is the prominent capped groove which bounds the *Main Overhang* on its left.
(5a). Ascend the lower wall past a holly to enter the groove. At the roof finish either left or right.

23 **Icarus**		10m	HVS	★ ★	1997

An improbable line demanding a forceful approach.

(5b). Start just left of *Spike* by the start of the *Yew Sculpture* and climb into a scoop and a peg in the roof. Blind moves over this lead to better holds and an easier finish up the groove on the left.

| 24 **Spike** | 10m | HS | | 1991 |

The big flake-crack splitting the *Main Overhang* is approached via a large dead wood mass, which forms a beautiful natural *Yew Sculpture*.

| 25 **The Ostrakon** | 11m | VS | ★ | 2008 |

(4c). Follow *Spike* to the overhang then pull out right to thin cracks. Step delicately right again and climb the centre of the crozzly wall direct on small holds.

Above: Flora Wharton is all go on **Green Light** (VS), Slape Scar. **Photo:** Nick Wharton

26 **Amazon**	11m	E2	★★	1991

(5b). Four metres right of *Spike*, climb a short right-facing corner to an awkward stance on a ledge on the left. Pull over the roof strenuously to gain better holds above and finish up the cracks.

27 **Axiom**	10m	F8a+?	☆☆	2000

The line of bolts over the *Main Overhang*, with the crux sequence turning the lip to gain a good hold on the top wall, is one of the hardest routes on South Lakes limestone. The hanger on the first bolt is currently missing.

28 **Jump for Joy**	9m	E3	★	2006

At the right end of the *Main Overhang* is a short groove.

(5c). Climb the groove onto an awkward small ledge on the left below the bulging wall. Difficult dynamic moves gain an obvious good flake at the lip. Use this to climb up then left, finishing more easily.

29 **It's My Party**	9m	E1		2000

Bordering the main overhang on the right is a hanging groove.

(5b). Gain the groove (runner at its base), then, using undercuts below, reach a good hold on the right of the groove and climb easily to the top.

30 **RB22**	9m	VS		1992

(4c). The next groove immediately right with a small overhang at three-quarters height.

31 **Stone Rose**	8m	HS		1997

Gain the open slabby groove 2 metres to the right. Finish direct, or better, move right and finish up the next groove.

Slape Scar Main Overhang Area Right Side

32	Little Yosemite Rib	VS		36	Broken Groove	VD
33	On Line	HVS		37	Scaredy Cat	E1
34	Worlds Apart	HVS		38	Tin Roof	E2
35	The Colostomy Kid	E2		39	The Badger	HVS
				40	Amber	VS

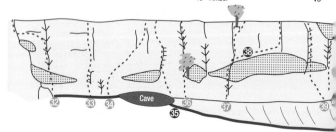

Election Special HVS 2000
(5a). Gain the right-hand finish to ***Stone Rose*** direct.

32 **Little Yosemite Rib**	8m	VS		1992

On the right is a jutting prow.
(4c). Climb the hanging corner right of this and finish up the prow.

33 **On Line**	8m	HVS		1997

Start 2 metres further right, at the right side of a bulge.
(5a). Gain a good flake hold with difficulty then finish direct.

34 **Worlds Apart**	7m	HVS		1996

Start immediately left of a low cave at ground level.
(5a). Climb to the bulge then move right and finish just to the left of
the blunt rib.

Above: Nick Wharton on **Little Yosemite Rib** (VS), Slape Scar. **Photo:** Flora Wharton

| 35 **The Colostomy Kid** | 8m | E2 | | 1992 |

(5b). From the right edge of the low cave climb up to a flake-crack on the right of the rib. Move left (hard) and finish on good holds.

| 36 **Broken Groove** | 7m | VD | | 1997 |

The unappealing broken groove on the right is full of broken rock.

| 37 **Scaredy Cat** | 8m | E1 | | 1992 |

Right of the broken groove is a crack.
(5b). Climb dubious rock to reach and follow the crack. Move right just below the tree to finish.

| 38 **Tin Roof** | 10m | E2 | | 2006 |

(5c). Climb *Scaredy Cat* to the crack at the bulge, then move right along the lip of the overhang, past one crack to reach the next crack in the upper wall, just left of the vague prow.

| 39 **The Badger** | 8m | HVS | | 1992 |

Five metres to the right is a birch tree.
(5a). From the tree, climb up and left to finish up the square-cut groove on the right of the roof.

| 40 **Amber** | 8m | VS | | 1999 |

(4c). Climb the hanging groove immediately right of the birch tree.

| **The Art of Limestone Rock Painting** | | | | |
| | 55m | HVS | ★★ | 1999 |

This traverse of the *Main Overhang* area is a good line on excellent rock and with ample protection, affording a surprisingly impressive route for such a small crag.
(5a). Start up the easy groove just left of the *Fallen Block* and follow a line rightwards above the overhangs with continuous interest. Belay as required (usually when gear runs out!), finishing at a holly a few metres past *The Badger*.

| **Treeline Traverse** | 23m | HVS | ★★ | 1992 |

(5a). The original traverse climbs *Pingora* to the roof then moves right to finish on the prow above the widest part of the *Main Overhang*.

Black Yews Scar (SD 439 867) is the northward continuation of *Chapel Head Scar*. Under the access agreement for *Chapel Head Scar* it has been agreed not to climb here.

Chapel Head Scar

Grid Reference: **SD 443 862**   Altitude: **70m**
Faces: **South-West**   Approach: **15 mins**

Chapel Head Scar is a steep limestone crag on the west side of the Whitbarrow Escarpment overlooking the idyllic Witherslack valley. The crag has a mixture of near-perfect smooth limestone and rough tufa formations. The rock is compact, offering little in the way of natural gear on most lines, resulting in the use of bolts for protection. Whilst there are a few routes that still require a rack of traditional gear, be under no illusion – this is a sport climbing venue and in fact by far the best of its type in the region. Many routes have been rebolted and some retro-bolted over recent years, leading to a far better climbing experience.

The crag does lie within the boundary of the Lake District National Park but is at a low altitude and well south of the rest of the Lakeland crags. Because of this, and with its steep nature, it is often in good condition when all other options are in the grip of the occasional bad weather that can occur in the region. However the crag may suffer from seepage after prolonged rain, with some areas being more affected than others.

The crag's south-westerly aspect means it gets the sun in the after-noon and evening, which is generally a good thing, though at the height of a summer heat wave it can get too hot. Midges can occasionally be troublesome but of more concern are the ticks. The whole area is infested with these parasitic arachnids, which like to attach themselves in warm moist nooks and crannies. They then feed on blood for several days until they become grossly engorged before dropping off – usually on the palest carpet. They are most likely to be found on dogs after a visit to the area, but humans will do just as nicely!

Approach:

The best approach (if coming from the east) is to leave the A590 at the Witherslack signs just after the start of the dual carriageway section. Drive through the delightful sprawling village, staying on the same road for about 3 miles, until you reach the entrance to Witherslack Hall School. A short track on the right leads to a parking area. The crag will be seen above the woods across the fields. Follow the path across the field, passing a football pitch on the left, to a gate into the woods. Follow the track up and right for 200 metres until a path branches off to the left. Follow this path through the woods, across a scree slope and up a short steep section to arrive at the crag between *Moonchild* (the steep groove on the right) and *Phantom Zone* (the steeper wall on the left).

The crag lies within an important nature reserve so access is delicate.

Great Gully

OUT OF
BOUNDS

Central Gully

Central Gully
Wall

Moonchild
Buttress

Interstellar
Area

Route of A
Evil Wall

Approach

**There will usually be a bird restriction from 1st March to
30th June due to nesting peregrines.** The climbing community
currently enjoys an excellent relationship with the National Park Rangers
but this could easily be ruined by any selfish disregard of the agreed
restrictions. In addition, certain reasonable rules apply to climbing at the
crag if access is to be maintained:

- No climbing is allowed left of *Central Gully*.
- Use only marked paths to and from the crag.
- No gardening is allowed on or above the crag; trees must not be
  damaged.

Chapel Head Scar Overview

Photo: Al Phizacklea

Up Town Wall

Great Buttress

- **Descent:** all routes finish at lower-off points. These **must** be used. **Do not top-out from any route.**
- Do not leave any litter including finger tape, chalk wrappers etc.
- If you really must relieve yourself (some of the routes can be intimidating!) – go well away from the path and leave as little evidence as possible.

The routes start 30 metres to the left of the point where the path arrives at the crag and are described from **left** to **right**.

Chapel Head Scar

Central Gully Wall

1	Cool Your Jets Mum	F6c
2	Le Flange en Decomposition	F6b

3	Gully Wall	F6b	
4	Gully Wall Direct	F6c	*
5	Winter Pincher	F6b	+
6	Odd Bods	F6b	
7	Strongbow	F6a	+
8	Comedy Show	F6a	+

Photo: Al Phizacklea

Central Gully Wall

At the furthest left end of the accessible part of the crag is the horribly vegetated **Central Gully** (VS, 1973). To the right of this is a wall with a number of short routes.

1	**Cool Your Jets Mum**	12m	F6c		1992

Just right of the gully is a smooth wall.
    Hard moves lead up the wall, then trend right to a belay.

2	**Le Flange en Decomposition**	15m	F6b		1986

You can think up your own translation, but do not get the wrong impression of this worthwhile short route.
    Climb the shallow groove, step left and climb up to the belay, passing an overlap.

3	**Gully Wall**	16m	F6b		1977

Climb the groove of *Le Flange en Decomposition* to the bulge and move right up a shallow groove to a belay.

Variation Start *F6b+*

Climb the smooth groove just to the right, direct to the traverse line.

4	**Gully Wall Direct**	15m	F6c	★	1985

Starting just right of the smooth groove, take a rising line up steep ground on fingery sidepulls until *Gully Wall* is reached at the end of its traverse right.

5	**Winter Pincher**	15m	F6b+		1985

Climb the shallow hanging groove.

6	**Oddbods**	15m	F6b		1985

The next short groove.

7	**Strongbow**	15m	F6a+		1979

The next hanging groove.

8	**Comedy Show**	15m	F6a+		1985

The fourth and last groove on this short wall.

The next three routes climb the barrel-shaped wall, either side of the large ash tree growing at the foot of the crag.

The Veil	20m	VS		1974

A couple of metres left of the tree is a shallow depression.

(4b). Climb a left-trending vague ramp to a horizontal break. Traverse right to a blocky ledge with a small tree. Climb the wall above to the trees.

Direct Start HVS 1985

Climb the thin crack direct to the blocky ledge.

Yashmak	21m	F6c		1996

Start just right of the ash tree.

Climb the wall and the blunt arête. Move up and right to a two-bolt lower-off.

Heinous Penis	21m	F6b+		1986

This can be quite stiff.

Start at a white patch and climb the smooth white rib through the bulge and up the smooth wall above to a lower-off.

Chapel Head Scar Interstellar Area

Photo: Al Phizacklea

Interstellar Area

This is the section of crag that lies immediately to the left of the point at which the path arrives at the crag. It is characterised by steep climbing on solid clean rock and gives some of the best routes on the crag.

9 **Starshine**	24m	E1			1974

(5b). Climb a shallow groove to a ledge heading for the nature reserve of the groove above.

10 **Jelly Head**	21m	F7a	★		1991

Start as for *Interstellar Overdrive* and follow that route as far as the dead tree beneath the upper wall. Climb up to the roof, over this leftwards, then up the wall.

11 **Interstellar Overdrive**	24m	F6c	★ ★ ★	1979

A great route, one of the best of the lower end sports routes on the crag. Start directly beneath the upper groove, a few metres left of the slanting groove/ramp of *Sun God*.

Climb the pocketed lower wall up a vague groove until the angle eases and a dead yew tree is reached. Clamber over this and use it to gain access to the wall above. Climb up to the roof then move right into the hanging groove. Follow this with increasing difficulty to the top.

Dune	39m	E4			1978

A left to right traverse of the *Interstellar Area* and *Moonchild Buttress*.
1   10m (5c). Follow *Interstellar Overdrive* to belay below a dead yew tree.
2   20m (6a). Head right across the wall as for *Combat Plumber* to reach *War of the Worlds*. Continue across *Bleep and Booster* to *Moonchild* and follow this to its lower-off.
3   7m (4b). Move right to the tree belay of *Lunatic*.
4   12m (5c). The final pitch of *Lunatic*.

12 **Sun God**	20m	HVS			1974

(5b). Climb the prominent flake-line that separates the slabby wall of *Interstellar Overdrive* and the steeper *Zantom Phone*. Follow the flake to the dead yew tree then continue up the groove and bulging flake behind.

13 **Cement Head**	21m	F7a+	★ ★	1989

Although this is only really half a route (the top half!), it does climb over superb rock. It can be climbed as a route in its own right but is perhaps better as an alternative finish to *Phantom Zone* or *Zantom Phone*. Before the upper groove of *Phantom Zone* was cleaned and bolted this was the preferred finish to that route, making an excellent combination.

Start on the ledge below the *Interstellar* tree – either by climbing this (bolts), or alternatively, *Sun God* (a couple of wires) - and step out right before heading up to the left end of the roof above. Surmount the roof then move up and right across superb smooth rock, eventually going right round the corner and up to a lower-off.

Combat Plumber	21m	F7a	★	

A worthwhile combination that allows easier access to the top of *War of the Worlds/Phantom Zone* by starting as for *Cement Head*. Good entertainment value.

From the ledge below the *Interstellar* tree, step out right as for *Cement Head* but keep going until beneath the upper groove of *Phantom Zone*. Climb the thin wall to the overlap then step right to climb the groove above.

14 **Zantom Phone**	26m	F7c+	★★	1986

Thin fingery climbing up the steep clean wall right of the groove of *Sun God*. Start below the wall and make hard moves, including a one-finger pocket, to eventually reach *Cement Head*: finish up this.

15 **Phantom Zone**	26m	F7b+	★★★	1986

Brilliant! Start at the toe of the buttress just left of where the approach path reaches the crag.

Make a hard rock-over move to reach a good tufa sidepull on the right. Move up and initially left then back right over steepening ground, to get through the bulge and into a vague groove. At the top of this is a small ledge offering a brief respite. In the past the route either finished here or traversed left to join and finish up *Cement Head*. Now you have the added option of continuing up the thin wall to gain and climb the smooth groove above to a belay on the left. This is the preferred option, but do also consider linking this route with *Cement Head* for a tremendous outing.

16 **Stan Pulsar**	27m	F7b	★	1986

A good route; start as for *Phantom Zone*.

Make the rock-over move to reach the tufa sidepull then swing steeply rightwards and pull up onto a small ledge at the foot of a groove. Climb the groove until a step left reaches a rest point on a ledge (as for *War of the Worlds*). Move back right and up to a hanging flake/groove. Climb this and the crack to a lower-off.

| 17 **Surfing with the Alien** | 12m | F8a | ★ | 1992 |

Even more steep and fingery than its neighbours! This route gains and then climbs the rib to the right of *Phantom Zone*. Start just to the right of *Phantom Zone* where the path meets the crag.

Climb the thin wall and steep rib to a lower-off just below the ledge on *Stan Pulsar/War of the Worlds*.

Moonchild Buttress

Right of where the path arrives at the crag, the steep buttress continues, now under the guise of *Moonchild Buttress*.

| 18 **Bleep and Booster** | 27m | F6c | ★★ | 1985 |

The shallow groove to the left of *Moonchild*. Start directly beneath the *Moonchild* groove, just right of where the approach path reaches the crag.

Climb a few metres up *Moonchild* to reach a good hold before moving left to reach the better holds at the bottom of the groove. This point can be reached more directly by making hard moves up and left from the start of *Moonchild* (F7a). Step up and right to something of a rest before pressing on up the groove until stopped by the capping bulge. Go over this on its left then back right to gain entry to the next groove. At the top of this stand up beneath the left side of the prominent prow to reach the lower-off on its left.

| 19 **Moonchild** | 24m | E4 | ★★ | 1974 |

A significant route in the early development of the crag which takes the most obvious striking line of the deep groove a couple of metres right of where the approach path arrives at the crag. The protection is good – where you can get it!

(5c). Start just right of the groove and climb the wall to gain the groove which is climbed to a scoop on the right. Pull up and left into another scoop then straight up, climbing the flake above. Finish up and left at the yew tree. Alternatively, step left at the second scoop and climb a crack leading to the yew tree.

| **Moon/Loon Connection** | 37m | E4 | ★★ | 1974 |

Two for the price of one!
1   23m (5c). Climb *Moonchild* until the second scoop then traverse right to the large ledge at the end of the first pitch of *Lunatic* and belay.
2   14m (5c). Climb the smooth groove of the second pitch of *Lunatic*. A great combination, though in truth the connecting climbing is not in the same league as the two individual routes.

Chapel Head Scar Moonchild Buttress & Route of All Evil Wall

10	Jelly Head	F7a *
11	Interstellar Overdrive	F6c ***
13	Cement Head	F7a+ **
15	Phantom Zone	F7b+ ***
16	Stan Pulsar	F7b *
18	Bleep and Booster	F6c **

19	Moonchild	E4
20	War of the Worlds	F6c+ **
21	62 West Wallaby Street	F7a+ *
22	War Hero	F7a
23	Tricky Prick Ears	F7b ***
24	Lunatic	E3 *

25	Darth Vader	E5
26	Maboulisme Merveilleux	F7c+ **
27	The Route of All Evil	F7a+ **
28	Eraser Head	F7b+ ***
29	Cyborg	E2 *
30	Mid-Air Collision	F7b ***
31	Omega Factor	F6c *

Not all routes shown.

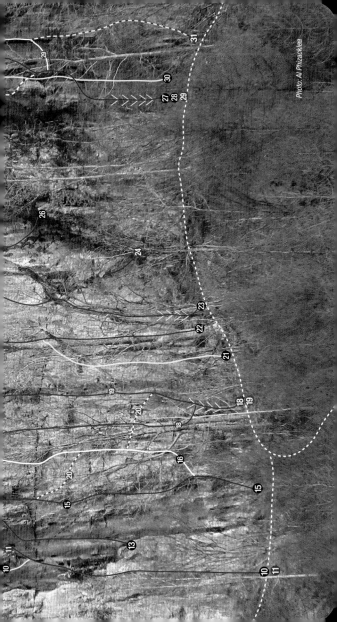

Photo: Al Phizackl¤a

| 20 War of the Worlds | 37m | F6c+ | ★ ★ | 1978 |

A long route that winds its way up and left across the buttress, taking in a lot of excellent climbing along the way.

Climb *Moonchild* into the groove proper where it is possible to swing left into *Bleep and Booster*, but keep traversing left to the groove of *Stan Pulsar*. Go up this to the resting place on the left. When you are ready, step down then head up and left above *Phantom Zone*, then up to the right-hand end of the roof, just left of the widest groove (this is the top groove of *Phantom Zone*). Pull right into the groove and follow it to the belay up on the left.

| 21 **62 West Wallaby Street** | 27m | F7a+ | ★ | 1997 |

The residents of this famous address would probably find some ingenious way of getting to the top – you will probably need to rely on power and technique! Start below the steep wall to the right of the *Moonchild* groove, a couple of metres down from the tree.

Climb the wall then the steep bulge, on small but very positive holds, to reach a good ledge. Continue up then trend rightwards to join the line of *War Hero*.

| 22 **War Hero** | 26m | F7a | ★ ★ | 1997 |

A great route. Start by the tree at the foot of the crag.

Climb the wall behind this, which becomes a shallow corner. At the bulge, head slightly leftwards before climbing up and right to gain first a small ledge, then up again to a larger ledge with the remains of a tree stump. Continue straight up the wall to the left of the corner on fantastic rock.

| 23 **Tricky Prick Ears** | 27m | F7b | ★ ★ ★ | 1988 |

A tremendous route with a lot of climbing. Start a couple of metres up the slope from the tree at a shallow blank groove.

Climb this to reach the obvious flake (*Lunatic*). Make a difficult move (crux) out left and up to easier ground. Move up and right, over the next bulge, to reach a resting position on the left. When you are ready, move up and right across the steep white wall to reach the hanging groove. Make hard moves to enter and then follow this groove to the top. Awesome!

| 24 **Lunatic** | 27m | E3 | ★ | 1974 |

Although not climbed very often these days, this classic route was a major ascent at the time and a fine sister climb to *Moonchild*. The climbing is still as good as it ever was, so dig out that trad rack, wind out your neck and get on it! Start below the obvious flake up on the wall of *Great Gully*, by a lower left-facing flake.

1   15m (5c). Climb this lower flake to gain the steeper right-facing flake then step left onto a ledge. Move up and left across the wall to reach the much larger ledge at half-height - probably best to belay here.

2   12m (5c). Climb up and right to gain the beautiful open groove on the right, which is followed to the top.

25 **Darth Vader**	25m	E5		1985

This route, while in an exciting position, now lacks independence. It makes an exposed traverse from the bottom of the *Lunatic* groove to join the top groove of *Tricky Prick Ears*.

(6a). From the belay ledge of *Lunatic* move right to a hollow flake. Go up and right to join *Tricky Prick Ears* and finish as for this to avoid the loose groove on the right and the top-out finish of the original line.

26 **Maboulisme Merveilleux**	16m	F7c+	★ ★	1986

A spectacular route up incredibly steep rock way out there above *Great Gully*. It can be slow to dry but once it is dry there are no excuses left; you just have to do it. Start at a ledge with a bolt belay some way up the gully, gained by a short scramble.

From the ledge traverse left across the gully, take a deep breath and fire yourself up the big holds. Keep heading outwards to a hard move on the lip. Pull over and finish more easily up and left.

Three routes once existed in and around the now completely overgrown gully. They are almost certainly best left to nature: **Great Gully** (VD, 1974), the gully itself; **Captain's Crack** (HS, 1972), the crack up the right-hand side of the gully leading into the cave; **Apollo's Exit** (E2 5c, 1980), the short crack through the roof of the cave.

Route of All Evil Wall

The next wall along is of solid compact rock with an amazing headwall.

27 **The Route of All Evil**	30m	F7a+	★ ★	1983

A great route that meanders up this excellent wall. Start at the foot of the corner/groove on the left.

Climb the corner/groove with a step right onto a small ledge. Move back into the right-trending groove and climb up the centre of the wall to reach a large break. Go up to another break, which is then followed leftwards to a reasonable rest. Step back right then finish up a shallow scoop up the left side of the headwall.

Chapel Head Scar
Route of All Evil Wall &
Great Buttress Up Town Area

Photo: Al Phizacklea

30a	The Borg	F7a+**
31	Omega Factor	F6c *
32	Rocinante	HS
33	Sad But True	F6c+
34	Half-Life	F6b+*

35	Up Town	F6c **
v1	Alternative Finish	F6c+
36	Atomic Bong	E2 *
37	Witherslack Alice	F6c

28 **Eraser Head**		25m	F7b+	★ ★ ★	1991

A more direct route up the wall, which includes the original direct finish to *The Route of All Evil* – known at the time as **True Path**.

Start up the initial corner/groove but, instead of stepping right to the ledge, move left slightly and follow a direct line straight up, crossing the traverse of *The Route of All Evil* and up the superb smooth pocketed rock of the headwall.

29 **Cyborg**		21m	E2	★	1975

Can just be done on bolts but would be a very sporting sport route!

(5c). Start up the corner/groove and step right onto the ledge as for *The Route of All Evil* (or start as for *Mid-Air Collision* and climb direct to the ledge). Continue traversing right then move up to a tufa pillar with an excellent natural thread on the left. Go up the pillar and the wall above to a small sapling and ledge with a lower-off up and right. A second pitch has been climbed up dodgy rock, which required going to the top of the crag - this is not allowed under the access agreement.

30 **Mid-Air Collision**		25m	F7b	★ ★ ★	1991

A companion route to *Eraser Head*, taking a parallel line to the right.

Start up the short wall to the right of the corner, to reach a small ledge. Make a start up the right-trending groove, but keep going in a straight line as far as *The Route of All Evil* traverse. Move up and right to a seemingly difficult move to finish.

A number of variations are possible, using sections of the above routes. For example, some say it is preferable to follow *Mid-Air Collision* to *The Route of All Evil* traverse then head left to finish as for *Eraser Head*.

30a **The Borg**			F7a+	★ ★	2011

Start up *Omega Factor*, climbing the crux moves of this before traversing left to the groove of *The Route of All Evil*. Follow this to the break then head right to climb the arête right of *Mid-Air Collision*.

31 **Omega Factor**		18m	F6c	★	1979

A good steep direct start to *Cyborg*. Start below a white groove with an open niche containing a holly tree.

Climb up into the niche then move steeply up and left to reach a good flake. Climb back right and up to join *Cyborg* (where the bolts run out!) to its ledge and lower-off. A second pitch (12 metres) moved right to climb a shallow depression – don't bother!

Left: Ian Cooksey starting the top wall of **Mid-Air Collision** (F7b), Chapel Head Scar.
Photo: Nick Wharton

Right of here the crag is heavily overgrown with a really impressive ivy "trunk" hanging out from the wall. **Garden of Eden** (VS 4b, 1979) lurks in here somewhere.

Great Buttress

This is the main part of the crag. It starts at a short steep groove with a yew tree sat at its top, 5 metres up the crag. The buttress starts off vertical then becomes steeper as it continues rightwards, eventually becoming quite undercut. The rock on the main part of the buttress is fantastic with tufa pillars to help in places and an essential tree!

The next routes all share a common start, up the right-facing corner/flake directly below the large yew tree growing 5 metres up the crag. The tree prevents a good view of the wall above, which provides some better climbs than might be expected from below, though route 32. **The Rocinante** (HS, 1979) is not one of them.

| 33 **Sad But True** | | 27m | F6c+ | | | 1996 |

The wall up and left of the yew tree - good climbing, though the rock becomes rather brittle in the upper section.

Climb the corner to the yew then move up and left across the wall. Harder moves gain the hanging groove up and right, which is followed to the top.

| 34 **Half-Life** | | 27m | F6b+ | ★ | 1977 |

A much better route than *Sad But True*.

Climb the corner and tree then onto the wall to a horizontal break. Move left and up into an open groove over some nice crozzly tufa. Go up the groove, then up and right to make an awkward move to stand below the steep upper bulge, joining *Up Town*. Move up and right into another groove with a lower-off at the top.

| 35 **Up Town** | | 25m | F6c | ★★ | 1984 |

An even better companion route to *Half-Life* with possibly the best small tufa formation on the crag.

Climb the corner and tree, then go up the wall to the horizontal break but move right and up, heading for the fabulous stalactite-like tufa (alternatively start up *Witherslack Alice* to this point). Go up the tufa and the groove above until a very delicate puzzling move gains a standing position below the steeper upper bulge (*Half-Life* comes in from the left here). Move up and right into another groove which is followed to a lower off.

v1 *Alternative Finish* F6c+

A slightly harder, worthwhile finish to either *Up Town* or *Half-Life*. From the awkward move to gain the standing position, head up and left through the final bulge before moving back right to the same lower-off.

36 **Atomic Bong**	36m	E2	★	1977

The original route up this part of the crag provides a good traditional outing. Although a little overgrown in the middle part, the climbing and the position at the top both make this really worthwhile.

(5b). Climb the corner and tree to the horizontal break as for *Up Town* and *Half-Life*. Traverse all the way right to a scruffy ledge with a few small trees, (possible belay on the lower-off bolts of *Shades of Mediocrity*). Alternatively climb **Witherslack Alice** or **Shades of Mediocrity** to the same point. Climb the yellow wall above the ledge via a flake on the right to a round scoop above (original and possible alternative belay). Hand-traverse right out of the scoop until a precarious step up can be made to reach a right-facing flake. Climb this to a ledge and bolt/peg belay.

Chain Reaction	50m	E3	★	1979

A high-level, left to right traverse of *Great Buttress*. A worthwhile excursion, possible on just the existing fixed gear but... – take plenty of slings.

1 21m (5b). Climb *Atomic Bong* as far as the scruffy ledge and belay.
2 26m (5c). Traverse right carefully along the break, past a sorry-looking tree and then a lower-off, to a flake on *Wargames*. Step down and move right to join *Android*. Traverse delicately right and up to reach the hanging flake. Move right past two lower-offs then make a few strenuous moves down to the left end of the large roof by the *Mangoustine* lower-off (the second may want to arrange a back-rope through the previous lower-off for this section). The moves right from here to the finish at the old chain of *Super Duper* are very delicate and well run-out.

Above: Neil Preston reaching the pinch tufa on **Up Town** (F6c), Chapel Head Scar.
Photo: Nick Wharton

Variation

The route originally finished direct above the hanging flake (known then as **Fast Breeder**).

| 37 **Witherslack Alice** | 26m | F6c | | 2004 |

Takes a line starting right of the *Up Town* tree.

> Climb straight up to and through the break to the right of the yew tree, watching out for loose rock. Follow the easier shallow corner to where the rock steepens again, gain holds in the horizontal break, and move up and right to good finishing holds.

| 38 **Shades of Mediocrity** | 20m | F7a | ★ | 1992 |

Start 6 metres right of the tree at the left hand of two tufa stumps.

> Stand up on the tufa then climb up, moving left at a small overlap. Continue, then drift back right over some excellent clean rock to a bolt belay.

| 39 **Gilbert Cardigan** | 20m | F7a+ | ★ | 1992 |

Start just to the right, at the right-hand tufa stump.

> Take a more direct line, this time moving slightly right then back left to a lower-off.

| 40 **Guloot Kalagna** | 21m | F7c | ★ | 1991 |

Hard and fingery climbing. Start 4 metres right of *Gilbert Cardigan's* stump beneath a tufa fin.

> Climb up to an overlap and over the bulge into the large scoop. Use tufas to climb the next bulge then up the steep thin top wall.

| 41 **Electric Warrior** | 12m | F7b | ★ ★ ★ | 1986 |

This is a superb if short route with big moves on fat tufas. Start a few metres right behind the ex-holly tree beneath a fat tufa that looks like a Rice Krispie cake.

> Climb the rough flutings until a big move up and right which allows access to a small ledge from where the lower-off is easily reached. Lower off here or continue up the next route.

Right: Matt Wright turns on the power for **Electric Warrior** (F7b), Chapel Head. **Photo:** Nick Wharton

Left: Cherrie Whiteley on the mantelshelf move on **Atomic Bong** (E2), Chapel Head. **Photo:** Nick Wharton

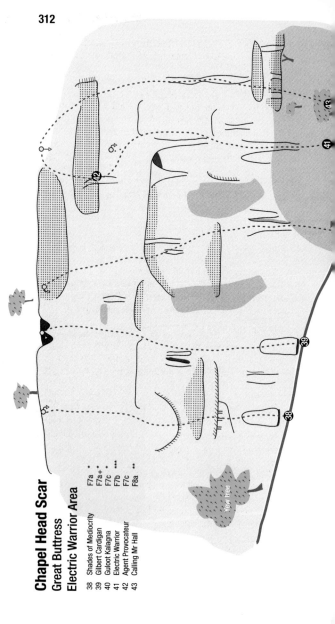

Chapel Head Scar
Great Buttress
Electric Warrior Area

38 Shades of Mediocrity   F7a   *
39 Gilbert Cardigan   F7a+   *
40 Guloot Kalagna   F7c   *
41 Electric Warrior   F7b   ***
42 Agent Provocateur   F7c   *
43 Calling Mr Hall   F8a   **

Yew tree

42 **Agent Provocateur**	21m	F7c		1987

The continuation of *Electric Warrior* - climb through the bulge using a very painful small hold.

Cosmic Dancer	38m	E5	★ ★	1986

A lower-level partner to *Chain Reaction*. It can be climbed as a sporty F7b on spaced bolts but sensible types take a rack.

1   24m (6b). Climb *Electric Warrior* to the belay ledge then traverse right, past *Wargames* and onto the left-to-right traverse on *Android*. Reverse this to reach *La Mangoustine Scatouflange* and take a hanging belay.
2   14m (6a). Follow *Mangoustine* up and right onto the small ledge but, instead of making the fingery moves up the steep wall, move into *Super Dupont*. Follow this to the roof then traverse right to the lower-off on *Super Duper Dupont*.

Alternative Start 21m F7a+ ★ ★ 1999

A more interesting start, tracing the line of the curving archway and more in keeping with the overall grade.

Start as for *Gilbert Cardigan* and climb as far as the third bolt. Traverse powerfully right on tufas towards *Guloot Kalagna*. More moves right lead to a span into the large bell tufa of *Electric Warrior* just below its belay ledge and chain. Continue as for the original route.

43 **Calling Mr Hall**	21m	F8a	★ ★	1990

Start at the other side of the ex-holly from *Electric Warrior*.

Climb up to an undercut in the fluting then make a series of hard moves through the bulge to gain a thin groove. Go up this and then the awkward bulge to finish.

44 **Wargames**	24m	F7b	★ ★ ★	1985

Probably the best route on the crag! Steep to start but on good holds then more delicate in the upper half. Great value. Start at a short, smooth lower wall below a tiny yew tree growing in the break (sometimes wet but don't let that put you off).

To the right of the fragile yew stump power up and outwards using tufas, sidepulls and pockets (not necessarily in that order) until you are forced into a big move right on undercuts to the base of the hanging groove. Go up the groove and onto the small ledge on the left. Draw breath, then climb the wall all the way to the overlap at its top. Overcome this then trend rightwards on good holds to reach the lower-off. Fantastic!

Chapel Head Scar
Great Buttress Android Area

43 Calling Mr Hall   F8a   **
44 Wargames   F7b   ***
45 More Games   F7b + *
46 Stretchy Perineum   F7b + **

47 Perverted Start   F7b+*
48 Android   E4   ***
49 Perverse Pépère   F7a   **
50 Song for Europe   F7b+***

Photo: Al Phizacklea

45 **More Games**	9m	F7b+	★	1992

A slightly harder direct start to *Wargames*, starting beneath the left end of the bulging roof at 5 metres and climbing up and leftwards to reach the base of the hanging groove.

46 **Stretchy Perineum**	10m	F7b+	★ ★	1987

Climbs the right side of the bulging overhang, providing an excellent direct start to *Perverse Pépère*. Start at the large tufa stump "stuck" onto the wall.

Gain the top of the tufa then move up and left past tufa flutings to achieve an awkward position beneath the right side of the roof. Make hard moves through the roof, past a short crack and up the wall, to reach a ledge from where *Perverse Pépère* leaves the *Android* traverse. Finish up *Perverse Pépère*.

47 **Perverted Start**	12m	F7b+	★	1986

A slightly harder right-hand variation to *Stretchy Perineum*.

Start up *Stretchy Perineum*, moving left to the flutings before climbing straight up and slightly right, with a hard fingery move to the junction with *Android*. Finish up *Perverse Pépère* or, if you are feeling stronger, *Song For Europe!*

In the middle of *Great Buttress*, right of the tufa stump of *Stretchy Perineum*, a tall dismal-looking ash tree grows from the base of the crag. This is the infamous *Android Tree*. The tree is in a very weakened state, supported by a length of rope. It should be treated with the respect and care that we give to gnarly old-timers that have given such good service. For the time being, and hopefully for at least a few more years to come, it will still provide the start for the next set of routes – some of the best on the crag.

Right: Nick Wharton prepares to step off the ailing Android Tree. **Photo:** Nick Wharton Collection

Left: Mark Greenbank on **Wargames** (F7b), Chapel Head. **Photo:** Nick Wharton

| 48 **Android** | 30m | E4 | ★★★ | 1979 |

A long circuitous route that works its way up this impressive buttress via the easiest ground. With care, this can be done on a single rope but double ropes will reduce rope drag.

(6a). Climb the *Tree* and step off the top onto the wall. Move up and left into the bottom of the large open scoop. Traverse left across the scoop. Move left at this level beneath a small overlap with a peg at the left end. From the peg, climb straight up into a vague groove with a thin flake (wires) until a scoop is reached below the next line of overhangs. Traverse delicately right and up to reach a large hanging flake. Climb this to reach a lower-off on the right.

Right: Android Tree Move – Mark 'Ed' Edwards leaves the precarious Android tree for the refuge of the rock. **Photo:** Nick Wharton

| 49 **Perverse Pépère** | 25m | F7a | ★★ | 1985 |

An excellent 'short-cut' variation of *Android*.

Climb up the tree and into the scoop. Traverse left and up to the next ledge as for *Android*. Instead of continuing left, take a deep breath and climb straight up with a big move to reach a massive hold. Continue up to rejoin *Android*. Climb the flake and step right to the lower-off.

| 50 **Song for Europe** | 23m | F7b+ | ★★★ | 1989 |

A magnificent route out of the top of the large scoop.

Climb the tree and into the scoop. Climb up to the top of the scoop on the right then continue up excellent tufas, through a small roof and the wall above, to reach a right-trending line up the top wall. Go straight up to the lower-off on *Perverse Pépère*.

| 51 **La Mangoustine Scatouflange** | 22m | F7a+ | ★★★ | 1986 |

A great route providing fingery climbing.

Climb the tree and into the scoop then move up and right to stand on a small ledge beneath the steep wall. A few hard finger-searing moves eventually lead to a tufa fluting. Follow this up and right until the lower-off is reached at the left end of the large roof.

Right: Toby Denny gets keyed up for **Song for Europe** (F7b+), Chapel Head Scar.
Photo: Nick Wharton

| 52 **The Witherslack Flange Finish** | 8m | F7a | | | 1987 |

From the lower-off on *Mangoustine*, pull over the roof and the wall above to another lower-off.

Sadly, one day the *Android Tree* will no longer provide an easy start to the previous five routes. However, in preparation for that day the following start will enable the routes still to be climbed – albeit at a harder grade.

| 53 **For When The Tree Goes** | 9m | F7b+ | ★ | | 1992 |

Climb the crozzly wall behind the tree (or above the tree stump, depending on when you are reading this!), through the bulge and into the scoop.

A couple of metres past the *Android Tree* is a thick tufa pillar. Right again there used to be a solid-looking holly tree which provided the start to the next few routes. Unfortunately, this tree clearly wasn't as solid as it appeared and has recently come away completely leaving this area of rock clear. This means a few extra moves are required to start the following three routes but should not affect the grades.

| 54 **Super DuPont** | 22m | F7b+ | ★ ★ ★ | 1985 |

Climb the wall using various tufa fins to a small triangular overhang. Make a hard boulder problem move to stand on top of the overhang then continue up into the broad scoop above. At the top of the scoop, where the rock steepens, make an initial move up into the right-trending groove, then pull out left to reach a ledge. Climb straight up from here, eventually reaching the lower-off at the left end of the large roof (as for *La Mangoustine Scatouflange*).

| 55 **Super Duper DuPont** | 24m | F7c | ★ ★ ★ | 1986 |

Start as for *Super DuPont*.

Make a boulder problem start up into the scoop and climb up to the right-trending groove but this time follow the groove past large tufa side-pulls until it is possible to climb straight up the steep grey wall, with a precarious mantelshelf move to get established on the top wall. Finish up and right at a chain at the right end of the large overhang.

| 56 **Prime Evil** | 24m | F7c+ | ★ ★ ★ | 1988 |

Amazing climbing up a steep wall made entirely of Rice Krispies – beware of finger tendons going "Snap, Crackle and Pop!"

Start as for *Super DuPont*, but head up and right using the tufa flutings and tiny crozzly finger edges to get established on the rough grey wall. Climb the wall on the small holds to reach a vague scoop up on the right, then climb the bulging wall above to the overhang. Hard moves over this gain the headwall which is followed to the chain at the right end of the large overhang (as for *Super Duper DuPont*).

| 57 **Unrighteous Doctors** | 24m | F7c+ | ★ ★ ★ | 1991 |

A fantastic route that provides a counter-diagonal to *Super Duper DuPont*. Start at the tufa just left of the yew tree.

Climb the wall on superb tufas, pockets and crozzly holds, heading leftwards higher up, to eventually reach a junction with *Super Duper DuPont* at the top of that route's right-trending groove. Pull up and left onto the upper wall and follow this to the break in the middle of the large overhang. Pull through the overhang at this point and up to a lower-off. Magnificent!

| **Doctor Evil** | 24m | F8a | ★ ★ ★ | 2011 |

This combination of the hardest part of *Unrighteous Doctors* followed by the hardest part of *Prime Evil* gives a very sustained route - albeit with no new climbing.

| 58 **Tufa King Hard** | 11m | F6c | ★ ★ | 1992 |

Not that hard! Start just right of the yew.

Climb parallel tufas then continue up the right-trending groove on big holds until a pull up and left through the bulge, plus one tougher move on smaller holds, gains the lower-off. Good climbing.

| 59 **Driller Killer** | 30m | F7a+ | ★ | 1985 |

To the right of the tufa pillars of *Tufa King Hard* is a small overlap at about 3 metres.

Climb up to and over this then up the scooped wall behind to reach good tufas below the next overlap. Traverse left at this level, across *Tufa King Hard*, to reach a ledge behind the yew tree. Make hard moves up and left through the bulges to reach easier ground.

| 60 **Videodrome** | 26m | F7b+ | ★ | 1987 |

A harder variation finish to *Driller Killer*.

From the ledge behind the yew tree step back right and make even harder moves up through the bulges up and left of *Tufa King Hard*.

| **Le Grand Traverse** | 85m | F7c | ★ ★ | 1994 |

A pumpy right-to-left traverse of *Great Buttress*.

Start up *Driller Killer* and follow this past the ledge until it moves up and back right. At this point swing up and left past a bolt to gain the traverse line. Follow this line strenuously, all the way across the buttress to reach *Wargames*. Finish up this.

Chapel Head Scar
Great Buttress
Tufa King Area

58	Tufa King Hard	F6c	**
59	Driller Killer	F7a+	*
60	Videodrome	F7b+	*
61	Warm Push	F6b+	
62	Reefer Madness	F6c+	
63	Doctor's Dilemma	F6c+	

Photo: Nick Wharton

| 61 **Warm Push** | 8m | F6b+ | | 1986 |

At the base of the wall, in its centre, is the left side of an 'archway'.
Climb up above the left side of this to stand on a large hold, then
follow the white streak to the overlap; lower-off up and right.

| 62 **Reefer Madness** | 9m | F6c+ | | 1991 |

Climb small but perfectly formed tufas where the right side of the
'archway' should be. Go straight up the wall heading left at the top to
the same lower-off as *Warm Push*.

| 63 **Doctor's Dilemma** | 7m | F6c+ | | 1992 |

Start at the right side of the wall by a triangular niche at head height.
Make a few hard moves up the short smooth wall to the overlap.
Either traverse left to the lower-off of the previous two routes
(doubles the length of the route!) or thread the bolt.

Left: Michael Kenyon not finding it **Tufa King Hard** (F6c). **Photo:** Ron Kenyon

Hell Moss Scar (SD 437 856) is a low, power traversing crag, situated on the wooded hillside opposite *Chapel Head Scar* (you can see parts of the crag from the road leading to *Chapel Head Scar*). It lies about 400 metres 'below' the car park at Witherslack Hall School. The moss of the name can be found above the crag and is unfortunately the source of much seepage. When it is dry however, the crag provides a long and hellishly strenuous traverse, rather like a tree-shrouded Dunnerholme, but without the big holds – useful training if you aspire to the big routes across the valley.

Low Crag (SD 447 850) lies somewhere on a long disjointed but broken outcrop, above steep scree heavily defended by dense woodland. It supposedly boasts about ten routes but could not be located.

Left: Great moves on the Great Buttress – Dave Parton on **Perverse Pépère** (F7a). **Photo:** Nick Wharton

Mill Side Scar

Grid Reference: **SD 451 845**
Faces: **South-East**

Altitude: **100m**
Approach: **10 mins**

Mill Side Scar sits at the southern corner of the Whitbarrow escarpment above the Mill Side area of Witherslack and is easily seen above the trees from the A590. Whilst there are not many climbs on this relatively small crag, the rock is sound and the climbing very good, and it is unlikely to be affected by seasonal bird restrictions, unlike its larger neighbours. Almost all the routes are bolt protected. The best route by far is *Cadillac*, which is readily identified from the main road by its prominent smooth slab and corner at the top.

Approach:

The crag is very accessible, being only 10 minutes from the A590. Pull off the A590 into Mill Side. Parking is available up the road between the village and the A590. It may be possible to park in the village by a junction with a telephone box where a minor road heads off right, but beware of causing

Right: Roger Chaldecott on **Pioneers' Cave** (HS), Mill Side Scar. **Photo:** Nick Wharton

Mill Side Scar

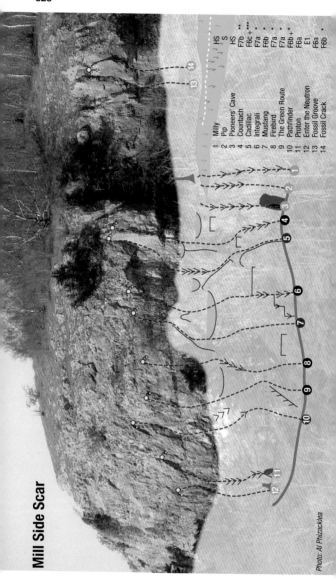

1	Milly	HS
2	Pip	S
3	Pioneers' Cave	HS
4	Countach	F7b **
5	Cadillac	F6c + ***
6	Integrali	F7a *
7	Mustang	F6b
8	Firebird	F7a *
9	The Green Route	F7a
10	Pathfinder	F6b + *
11	Proton	F6a
12	Enter the Neutron	E1
13	Fossil Groove	F6a
14	Fossil Crack	F6b

Photo: Al Phizacklea

any obstruction for local residents or the milk tanker! Walk up the small, steep road on the right past a path junction at its top on the left, which leads to Beck Head. The road/track flattens out here. Follow the road for another few hundred metres until another path leads up into the woods on the left. Climb up through the woods on this path for about 200 metres until a less obvious path heads back to the left. Follow this over a narrow scree chute to reach the foot of the crag at the tall narrow *Pioneers' Cave*.

Descents are from lower-offs or by abseil.

The routes are described from **right** to **left**.

Main Crag

1 **Milly**	10m	HS		2009

A couple of metres right of the cave is a pleasant open groove.
    Climb the groove to the top.

2 **Pip**	10m	S		2009

Just right of the cave is a buttress with a vague groove.
    Climb the groove direct, taking care at the top.

3 **Pioneers' Cave**	10m	HS		1972

The obvious tall thin cave at the right end of the crag provides the line for this route.
    Bridge up the entrance to the cave, past a small tree and into the smaller upper cave. Up this, then exit right, with great care, onto a large ledge and tree belay. Once upon a time a second pitch continued up the now completely overgrown gully.

4 **Countach**	23m	F7b	★★	1985

A powerful route up the left side of the bulging buttress left of the cave. A few metres left of the cave is a slim groove with a fine crack.
    Climb the groove and crack then step left onto the ledge. Make hard moves up the thin crack above, through the overhang (crux), then pull up to good holds below the next bulge. Get your breath back, then launch up over the next bulge and into the flaky groove, and so to the top. Excellent.

5 **Cadillac**	24m	F6c+	★★★	1982

A great route with some fine technical climbing. About 6 metres left of the cave is a large pinnacle.
    Start by climbing the crack which forms the right side of the pinnacle and up onto the top. Climb up a shallow scoop to another, smaller

ledge on the left. Move up and right to a bulge. Pass underneath this then move out right onto a superb smooth steep wall using flakes, small edges and good footwork, to reach a hanging groove which leads to the top. Fantastic.

| 6 | **Integrali** | 22m | F7a | ★ | 1995 |

A few metres left a small pedestal sits within a square-cut corner.

Climb easily up the right-hand side of the short pedestal to the horizontal break. Climb the bulge above, with a hard move, and up a flake to reach a thin right-leaning yellow corner. Go up to the top of this, moving right to finish.

| 7 | **Mustang** | 21m | F6b | ★ | 1991 |

Climb the wall just left of the short pedestal to the horizontal break. Climb up to a small niche then left to a small tree. Step up and right onto ledges then straight up the steep top wall. Good climbing but a bit of a disappointing finish as the lower-off feels like it is too low.

Left of the pedestal-filled corner, the crag is split into two, with a lower wall leading to a vegetated ledge. The following three routes start by climbing this lower wall to the ledge.

| 8 | **Firebird** | 20m | F7a | ★ | 1995 |

Start by the left side of a large white patch of lichen.

Climb the lower wall to the ledge by a small low cave. Climb up into a short thin groove above, then continue up the wall above.

| 9 | **The Green Route** | 20m | F7a | ★ | 1995 |

Start just to the left of the white patch on the lower wall and climb this to the break.

Climb the bulging wall just left of the small low cave to another bulge at half-height. Over this then up the wall above with sustained difficulty on fingery holds, including two small very sharp resin holds.

| 10 | **Pathfinder** | 18m | F6b+ | ★ | 1974 |

Start directly below the large groove higher up the crag.

Climb the scruffy lower wall to the break. Harder moves lead up and left across the wall (do not get drawn into the groove on the right – it will not help!) to reach the ledge at the bottom of the upper groove. Climb the excellent groove above.

Right: Ian Cooksey on **Countach** (F7b), Mill Side Scar. **Photo:** Nick Wharton

As you move left, the lower wall of the crag peters out. The next two routes start at the next level up by an ash tree growing at the base of the crag on a narrow ledge reached from the left.

11 **Proton**		8m	F6a		1995

Start just right of the ash tree at a small scoop with an obvious natural thread. Climb the bulging wall and grooves above.

12 **Enter the Neutron**		17m	E1		1983

(5b). Climb the wall immediately left of the ash tree to a small roof. Step right into the groove and climb this, exiting right at the top, then go up the wall above.

Upper Right Tier

Up and right of the *Main Crag* is a grassy ledge with one area of clean solid rock sporting two short routes. This ledge can be reach by scrambling up from back along the approach path. The more adventurous may be tempted to climb the first section of *Pioneers' Cave* to reach the ledge.

13 **Fossil Groove**		9m	F6a		1982

The left-hand line. Start in the centre of the wall.
Climb a short wall past a small yew. Pull up into the left-hand groove above, then step right into the flake/groove to finish at the tree.

14 **Fossil Crack**		12m	F6b	★	1982

The right-hand line. Start a couple of metres to the right.
Climb the technical lower wall before making a long move to reach the bottom of the hanging crack. Climb this to the tree at the top.

White Scar

Grid Reference: SD 459 853   Altitude: **100m**
Faces: South-East   Approach: **5 mins**

White Scar is the amazing-looking crag forming the south-eastern flank of the Whitbarrow plateau. It dominates the view from the A590 west of Gilpin Bridge. The climbing is steep and precarious – and that is just the approach! Whilst some of the routes are bolt protected they still present a significant and serious undertaking.

The owners of White Scar have banned climbing for over ten years, following attempts by a few individuals to make access to the foot of the crag safer by

installing a metal ladder. Unfortunately there was also considerable damage to rare vegetation so perhaps the ban was justified. However the agreement was that the ban would be lifted after ten years but the owners have since refused to honour this. After repeated negotiations the BMC has recently (August 2011) written to the National Park Authority and Natural England to advise that they can no longer support a voluntary ban on climbing except to protect peregrines and rare vegetation.

Natural England have stated that their only objection to access is either due to breach of bird restrictions or removal of vegetation in the SSSI. They say, "At the instigation of the ban we supported the landowners as there had been extensive vegetation removal (including the sawing down of very rare whitebeams) and trundling of masses of scree and stone which damaged both grassland and scree vegetation. The amount of fixed gear there was not a issue in its own right but more that it was encouraging more and more vegetation removal. If the Peregrine restriction is followed, there is no vegetation removal and no more fixed gear (we would be happy with replacement bolts and lower-offs) then we have no objection to climbing there. New routeing could be contentious as it would need vegetation removal and new fixed gear at the crag base."

So on the question of whether climbing is allowed at White Scar or not, officially it is not. However if you do climb there, please respect the peregrine restriction and do not remove any vegetation whatsoever or damage any trees.

Because of the ban, it has not been possible to properly check route descriptions nor the current state of climbs prior to the writing of this guide. Much reliance has had to be placed on the good work of previous guide-book writers and the fading memories of the current author and first ascensionists. With this in mind, even greater care should be taken. It does however add to the adventurous nature of the venue. Lack of recent activity due to the ban has allowed much vegetation to encroach onto some of the established routes – particularly those to either side of the main buttress.

Approach:

Travelling west along the A590 dual-carriageway, take the first right after the A5074, Gilpin Bridge turning. After a few hundred metres turn right again down a narrow road that leads to Raven Lodge Farm. Follow the track round the bend at the farm and park on the left. A short walk leads up a track through a gate and eventually opening out onto a large very easy-angled smooth slab. The crag and its approach slopes are above you. Routes have in the past been reached by precarious scrambling up the approach slopes or by terrifying abseils from above. It is hoped that an approved method of approach will be tied into any future access agreement – if such a thing should ever happen.

The current recommendation would be to scramble up the scree rather than abseil, to avoid damage to sensitive cliff-top vegetation.

White Scar

1	Puppy Dog Pie	VS*
2	Air City	E2
3	Book of Invasions	E3***

4	Zone Norte	F7b**
5	Introducing the Hardline	F7b**
6	Men At Work	F7b*
7	Ten Years Gone	F7c*

Space Buttress

Photo: Nick Wharton

Above: The Whitbarrow Escarpment and distant Lakeland Fells, as seen from the Kent Estuary. The prominent crag is White Scar. **Photo:** Karl Lunt

There will usually be a bird restriction from 1st March to 30th June due to nesting peregrines.

Descents are exciting!

The routes are described from **right** to **left**.

Space Buttress

This is the main, impressive, barrel-shaped, towering buttress that dominates the front of the Whitbarrow escarpment. Beneath the actual rock is a similar height of extremely unstable, fine scree. Both extremities of the buttress have been invaded by vegetation; however the face's central section is too steep and hard for even the ivy to climb it!

| 1 | **Puppy Dog Pie** | 29m | VS | ★ | 1977 |

(4c). At the far right of the buttress is an obvious deep crack – this leads to completely impenetrable jungle.

| 2 | **Air City** | 51m | E2 | | 1968 |

Start just left of the toe of the buttress beneath a groove.
1 27m (5b). Climb the groove to a small ledge (peg) then continue to a larger ledge and peg belay.
2 24m (5a). Swing left onto the wall, then move up for 3 metres and traverse right to a shallow groove. Climb this and a steep wall above, then traverse easily left to the top.

| | **TMA** | 53m | E1 | | 1979 |

The easiest way up *Space Buttress* – but no less exciting. Start left of the toe of the buttress, at the foot of the large curving groove.
1 21m (5a). Climb the groove to a hanging stance by a holly.
2 8m (5a). Traverse right along a fragile break to a peg belay on *Air City*.

3   24m (4c). Follow *Air City* for 9 metres to below the shallow groove, then traverse right across the steep wall to an easier-angled groove and follow this to the top.

| 3 **The Book of Invasions** | 42m | E3 | ★ ★ ★ | 1968 |

The obvious line up the centre of the buttress, with a spectacular top pitch. Start as for *TMA*, left of the toe of the buttress, at the foot of the large curving groove.
1   21m (5a). Climb the groove to a hanging stance by a holly (as for *TMA*).
2   21m (6a). Move left to a ledge then climb the wall and overhang to a flat hold (peg and threads), reach up left to a small hidden sidepull, and climb the wall (peg) to a depression below the final bulge (poor peg). Climb the thin crack above until it fades out, then make a hard move right to gain an easy groove above.

| 4 **Zona Norte** | 42m | F7b | ★ ★ | 1996 |

A superb route with two great pitches. The first is fingery and steep, whilst the second is more powerful, climbing the bulges on the top wall. The route is bolt-protected, though they are well spaced!
1   21m. From the bottom of the central groove, follow a line of bolts up the wall 3 metres to the left of the groove, until the holly tree belay can be reached (trying to avoid traversing onto easier ground at the top).
2   21m. Fire yourself at the overhang above the stance, using whatever small holds you can find, to reach a break. Get stood up above the roof then continue to layback the shallow groove to the final bulge. A final hard move on the right brings the belay. Abseil descent.

| 5 **Introducing the Hardline** | 42m | F7b | ★ ★ | 1988 |

Historically, the first of a series of hard face climbs. Start as for *Zona Norte*, left of the central groove.
1   21m. From the first bolt of *Zona Norte*, head diagonally left to another line of bolts, which is followed up steep ground to a hanging groove. Follow this rightwards to reach the hanging stance on *The Book of Invasions*.
2   21m. Move up and right (peg) from the tree to a tape and then to a bolt. Climb through the bulge above to a second bolt then traverse right for 2 metres before pulling over the next bulge to another bolt. Step up and right (peg on left) and finish up the right arête.

| 6 **Men at Work** | 42m | F7b | ★ | 1996 |

An impressive line up the main face, sporting well-spaced bolts. Start at the left end of the large ledge below a right-facing groove.

Left: Chris Gore and Mick Lovatt on **Men at Work** (F7b), White Scar. **Photo:** Steve Wilcock

1   21m. Climb the shallow groove to a bulge which is turned on the right, then step left and make a hard fingery pull to better holds. Continue in a direct line, past the traverse of *The Prometheus Crisis*, to a bolt belay at the break.
2   21m. Move right from the belay and pull through the bulge to join the line of *The Prometheus Crisis*. Follow this for 3 metres then continue in a straight line up a thin intermittent crack to the belay. Lower off.

7 **Ten Years Gone**	42m	F7c	★	1996

A sustained technical first pitch followed by an easier but fantastically positioned second. Start at the end of the ledge as for *Men at Work*.
1   21m. From the ledge, head a few metres left on poor rock to reach the first bolt. Climb the bulging wall above, then up a sustained fingery section to a rest in a shallow groove. Follow the groove to where it peters out at the *The Prometheus Crisis* traverse and continue up the smooth wall above to a ledge and bolt belay.
2   21m. Move right from the belay and through the bulge as for *Men at Work* but then follow a line of bolts leftwards, then straight up the centre of the wall in a fantastic position. Make the last moves past the lower-off to great finishing holds.

8 **The Prometheus Crisis**	48m	E3	★	1982

A great looking traverse of the left side of the *Space Buttress*. It starts down and slightly right of the vegetated gully on the left side of the buttress. Approach by a dodgy scramble up or a dodgy abseil down - take your pick! The start is a little overgrown.
1   24m (5b). Step right round the arête and climb a short groove to a horizontal break. Follow this rightwards for 8 metres (peg), then move up to a shallow depression (thread) and up again to a spike below the overhang on *The Book of Invasions*. Move right to the hanging belay.
2   24m (5b). Move back left past the spike for 6 metres to a thread then pull over the overhang to a good flake. Move up for a few metres then traverse right round a vague rib to the junction with *The Book of Invasions*. Follow the thin crack above with a hard move right to finish up a groove. Abseil descent.

9 **Aqualung**	30m	VS		1978

This is the very vegetated gully/chimney that forms the left extent of *Space Buttress* before it curves back left.
    (4c). One would need to be armed with machete, strimmer and 'Roundup', get to the foot of the chimney, never mind climbing it. Alan Titchmarsh might have a few tips.

Tapestry Buttress

| 10 **The Turin Shroud** | 36m | HVS | | 1981 |

If you have coped with the horticultural delights of *Aqualung*, you might fancy the even greater challenge of this route. It starts at the right hand end of a broad terrace.

1   24m (4c). Somewhere under the ivy there is rumoured to be a groove/corner which leads to a ledge below the arched overhang. Peg belay.

2   12m (4c). Climb the crack to the overhang, traverse right, then pull over onto a short headwall.

| 11 **The Malacia Tapestry** | 51m | E2 | ★ | 1980 |

A good route that weaves its way up the centre of the wall: as gripping as the novel it is named after. Start at a bolt belay at the left end of the broad terrace.

1   12m (5b). Move left to an obvious groove and follow it past a bulge to a small stance.

2   24m (5c). Traverse right to a perched block at the foot of a steep wall. Climb this on small holds then trend right to below an overhang. Pull round (peg on left) to a superb jug then move right (crux) to the *Porthole*. Climb up to a horizontal break and hand-traverse left (peg – hard to clip) to a ledge and belay around the arête.

3   15m (5c). Step right and climb a short wall to the top.

| 12 **Torn Curtain** | 27m | HVS | ★ | 1980 |

Start about 20 metres left of the broad terrace below the obvious steep crack at the left end of the large roof.

    (5b). Climb delicately to the ledge, then pull over the overhang and onto a long flake which is followed strenuously to the top.

| 13 **Sidewinder** | 255m | E3 | | 1996 |

A right to left girdle traverse of the entire crag following, for the most part, the mid-height horizontal break.

    (up to 5b). Start right of *Puppy Dog Pie* and keep heading left, with belays as found to be appropriate. The line dips down underneath the large roof of the *Tapestry Buttress* to gain the start of *Torn Curtain* before bushwhacking further left to eventually reach and climb the wide crack on the right of the *Stride Pinnacle*. If setting out on this route you will need the following: a sense of adventure, a very understanding (or completely ignorant) partner and plenty of provisions (it could take some time!). Be sure to make your farewells to loved ones before setting out – who knows what the outcome might be?! It may be worth thinking about an escape plan before starting this route – but that shouldn't be too difficult as you must have already successfully escaped from the asylum!

Stride Pinnacle Area

Left of *Tapestry Buttress* is a deep wide bay. At the left end of this is a large pinnacle – *Stride Pinnacle*. The following routes climb this feature – the first up the front and the second up the left-hand side. Access will always present as much of a challenge as the climbing, with abseil from above probably being the only reasonable option. Only limited details are provided in order to allow the maximum feeling of adventure.

Big Strides	25m	E1			1996

(5b). From the left end of a ledge beneath the right side of the pinnacle, move left to a loose spike level with the ledge. Climb the widening crack running up the front of the pinnacle.

Stride Pinnacle	70m	VS			1973

Climbs the left side of the pinnacle.

(4b). Gain the deep crack via a short wall. Follow the crack to the saddle between pinnacle and face. Step onto the wall and climb the right-slanting weakness to a tree.

Wilf's Crag

At the top of the large smooth slab of rock below and left of the main crag is a short wall that has the following routes.

Tormented Shower	8m	HVS			1993

(5a). The deep crack that forms a groove at the right side of the crag.

Summer Lightning	8m	F6a			1993

The line of bolts 2 metres to the left.

Anniversary Waltz	6m	F6a+			1993

At the left side of the buttress, at a higher level, a line of three bolts leads rightwards.

Anaconda Adams	6m	F6a+			1993

Climb the three-bolt line immediately to the right of the angle of the crag.

Yewbarrow (SD 405 782) is a small limestone crag in the woods above Grange-over-Sands with a handful of climbs but nothing to get excited about.

Humphrey Head

Grid Reference: **SD 390 740**   Altitude: **0m**
Faces: **West**   Approach: **1 min**

Humphrey Head is a small headland that protrudes south into Morecambe Bay, west of Grange-over-Sands. Whilst technically a sea cliff, it is non-tidal and is blessed with a large flat sandy (muddy) foot, ideal for picnics, barbecues and family fun. The crag is rather overgrown at the time of writing and has seen little activity recently, and the quality of the rock varies greatly from good and solid to snappy and loose. The top of the crag tends to disappear into the hillside and vertical grass, so in most cases bolt lower-offs are recommended. There are a few good routes that make a visit or two worthwhile, particularly on a winter's afternoon when the sun is on the crag and the leaves are off the trees.

Beware how you these Rocks ascend
Here WILLIAM PEDDER met his end
August 22nd 1857 Aged 10 Years
                    By permission

Above: You have been warned! **Photo:** Al Phizacklea

Humphrey Head Main Crag

1	Sniffin' The Saddle Direct	E2
2	3-2-1	E2
3	Sniffin' The Saddle	E2
4	Fusion	E3 **
5	Triggerfinger	E3 *
6	Shot by Both Sides	E3 *
7	The Firing Squad	F7b *
8	Virility	E1
9	Hammerlock	E4
10	Live Rounds	F7a+
11	Shooting the Load	F7a+
12	Humphrey Hymen Met a Sly Man	F7b+ **
13	Stymen	F6b
14	Noda	E1
v1	Noda Alternative Start	E1
15	Pork Pie	F6a+
16	Humphrey Bogart	F7b
17	Sunflake	HVS

Photo: Al Phizacklea

Approach:

The crag is very easy to reach. Drive through Grange-over-Sands to Allithwaite. Just after the end of the village there is a signposted turning on the left. Follow the narrow road, turning left after the level-crossing, until the road ends at the beach. The *Main Crag* is up on the left.

There will usually be a bird restriction from 1st March to 30th June due to nesting peregrines.

The routes are described from **left** to **right**.

Landward Buttress

The first two routes are on a small isolated wall 200 metres left of the *Main Crag*, reached by walking along the top until a large square-cut fence post is found. The tops of the routes are 30 metres beyond this and fairly obvious – it is probably best to abseil as the slope down to the bottom is very steep and overgrown.

The Left Hand of Darkness	10m	HVS		1978

(5a). Climb the right-leading flake to the overlap then follow good holds on the right. It is also possible to move left, then over the overlap – slightly harder.

Right-Hand Man	10m	HVS		1997

(5b). Gain the left-leading flake, then go up the right wall and short groove.

Half a dozen routes have been recorded on slabby rock approximately 30 metres left of the **Descent Gully/path**. The area is now really quite overgrown, verging on the impenetrable.

Main Crag

This is the most obvious and largest wall and is reached by a path from the beach. The foot of the wall can be followed leftwards and up to an overgrown ledge which is where the first routes start.

1	**Sniffin' the Saddle Direct**	21m	E2		1991

Start towards the left end of the ledge.

(5c). Climb the bulging wall past a bolt, then up and right to reach a good flake on *Sniffin' the Saddle*. Finish up this.

2 **3-2-1**	20m	E2		1989

Start in the middle of the ledge below a left-facing corner.

(5b). Climb the corner and the one above then move left and follow a shallow groove to a bolt belay.

3 **Sniffin' the Saddle**	18m	E2		1986

Start below the left-facing corner, as for *3-2-1*.

(5c). Climb the corner then move right past a peg to reach a shallow niche. Climb this to the ledge. Step left to gain a good flake then use sharp pockets to reach a good hold. Finish at the bolt belay above.

4 **Fusion**	15m	E3		1967

(6a). Follow *Sniffin' the Saddle* to the large ledge then climb the thin crack above.

Girdle Traverse	38m	E1		1968

1   10m (5b). As for *Sniffin' the Saddle* to the ledge.
2   18m (5a). Traverse right across the wall to a deep recess with an unpleasant thorny bush. Climb past this to belay on the loose pinnacle.
3   10m. Move right and climb loose rock to the top.

The Fertility Variation 1966

3.   Climb the steep wall above the belay with two pegs for aid and loose rock to the top. Sounds great!

5 **Triggerfinger**	18m	E3+	★ ★	1978

One of the better routes and quite hard for its grade. Start by a shallow scoop at the right end of the ledge behind the large tree.

(6a). From the scoop swing right onto a small ledge below a small tufa pillar. Move up and left over the bulge and onto the ledge above with difficulty. Climb up to a peg then climb the upper wall direct to a bolt belay.

6 **Shot by Both Sides**	8m	E3	★	1986

(6b). From the large tree at the right edge of the ledge, climb directly up the wall to the first ledge of *Triggerfinger*. Climb up to and over the bulge then continue to a peg below the overlap. Move up steeply to the flake in the upper wall then make fingery moves left to reach a pocket on *Triggerfinger* just below the belay.

7 **The Firing Squad**	19m	F7b	★	1984

Given the choice of facing the firing squad or *The Firing Squad*, it might be quicker, easier and less painful to opt for the former! Start down and right of the ledge a few metres right of the large tree.

Climb the steep fingery wall to a small ledge. Continue in the same line past a long reach to gain a ledge and easier climbing (briefly) before attacking the desperate shallow crack and hard finishing move.

8 **Virility**	24m	E1		1966

Start at the base of the steep wall, right of the upper ledge, where a right-trending gangway starts.

(5b). Follow the gangway to a shallow niche at its end. Step up and right, around the arête and climb the none-too-solid wall to a bolt belay out right.

9 **Hammerlock**	22m	E4		1968

(5c). Halfway along the *Virility* gangway is a very dodgy left-trending groove – this has been climbed.

10 **Live Rounds**	20m	F7a+		1989

A direct line crossing the *Virility* gangway. Start just left of where the path arrives at the base of the wall.

Follow a limited number of bolts and a peg in the break.

11 **Shooting the Load**	20m	F7a+		1989

Start below the niche that forms the end of the *Virility* gangway.

Climb directly to the niche, then continue above, trending left to finish as for *Live Rounds*. It is also possible to traverse left at half-height past a couple of pegs to join and finish up *Live Rounds* – known as **Humphrey Cushion** (F7a).

12 **Humphrey Hymen (Met a Sly Man)**	16m	F7b+	★ ★	1986

A good steep fingery route up the grey wall.

Climb the steep bulging rib and the steep wall past several pairs of bolts.

13 **Stymen**	16m	F6b		1991

An obvious feature round to the right is a sentry box several metres up the wall.

Start one metre left of the sentry box and climb the wall to a scoop, then up the wall above.

14 **Noda**	16m	E1		1967

(5a). Climb up into the sentry box then, using a suspect flake on the left, move up and right into a short groove. Climb this and the crack above. All a bit loose.

v1   *Alternative Start* E1

(5b). Climb the first section of *Humphrey Hymen* to a ramp which is followed rightwards to the bottom of the short groove.

15 **Pork Pie**	16m	F6a+		1991

From the sentry box move up and right, then straight up the wall.

16 **Humphrey Bogart**	16m	F7b		1991

Several metres right of the sentry box is an overlap just above head height. Surmount the overlap and go up the scooped wall above.

17 **Sunflake**	15m	HVS		1968

At the right-hand end of the wall a large flake can be seen at the top.
(5a). Climb up to, then up the flake – a bit overgrown in the lower section.

Humphrey Dumphrey Buttress

From the beach a large clean rocky depression can be seen in the hillside 40 metres right of the *Main Crag*. Down and left of this, the following routes lie above a deep cave with a central pillar. This area is reached by a rather overgrown path starting down and right of the depression.

Humphrey Dumphrey	8m	F5		1992

The bolt line just left of the cave.

Englebert Humphreding	8m	F7b		1994

The central bolt line above the cave, starting just right of the pillar.

Mr Self-Destruct	12m	F7b		1997

The right-hand bolt line, just right of the cave.

Edgar's Arch

Further right again is a large blow hole which has created a large rock arch – this provides some steep climbing. It can be reached by a dodgy path from the beach – it may be easier to walk along the top and make an easy scramble down into the roofless *Cave* behind the arch. The routes are described clockwise from the left of the arch (looking inwards).

Mindfields	15m	F7a+		1998

Start underneath the arch and climb past two bolts to the roof. Follow the line of pockets running up and right beneath the roof to reach the deep hole on *Slightly Shoddy*, then up the overhanging wall above.

Head Like a Hole	15m	F8b+		2005

As for *Mindfields* to the roof, but where that route goes right, take a line of bolts across the roof following a vague V-groove and heading for a hole in the inner arch and a lower-off.

Hollow Lands	12m	F6c		1989

Start inside the *Cave* and climb the steep wall past a couple of bolts to a peg. Move up and left over the roof then step left to a large hole and finish at the lower-off above.

Slightly Shoddy	11m	F7a		1991

Not so much of the "Slightly"! Start in the corner on the back wall of the *Cave*. Climb the rounded tufa pillar to reach the deep hole then up the overhanging wall above.

The Job	22m	E1		1986

Start on the other side of the *Cave*, just right of the scramble down from the top. (5c). Climb the short left-leaning crack.

Back to the Future	11m	F8a		1977

Climbs underneath the arch from the inside to the outside. Start just right of the crack of *The Job*.

Head up to a bolt then right, following a line of holds underneath the arch, along a prominent flake-crack to a hanging flake on the lip. Now change direction and start climbing up (instead of down) to reach the top.

Direct Variation F7c+ 2005

Climb straight up where *Back to the Future* goes right and finish at the lower-off of *Head Like a Hole*. The bolts currently do not have hangers and it's described as poor, which gives you two reasons not to try it.

Sir Edgar's Crack	10m	VS		1997

A route outside the arch on the right side.

(4c). Climb the left-slanting crack. There are no belays so folklore suggests that the leader be lowered down the inside of the arch to belay the second who is subsequently lowered back down the outside. Sounds like the most interesting part of the day!

"A nasty fall on Humphrey Head about two years ago… One of his favourite haunts was Humphrey Head…" HBL recalls an early pioneer of South Lakes Limestone in his obituary to 'Jack Herbert', **FRCC Journal** 1924 (and long before any recorded routes)

Humphrey Head Forgotten Walls

18	Adela	F6c
19	January	HVS
v2	September Arête	
20	Where Bolters Fear to Tread	HVS

Photo: Al Phizacklea

Forgotten Walls

Right again is a clean area of rock with a large right–facing corner in its centre and a grassy ledge below.

Up to the left of here, starting at a tree at a higher level, **Wolfman** (E2 5b, 1997) climbed the groove and crack before heading right. However, the lower half is now completely overgrown. The following route originally started as for *Wolfman*, but is now described with an alternative start to allow the better upper part to still be climbed.

18 **Adela**	18m	F6c		1997

Climb the deep corner and step left onto the ledge. Climb up past a bolt to the horizontal break. Continue up, then left, using pockets to reach a thin diagonal crack on the left. Step up to a good jug then make a long step back right to finish.

Right: Flora Wharton soaks up the golden glow of sunset on **January** (HVS), Humphrey Head.
Photo: Nick Wharton

| 19 **January** | 22m | HVS | | 1981 |

(5a). Climb the easy right-facing corner to a ledge on the left, then back right and up the depression above on lovely bubbly rock. Climb past a short slab to a peg belay.

v2 ***September Arête*** 1997

The left arête of the corner gives an alternative start at about the same grade as the corner.

| 20 **Where Bolters Fear to Tread** | 23m | HVS | | 1997 |

Its not that they fear to tread here, but would just rather not!

(5a). Start below the corner and climb out to the arête on the right via the flake-crack. Follow the arête and the rock on its right side until a step left onto a short slab at the top.

| **Oktoberfest** | 30m | HVS | | 1997 |

Ten metres right of the corner is a huge flake sticking out of the ground.

(5a). From the left side of the flake climb the slab and groove above to a large ledge. Step left and up to a thread beneath the overhang. Traverse left to a peg then round the overhang to a peg belay at the top.

Brant Fell (SD 409 962) is just south of Bowness and is reached from the B5284. There is a slate crag near its summit with some good bouldering, including a 6b traverse. Unfortunately some misguided individual has been modifying the holds with a chisel recently, presumably because they can't climb 6b – this is not, however, the accepted way to achieve this grade.

Bow Mabble Breast (SD 428 938) is a steep slate crag a mile and a half south of Crosthwaite. It is rumoured to have one 5a route up the groove high in the centre of the diamond-shaped buttress – probably one was enough.

White Stone by Roger Wilkinson

Grid Reference: **SD 390 848**   Altitude: **200m**
Faces: **West South-West**   Approach: **10 mins**

Although the traffic on the A590 can be intrusive, this is a pleasant little crag, easily reached, ideal for an evening, and often climbable when it is raining over the high fells. The Silurian siltstone, which tends to provide incut pockets, is generally good and protection is usually (though not always) plentiful.

The crag lies in an elevated position about 2km south-east of Newby Bridge, overlooking the A590 road and the Cartmel Peninsula, and just above the north-west end of the dual carriageway Newton by-pass. There is a disused stretch of road for parking, reached by entering the minor road towards Staveley-in-Cartmel and immediately turning right.

Approach:

Both the crag and its approach are on Access Land. Take the public footpath starting 250 metres south-east from the Staveley-in-Cartmel junction. After 60 metres leave the main path and take a right fork parallel to the road. This path crosses a small beck (sometimes dry) and then ascends steeply through bracken until a boulder field is reached below the *Main Crag*. Climb the boulder field until zig-zags lead rightwards to the gearing-up point below the steep pillar of *Moose*. From the foot of the boulder field a path leads rightwards to the *Easy Slabs* and, from the top of the boulder field, a path leads under a yew to *Lower Crag*.

There may be a bird restriction from 1st March to 30th June due to nesting peregrines.

The routes are described from **left** to **right**.

Lower Crag

Rather an unprepossessing piece of rock, this is the inferior part of the crag in both senses. Neither the rock nor the protection is such as to give great confidence.

The routes start just above and left of the prominent yew tree.

| 1 | **Long Ridge** | | 100m | D | | |

This long ramble is on the left of *Lower Crag*. Start left of the steep buttress, about 10 metres left of the yew.

Take the most appealing line up a succession of small outcrops.

White Stone

1	Long Ridge	D
2	Two Overhang Route	HS
v1	Cartmel Groove	HVS
3	Elk	VD
4	Stag	S
5	Missing Words	VS

6	The W	HVS
7	The V	HVS *
v2	Golf variation	HVS
8	Direct Route	HS *
9	Jess	S *
10	High Level Girdle	HS *
11	Chimney Route	VD *
12	Wild Winds	HVS
13	Moose	VS **
14	Cracked Wall	MVS *
15	Ridge	MS

Photo: Roger Wilkinson

2 **Two Overhang Route**	17m	HS		1983

Start beneath the lower overhang, passing it on its left up a slanting corner-crack. Hand-traverse boldly right between the two overhangs and climb up untrustworthy-looking rock to a ledge on the right. Move back left above the second overhang on better rock and finish up the arête.

v1 *Cartmel Groove* HVS 1987

(4c). It is possible to take the first overhang direct on horribly fractured rock with no meaningful protection. Finish direct up a slight groove.

3 **Elk**	15m	VD		1986

Low in the grade technically, but with no reliable protection until 12 metres. Better than it looks. Start 2 metres right of the first overhang at a stumpy pillar.

Climb the pillar and the steepening wall above. It is best to choose the right-hand options where a choice appears.

Main Crag

The crag is characterised by a mid-height overhang which rises left-wards, a right-leaning groove left of the overhang and a deep cleft right of the overhang.

Descent from the *Main Crag* is to the right.

4 **Stag**	26m	S		pre-1969

Though the second pitch is good, unfortunately the first pitch is poor and vegetated. It may be preferable to start up the first pitch of *Jess* or the first part of *The V*. The spike belay at the top of pitch 1 is loose. Start at the large right-facing corner at the left end of the crag.

1   12m. Climb the corner and awkward V-groove to emerge through a hawthorn. Continue on grass to belay below the large leaning groove.
2   14m. Climb the bulging wall split by two cracks right of the groove. Continue easily up the slab above.

5 **Missing Words**	20m	VS/HVS		1983

Rather an unsatisfying route, being artificial in nature and struggling continually to avoid much easier climbing. The grade depends on the exact line taken. Start one metre right of *Stag*.

(4c/5b). Climb the wall to a ledge and then on to two doubtful-looking flakes. Climb (or walk past) the unprotected rib and continue up the wall above, just left of the overhang and right of pitch 2 of *Stag*. From the break, climb directly over the overhang (or round its edge) and so to the top.

The next two routes are only distinct in their upper halves, and share virtually the same crux, which involves a strenuous and intimidating (though reasonably protected) overhang.

6 **The W**	25m	HVS		1992

Rather a one move wonder, inferior to its neighbour. If the initial slab is wet it can be started as for *The V*.

(4c). Climb the pocketed slab left of the left-facing corner direct to a small block below a prominent V-notch (the left-hand of two). Step off the block and pull strenuously into the smaller V-notch using a good pocket. Follow the easy groove to finish slightly rightwards on slabby rock, passing a prostrate oak.

7 **The V**	25m	HVS	★	pre-1969

Start below the right-hand end of the main overhang where a projecting block creates a left-facing corner.

(4c). Climb the corner and move left below the overhang to stand on a small block below a prominent V-notch (the left-hand of two). Climb the overhang (easiest between the two notches) and climb the crack up the slab to a finish up the wide twisting crack.

Variation Start

Climb the pocketed slab (as for *The W*) direct to the V-notch. Often wet or greasy.

v2   *Golf* HVS 2007

(5a). A variation finish up the front of the pillar, left of the wide crack, on improving holds.

8 **Direct Route**	25m	HS	★	pre-1969

A route with one overly hard, albeit well protected, move. Start as for *The V*, below the right-hand end of the main overhang where a projecting block creates a left-facing corner.

Climb the corner and step up right on to the hanging block. Climb the overhang between the two grooves (good wire in right-hand groove) and continue direct up slabs to finish by the prostrate oak.

Right: James Bumby locks horns with **Moose** (VS), White Stone: in the distance, a fine backdrop of Dow Crag and the Coniston Fells. **Photo:** Nick Wharton

9 Jess	37m	S	★	1988

A low level girdle and a worthwhile route; better than it looks, though a little vegetated in places.

1   23m. Climb the slabs of the start of *Chimney Route* then traverse, awkwardly at times, below the full length of the central overhang until a tricky slither leads to a belay (shared with *Stag*) at a loose spike.

2   14m. Climb the steep slabby chimney groove above, to the left of *Stag*, passing an awkward small overlap. Easy slabs remain.

10 High Level Girdle	30m	HS	★	

Varied climbing and good positions make this right to left girdle a worthwhile little adventure. Rope drag can be a problem, so splitting it into two pitches may be a good idea.

Follow *Chimney Route* until the slab move. Continue left above the overhangs following a rising line to below the final bulge of *Missing Words*. Step down (possible belay) and traverse to the groove of *Jess* pitch 2 (finishing up this route reduces the grade to S). Cross the chimney-groove boldly (crux) to stand on an overhung glacis. Climb the steep juggy wall above to finish.

11 Chimney Route	25m	VD+	★	pre-1969

This route, which demands a variety of techniques, follows the deep cleft to the right of the mid-height overhang.

Trend left up a pocketed slab which lies beneath the projecting pillar of *Moose*, stepping left into an overhung V-niche. Bridge up past the overhang and pass the flake chockstone above by a move on the slab. Continue up the cleft to finish on jugs up the steep crack in the right wall.

12 Wild Winds	25m	HVS		1981

This bold route climbs the left edge of the central pillar and has a poorly protected crux.

(4c). Follow *Chimney Route* to the V-niche, step right and climb the rib (junction with *Moose*). Continue steeply up the wall (crux) right of the arête, quickly reaching good pockets and gear. Don blinkers and stick to the line, right to the top.

13 Moose	25m	VS	★ ★	pre-1969

The route of the crag. It accepts the challenge of the steep central pillar via a bold crux. Start at a pocketed slab directly below the pillar.

(4b). Climb the slab easily then follow a short diagonal crack leading to a niche below the overhang. Step up and left, then make a difficult

Right: Kerry Bumby cruising **Cracked Wall** (MVS), White Stone. **Photo:** Nick Wharton

move right (crux) onto a glacis above the overhang. Continue, still boldly at first, up the pillar near its right edge.

14 **Cracked Wall**	23m	MVS	★	pre-1969

To the right of *Moose* a steep wall gives way to a slab sporting a large triangular niche. This good route sets out to follow the groove between wall and slab, but it is hard not to stray onto the slab, which is easier, and the route is marred somewhat by this artificiality and lack of definition. The grade given is for the pure line.

(4b). Follow *Moose* to the niche below the overhang but then step right. Awkward climbing, but with good protection, leads diagonally right up the groove, or more easily via the large triangular niche, finishing over (or avoiding?) a suspicious-looking flake block.

Cracked Moose HVS 2007

An enjoyable if somewhat eliminate variation finish.

(5a). Climb the groove almost to the top then pull up the steep left wall to good holds and the finish of *Moose*.

Below the slab of *Cracked Wall* is a sloping field and a vegetated arête. To the right again is an easy-angled, left-facing, rightward-leaning corner. This sadly vegetated line used to be **Easy Chimney** (D, pre-1969).

15 **Ridge**	15m	MS		pre-1969

This pleasant excursion is not technically hard but not easy to protect. Start where a rowan tree splits a block at the foot of an arête right of *Easy Chimney*.

Climb the arête to a ledge. Step right then regain the arête and climb it to the final tower where there is a choice of finishes.

Easy Slabs

This part of the crag, which is popular with outdoor centre groups, provides pleasant easier climbs on good rock, though unfortunately protection is not abundant. Grades reflect this. The best climbs are these four (described from **left** to **right**) on the *Main Slab* which lies below and left of the prominent nose at the top of the crag. Some inferior routes may be found on the more vegetated *Left Slab*.

Grubby Groove	12m	VD		

Start at a shallow groove at the left edge of the *Main Slab*.

Climb the groove and the left corner of the slab to finish over a jammed flake in the upper wall.

| **Overlap Route** | | 12m | VD | | |

Start below the middle of the *Main Slab* below a crack running through the overlap at 4 metres.

Climb direct to and up the crack and continue up the slab above (easy but gearless). Finish as for *Grubby Groove*, via the flake.

| **Slab and Corner** | | 12m | D | | |

Start below the prominent nose.

Climb the pocketed wall and slab above, finishing up the corner left of the nose. Poorly protected.

| **Nose Direct** | | 12m | VD | | |

Start at the right edge of the *Main Slab*.

Climb direct up steepening rock just left of the small hawthorn tree. Finish up the groove in the right flank of the nose.

Lindale Slabs (SD 418 817) are the clean open slabs seen clearly from the A590 Lindale by-pass on the slopes of Newton Fell. They are reached from Lindale village by taking the narrow road next to the pub at the bottom of the hill. The slabs are 15 metres high and offer a handful of D and VD routes which are used regularly by local outdoor centres. The routes lack both line and protection but are good for top roping and there are bolt belays. In order to prevent congestion any groups intending to visit the crag are asked to ring Castle Head Field Centre (015395 34300) prior to their visit. Individuals should ask permission from the farmer, who lives just north of the crag.

Barker Scar (SD 334 783), a broken crag next to the Leven Estuary, has two routes: **Crocodile** (9m, E2 5b), a snappy climb up the centre of the first big clean wall (one bolt) and **Harry Worth Goes to Hollywood** (A2), which crosses the roof of the cave further right on large Friends, to finish back on the floor.

Kettlewell Crag (SD 504 933) is a small scrappy limestone outcrop on the edge of Kendal, below the golf course. It has been used for bouldering.

Meathop Quarry (SD 433 798) is a tottering pile of choss that has been climbed on in the past and has a few routes recorded but none worth a visit. There is some bouldering on natural rock on the other side of the railway line.

High Newton Crag (SD 404 828) is a 12 metre high overgrown disused quarry. This roadside attraction has two recorded routes: **Cat o' Nine 'Tales'** (HVS 5b, 1981) follows the obvious right-slanting crack and **The Wall** (E1 5c, 1981) takes the wall to its left. Various easier routes also exist.

The Furness Peninsula

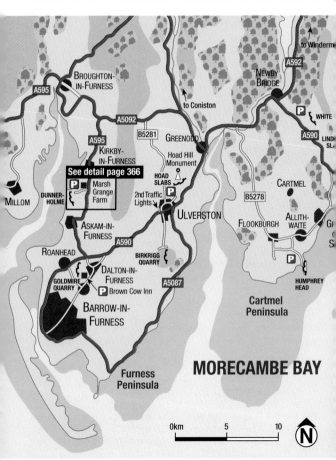

The Furness Peninsula is conveniently identified as the land lying between the Rivers Leven and Duddon and to the south of the A5092 Broughton to Greenodd Road. It has produced many fine climbers, but hasn't been known as a destination for climbing. The development of *Goldmire Quarry* and kinder weather than the central Lakes may change that. The crags and quarries are listed here from north-east to south-west.

Stott Park Heights (SD 370 895) is used by the YMCA at Lakeside and is best left to them.

Hoad Slabs

Grid Reference: **SD 296 790**	Altitude: **80m**
Faces: **East**	Approach: **3 mins**

Clearly seen from the A590 just north of Ulverston, these clean slate slabs are a popular practice ground. Park in the steep lane below the hill.

The most obvious line is the central crack of *Devil's Armchair*. Just five climbs are described, but locals have been varying and combining routes here for decades and every conceivable possibility will have been climbed, including many inferior lines - feel free to ad lib. There are an astonishing number of bolt belays at the top of the crag.

Descent is possible on either side but easier at the town end.

The routes are described from **left** to **right**.

1 **Hoad Way**	25m	HS		

Start from the lowest point of the slab and climb up to a large ledge. Move right and up an easy-angled groove to an obvious slightly rising foot ledge and follow this boldly across the slab to the sentry-box on *Devil's Armchair*. Move right around the top arête and finish up a groove.

Hoad Slabs

1	Hoad Way	HS
2	Airway	VS
3	Hoad Road	HVS
4	Devil's Armchair	HS *
v1	Armchair Finish	MVS
5	Railway	HS

Photo: John Holden

2	**Airway**		22m	VS		

Start 5 metres left of *Devil's Armchair*.
  (4b). Climb the thin crack to the ledge. Move right on good holds and, either finish direct up the left arête of the top slab, or move left and climb the short slab and overhang direct.

3	**Hoad Road**		22m	HVS		1978

A straight eliminate starting midway between *Devil's Armchair* and *Airway*.
  (5a). Climb the slab direct via a vague crack. The thin top slab is the crux.

4	**Devil's Armchair**		20m	HS	★	

  Climb the central crack to the sentry box and finish direct. Classic!

v1   ***Armchair Finish*** 8m MVS
  (4c). From the sentry box on *Devil's Armchair*, move left and finish up the slab with difficulty.

5	**Railway**		20m	HS		

  Climb the right-hand side of the slab, then finish right of the top arête.

Right: Jenny Holden looking comfy on the **Armchair Finish** (MVS), Hoad Slabs.
Photo: John Holden

Birkrigg Quarry

1	The Slab	VB
2	Bolt Wall	V1
3	Jug Bug	VB
4	North Crack	V0
5	Gurt Wall	V1
6	Swinging Groove	V0
7	Hole Wall	V0
8	Pincher	V0 +
9	Old Clem	V0
10	Burke Rigg	V1
11	Chopping Block	V2
12	Lunatic	V1
13	Ankle Breaker	V2
14	Space Cowboy	V2
15	Ziggy	V2

Birkrigg Quarry

Grid Reference: SD 282 747   **Altitude: 90m**
Faces: West   **Approach: 30 secs**

The quarry is on Birkrigg Common, a low rounded hill 3km south of Ulverston. Make sure that you take the trouble to go to the trig point at the top; the panoramic view is magnificent. The best rock is in the low quarry, below the road level just left of the main face.

It is a popular bouldering and training area, often viewed from the 'galleries' by the public. The rock is limestone, which has been highly polished in some areas, whereas the unpolished stone is friable and loose.

The usual test-piece is the low-level traverse which runs from left to right (5c). There is also a very bold upper traverse along the horizontal break near the top of the quarry, along the left and central walls (5c).

Of note are the superb boulder problems on the left wall. Use your imagination and fingers! Some of the more popular routes are top-roped on first visits, as they reach a height of around 8 to 9 metres. Not top-roping has had a detrimental effect on a number of climbers' ankles.

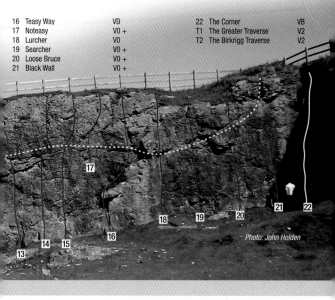

Photo: John Holden

Donkey Rocks (SD 211 867) is a steep quarry half a kilometre south of Broughton on the Foxfield road. The rock is smooth slate of a most unusual blistered architecture. Routes have been climbed here in the past but, because of its unique geology, the site has been designated an SSSI. **Please do not climb here.**

Dunnerholme

Grid Reference: **SD 211 799**　　Altitude: **5m**
Faces: **West**　　　　　　　　Approach: **10 mins**

Dunnerholme is a collection of small limestone crags set in a beautiful location. An excellent bouldering and sport venue for very strong climbers with young families. A total arm pump can be achieved in half an hour and then competitive sand castle building can be indulged in for the rest of the day.

There are four separate sections described in the order they are approached by going from south to west; *The Slabs*, *The Monster Traverse*, *The Arêtes* and *The Cove*.

There are two possible approaches. The first, via Marsh Grange, takes 5 minutes, but there is very limited parking. The alternative is to take a pleasant stroll from Askam (15 minutes).

Dunnerholme The Arêtes

1	The Traverse	V3	3	1st Crack	V1
2	1st Wall	V2	4	Problem 5	V4
			5	2nd Crack	V1
			6	Problem 7	V1

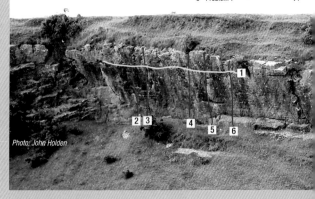

Photo: John Holden

1	The Slabs	
2	The Traverse	
3	The Arêtes	
4	The Cove	

Marsh Grange

Dunnerholme Golf Club

P Limited parking

to Askam

The Slabs: Useful to practice footwork on. The odd spot of blue paint is still visible from problems marked up in the '80s.

The Monster Traverse: There ought to be a free pint for anyone who can complete it. Finger shredding climbing; taping up is recommended.

The Arêtes: A good set of problems. The three furthest left (2, 3 and 4) and three furthest right (12, 13 and 14) give most fun if done with a sitting start.

The Cove: Rather shattered limestone, so it is reassuring to know that the bolts are M12 stainless steel, Hilti resin anchors, a minimum of 15cm long. There are a number of belay stakes at top. The routes are described from **left** to **right**.

Above: John Holden on **The Monster Traverse** thinking that golf would be an easier option.
Photo: Al Phizacklea

Dunnerholme The Cove

1 Power Windows (1993)   F7a
2 Grace Under Pressure (1993)   E3
3 Caress of Steel (1996)   F7b
4 Permanent Waves (1994)   F7b +

5 Natural Science (1996)   E2
6 Different Strings (1985)   E1
7 La Villa Strangiato (1993)   E2

Photo: John Holden

Goldmire Quarry

Grid Reference: **SD 219 739**
Faces: **West**

Altitude: **60m**
Approach: **10 mins**

This quarry lies one kilometre west of Dalton-in-Furness, 5km from Barrow, at the southern end of the Furness Peninsula. The quarry provides a wet weather alternative for middle grade climbers who find *Chapel Head Scar* too challenging.

Goldmire Quarry is an extensive limestone quarry, with typically shattered and loose walls of unstable blocks, except for one stunning feature. This is the *Grey Slab*, a solid sweep of limestone, 30 metres high, and set at an angle which increases from 60° to 80° at its steepest end. This slab is a natural fault line laid bare by quarrying: it displays few features and is quite unlike any other limestone wall in the country. The face of the slab is covered in some areas by calcite crystal formations. These are loose and brittle, often snapping off with alarming results, but the underlying rock is basically sound.

Unfortunately, the owners of *Goldmire* have planning permission to use it as a tip. Efforts are being made to see if the owners will leave

Grey Slab alone, but if you climb there whilst work is in progress you will be asked to leave. **Currently there is no permission to climb at Goldmire Quarry and the following descriptions are included only for completeness of the guide and in case access is ever allowed in the future.**

To reach *Goldmire*, follow signs for Dalton-in-Furness. Drive through the centre of Dalton, following the main road towards Barrow (the old A590) to the outskirts of town, where an excellent pub called The Brown Cow will be found set back from the road on the right. From the large car park, take a path alongside the beck until a field is entered just beyond some cottages. Walk uphill, aiming slightly leftwards. Take the path down the side of the workings to enter the obvious level containing the *Grey Slab*. It is imperative that you do not approach the slab through the quarry buildings.

There are three easily identified routes: *Black Gold*, *The Pipe* and *Gold Digger*. *Black Gold* takes the prominent crack system that reaches the ground at the left-hand side of the curving overlap. *The Pipe* is the obvious very grassy diagonal break that runs up from left to right.

Descent: Follow the fence rightwards, taking great care where the quarry edge gets close to it, until a track is reached which leads back down rightwards.

The routes are described from **right** to **left**.

The first route starts about 50 metres left of the main shattered corner of the quarry, just right of a prominent curving overlap and roof halfway up the crag.

1	**Midas Touch**		28	HVS?	★	1999

This route takes a line of runnels 16 metres right of *Black Gold*. The spoil heap at the start has been removed, since when it hasn't been repeated.

(5a). Climb the steep wall to the first runnel via a bolt and a good peg, then step left and climb small ledges to gain the next runnel. Move left again to a long runnel (peg) and climb this to an exit up flakes on the right at the top.

2	**Goodbye, Cruel World**		30m	E3?	★	1993

A good sustained climb which powers directly over the prominent roof. Start 8 metres right of *Black Gold*, but the starting spoil heap has been removed and the route has not been repeated since.

(5c). Climb up to reach a thin left-facing flake at 7 metres and follow this to a horizontal crack at 10 metres, then step left to a good hold. Stand on this and then delicately climb left to reach an excellent crack below the roof. A fingery swing directly over the roof leads to a good break (Friend 2½). Step right and continue up the headwall to finish on good holds.

Goldmire Quarry

1	Midas Touch	HVS *
2	Goodbye Cruel World	E3 *
3	Welcome to Barrow, Gateway to Oblivion	E2 *

4	The Gold Standard	E1 **
5	Black Gold	E2 **
6	Crystal Dancer	E1 *
7	Caught by the Fuzz	E1
8	Baedecker for Metaphysicians	E1 *
9	The Pipe	HVS

3	**Welcome to Barrow, Gateway to Oblivion**			
	30m	E2	★	1993

A good steep route, with a loose start and finish, but with excellent rock and protection between. Start 3 metres right of *Black Gold*.

(5c). Gain a shallow groove using pockets and continue up a crack to the overlap. Pull through this strenuously on brilliant holds to reach a fine crack system above. Follow this, slightly right, to the final roof. Pull carefully over this to reach the top.

4	**The Gold Standard**			
	26m	E1	★ ★	2011

Start as for *Black Gold*.

(5b). Climb up to the roof and traverse rightwards until a hard move gains a small ledge and lower off just beyond the right-hand end of the overhangs.

5	**Black Gold**			
	30m	E2	★ ★	1993

A superb route, with a good variety of climbing. Start below the prominent crack system that reaches the ground at the left-hand side of the curving overlap.

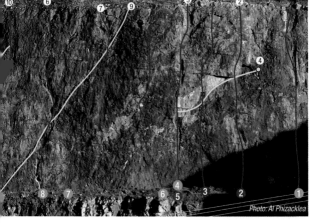

Photo: Al Phizacklea

(5c). Follow the cracks over the overlap to gain a shallow snaking runnel in the wall above. Climb this delicately past an excellent nut slot to reach a horizontal crack below the final dirty scoop. Avoid this by climbing the clean nose on the left to finish.

| 6 | **Crystal Dancer** | 30m | E1 | ★ | 1999 |

Start 5 metres left of *Black Gold*.

(5a). Follow a left-leaning crack to a quartz patch. Move rightwards for 3 metres up a narrow ramp to gain another left-leaning crack and follow this for about 4 metres until it thins out (runners). Step right, then climb up until forced right (Friend 0 in finger slot) and continue up to reach a good jug. Finish direct.

| 7 | **Caught by the Fuzz** | 30m | E1 | | 1993 |

This route takes a line parallel to, but 3 metres lower than the obvious grassy break for its first half, before climbing directly to the top. Start a couple of metres right of the runnel of *Baedecker for Metaphysicians*.

(5b). Climb up a clean slab to a flake, move up and right to about 3 metres below a grassy pock-marked overlap, then trend diagonally right into a small vague scoop. Continue up and right, past two good runners to a ledge. Climb leftwards on calcite flakes to a cleaned break in the diagonal grassy line and step onto the wall above. Pull up to a thin crack and climb this directly to the top.

8	**Baedecker for Metaphysicians**	28m	E1	★	1993

This pleasant route with spaced protection follows the obvious winding runnel 4 metres right of *The Pipe*.

(5a). Enter the rounded niche at 3 metres and continue, crossing the diagonal grassy line, following the runnel until it fades. Climb the wall above, keeping right of the grassy area, then trend left to a dirty finish.

9	**The Pipe**	35m	HVS		1998

The obvious very grassy diagonal break that runs up from left to right.

(4c). Follow the break until 3 metres right of *Baedecker for Metaphysicians'* runnel. Step right to a small ledge and climb the wall to rejoin the break. Follow it to the end.

10	**The Insular Peninsula**	20m	E2	★ ★	1993

Pleasant delicate climbing with a rather bold beginning. Start below a smooth slab one metre left of *The Pipe*.

(5b). Climb the slab to reach a good pocket where an unprotected delicate move left leads to a thin crack. Follow this until the centre of the clean slab is reached. Climb straight up the slab to a horizontal break and bolt (possible lower-off, or continue up loose rock). The crack on the left gives an alternative start.

11	**Goldsmith**	27m	HVS	★	1999

Six metres left of *The Pipe* there is an obvious crack/runnel.

(5a). Climb this until it peters out at 10 metres and the rock steepens (small ledge). Move up and left to reach a handrail and traverse left using this to reach a prominent left-leaning curving crack. Follow this to its end, then make a couple of awkward moves left to a finish up a shallow runnel.

v1   *Variation Finish* ★ ★
(5b). From where *Goldsmith* traverses left, climb the wall above and trend right to the bolt on *The Insular Peninsula*.

Right: Al Phizacklea on the first ascent of **The Insular Peninsula** (E2), Goldmire Quarry.
Photo: Andy Rowell

12 Au	29m	VS		1998

Starts 13 metres left of *The Pipe* at a short broken runnel.

(4c). Climb the runnel and the continuation flake past a slight bulge until it is possible to step left. Climb the short wall and depression above to the top.

13 **The Glassbead Game**	29m	VS	★★	1993

Good climbing. Start as for *Au*.

(4b). Climb the runnel then go left and up a pocketed slab directly to reach a good hold. Continue straight up a vague depression to a steepening, step left and climb straight to a dirty finish.

14 **Ealasaid**	27m	E1	★★	1999

Start directly below thin slanting cracks at 4 metres, 3 metres left of *The Glassbead Game*.

(5a). Take a direct line line past the cracks to finish up a scoop.

15 **Paranoid Man**	28m	HVS	★	1993

This pleasant delicate route starts 7 metres right of *Gold Digger*.

(4c). Climb the scalloped crack to a small ledge at 9 metres and continue direct, just left of a small bush, to pass a prominent white rock scar. Move right across a delightful slab and climb the shallow runnel to its top. Move carefully left and pull over the top at the same point as *Arrested Development*.

16 **Arrested Development**	28m	E1	★★	1993

Another fine delicate route which starts one metre right of *Gold Digger*.

(5b). Follow a thin crack rightwards up the slab to a good hold. Continue directly to reach a peg, where thin moves lead to a small overlap. Pull over onto the slab and climb the delicate scoop above, pulling over the final block to finish on top.

17 **Gold Digger**	24m	MVS	★★	1993

Start below a prominent scooped runnel, the most obvious feature here.

(4a). Climb the narrow runnel which soon opens into a fine deep scoop, and move up to where the angle eases. Avoid the deep grassy slot by taking a shallow line on the right, parallel with the grassy slot, to a slab below the headwall. Stride left across the grass and move up to a spike lower-off. The runnel has been climbed direct but is very dirty. A direct start has also been made but utilises much of the start of *Arrested Development*.

| 18 **Hunding** | 20m | MVS | ★ | 1993 |

This worthy route starts at the highest point of the grass, 2 metres left of *Gold Digger*.

(4b). Step left and follow a narrow vertical runnel to a horizontal line at 8 metres. Move diagonally right, crossing the peach-coloured streak on the slab, then climb directly over the rounded grey bulge to join *Neibelheim* just below the lower-off.

v2 **Variation Start**

(4c). From the foot of *Gold Digger*, climb up to a foothold at about 3 metres, then continue past crozzly rock to gain *Hunding* at the end of its traverse.

| 19 **Neibelheim** | 20m | HS | ★ | 1993 |

A pleasant route requiring a delicate touch. Start 4 metres left of *Gold Digger*. Climb into an open hole just above the spoil heap and continue directly to reach a thin crack at 8 metres. Follow this slightly rightwards, past an ancient peg until the angle eases, then cross delicately right to join the upper section of *Gold Digger*, just left of the grass. Climb up to a spike lower-off.

| 20 **Bypass to Nowhere** | 23m | E1 | ★ | 1993 |

A good sustained route starting off a small perched block below the smooth slab, 7 metres left of *Gold Digger*.

(5b). Climb directly up the slab to a nut slot then follow a short ramp on the left which leads up to a wide crack. Continue straight up the easier slab to a spike runner just left of a grassy crack. Climb the wall above this to a nut slot, then move left and up to a peg, and continue directly up the headwall to finish on good holds.

| 21 **The Last Train to Millom** | 26m | E2 | ★ | 1993 |

This route takes the wall between the two vertical cracks marked by conspicuous pot-holes high up the face - it improves to a good fingery finish. Start 5 metres left of *Bypass to Nowhere* at the base of the stack of blocks resting against the face.

(5c). Climb onto the lower right edge of the blocks and pull onto the wall to a flake pocket (Friend 3). Climb up and slightly right, following a shallow groove, to reach a nut by the right-hand crack. Traverse diagonally left into the centre of the face to a conspicuous hole, then climb the fine wall above, past a peg, to reach the short finishing crack.

Ormsgill Quarry (SD 199 717) in Barrow is home to a few routes but is terribly loose, overgrown and sandy. To add to the delights of the place, the glue sniffing vandals have been forced out by the smackheads.

Useful Contacts

Climbing
British Mountaineering Council
0870 0104878   www.thebmc.co.uk
Fell & Rock Climbing Club   www.frcc.co.uk

Lake District Weather
Weather Forecast
0844 846 2444   www.lake-district.gov.uk/weatherline/home/index.php

Lake District National Park Authority   www.lake-district.gov.uk
Bird Restrictions
017687 79633   www.frcc.co.uk/conservation_birdrestrictions.asp
Brockhole National Park Centre
015394 46601
Head Office
01539 724555

Above: Welcome to the Eden Valley! Alan Beatty scares Stew Wilson away from his new route.
Photo: Phil Rigby

Tourist Information
Cumbria Tourism
01539 8222 222   www.golakes.co.uk

Appleby	017683 51177
Barrow in Furness	01229 876505
Bowness-on-Windermere	015394 42895
Brampton	016977 3433
Brough	017683 41260
Carlisle	01228 625600
Glenridding	017684 82414
Grange-over-Sands	015395 34026
Kendal	01539 735891
Keswick	017687 72645
Killington Lake (M6 Services)	015396 20138
Kirkby Stephen	017683 71199
Penrith	01768 867466
Rheged (Junction 40)	01768 860034
Sedburgh	015396 20125
Southwaite (M6 Services)	016974 73445
Windermere	015394 46499

Journey Planners
Cumbria County Council
www.cumbria.gov.uk
Public Transport Information – Traveline
0871 200 2233   www.traveline.org.uk

Crag Guide

Crag Name B – bouldering S – sport T – trad	Access Restrictions	Aspect	Alt (m)	Approach Time (mins)	
North Cumbria & The Eden Valley					
Headend Quarry		S	295	2	
Seat Quarry		E	310	5	
Spadeadam Crag		S	215	10	
Gelt Boulder		S & E	150	10	
Cumrew – **T**		W	350	15	
Cumrew – **B**					
Armathwaite – **T**		SW	50	10	Fas
Lazonby	Restricted	E	60	15	
Scratchmere Scar – **T**		SW	220	10	Fas
Scratchmere Scar – **B**					
Cowraik – **T**		S	200	5	Fas
Cowraik – **B**					
King's Meaburn		W	150	3	Fas
Hoff	Restricted	W	160	3	
Coudy Rocks – **S**		W	160	3	
High Cup Nick		W	550	60	S
Murton Scar		SW	470	15	F
White Mines		N	450	25	S
Helbeck Wood Crag	Restricted	SW	380	25	
Brough Scar		SW	380	15	F
Windmore End – **T**	Part	SW	410	5 - 10	F
Windmore End – **B**					
Aisgill		S	370	8	Me

	Total Routes 1112	M D VD	MS S HS	MVS VS	HVS E1	E2 E3	E4+
		To 5+	F6a/a+	F6b/b+	F6c/c+	F7a/a+	>F7a+
		<V0(5a)	V0(5a/b)	V1(5c)	V2(5c/6a)	V3(6a)	>V3(6a)
		83	250	237	259	183	100
		(Grades columns are not intended to be mutually comparable)					
	33	7	11	11	4		
	41	1	13	15	10		
	17		4	7	4	2	
	10		6	2	2		
	20	2	7	5	3	3	
	9		5	2	1		1
	97	6	9	15	17	22	28
	79	1	16	17	26	14	5
	37	12	5	8	8	1	3
	10		2	3	3	1	1
	22		6	9	6	1	
	38	2	15	6	7	5	3
	56	3	10	11	20	9	3
	28	2	17	6	2	1	
	16	4	3	3	3	2	1
	6	1	1	2	2		
	19		2	5	4	8	
	2				1		1
	18		4	3	5	5	1
	8				3	3	2
	186	17	46	45	43	30	5
	31		18	8	3	1	1
	10			5	2	3	

Crag Guide

Crag Name B – bouldering S – sport T – trad	Access Restrictions	Aspect	Alt (m)	Approach Time (mins)	
South Lakes Limestone					
Hebblethwaite Hall Gill		SE & N	220	20	
Scout Scar – **S**		W	200	10	
Scout Scar – **T**					
Slape Scar		W	180	40	
Chapel Head Scar – **S**	Seasonal	SW	70	15	
Chapel Head Scar – **T**	Seasonal				
Mill Side Scar – **S**		SE	100	10	Fas
Mill Side Scar – **T**					
White Scar – **S**	Restricted	SE	100	5	Fas
White Scar – **T**	Restricted				
Humphrey Head – **S**	Seasonal	W	0	1	Fas
Humphrey Head – **T**	Seasonal				
White Stone	Seasonal	WSW	200	10	Fas
Furness Area					
Hoad Slabs		E	80	3	
Birkrigg Quarry		W	90	0.5	
Dunnerholme – **S**		W	5	10	F
Dunnerholme – **T**					
Dunnerholme – **B**					
Goldmire Quarry	Restricted	W	60	10	Me

	Total Routes 1112	M D VD	MS S HS	MVS VS	HVS E1	E2 E3	E4+
		To 5+	F6a/a+	F6b/b+	F6c/c+	F7a/a+	>F7a+
		<V0(5a)	V0(5a/b)	V1(5c)	V2(5c/6a)	V3(6a)	>V3(6a)
		83	250	237	259	183	100
		(Grades columns are not intended to be mutually comparable)					
	9			1	6	2	
	23	2	3	2	4	9	3
	15	5	2	3	2	3	
	46	1	8	13	16	7	1
	58		2	7	12	13	24
	12			1	2	4	5
	10		2	3	1	3	1
	4		3		1		
70	8		3				4
	12			3	5	5	
24	16	1	1	1	2	4	7
	18			1	10	6	1
25	19	7	6	2	4	9	3
2	4	2		1	1		
10	24	4	10	4	6		
10	3		3			1	2
	4					3	
	14		2	4	4	3	1
30	21		1	4	11	5	

Crags Suitable
for Groups

Head End Quarry (NY 249 408)
Described in the text on page 42.

Scratchmere Scar (NY 516 380)
Described in the text on page 142.

The Hoff (NY 675 180)
Described in the text on page 187. **However access is currently banned.**

Hutton Roof Crags (SD 565 782 and SD 554 781) are short west-facing limestone crags in an idyllic situation on top of Farleton Fell and usually accessed from the nearby village of Hutton Roof. Although in Cumbria, they are described in full in the Lancashire guidebook. They are popular for group instruction, possibly too popular, a fact that is apparent from the horrendous polish on some lines!

White Stone (SD 390 848)
Described in the text on page 351. *Easy Slabs* is much used by groups.

Lindale Slabs (SD 418 817)
Described in the text on page 359. In order to prevent congestion any groups intending to visit the crag are asked to ring Castle Head Field Centre (015395 34300) prior to their visit.

Hoad Slabs (SD 296 790)
Described in the text on page 361.

Above: Chris Gore getting to grips with **Witherslack Alice** (F6c), Chapel Head Scar.
Photo: Nick Wharton

Climbing Walls

There is a good range of climbing walls available to those living in or visiting the Lake District. They are described here for use on those occasional rainy days and dank evenings:

Ambleside: Ambleside Climbing Wall (Adventure Peaks)
Climbing wall and bouldering area available to anyone who wants to try it. Location 101 Lake Road, Ambleside – Open 10:00 to 21:30, seven days a week.
Access check – tel: 015394 33794, www.adventurepeaks.com

Ambleside: University of Cumbria (ex-Charlotte Mason's College)
Low cost revamped wall at the college, with good bouldering but no leading. At the time of publication of this guide the Wall was open only to students at the College.
015394 30274

Barrow in Furness: Park Leisure Centre
Good access and low cost, but very limited lead climbing and a cramped bouldering area. Excellent other facilities. Open all day until 21:45 weekdays, 10:00 to 18:00 weekends.
Access check – tel: 01229 871146, www.barrowbc.gov.uk

Carlisle: The Sands Centre
Reasonable low cost climbing facility in a large sports centre. Good bouldering and leading. Very good access and excellent general facilities. Open 09:30 to 22:30, seven days a week.
Access check – tel: 01228 625222, www.thesandscentre.co.uk

Carlisle: Richard Rose Central Academy
Open for 8 – 21 year olds with club evenings.
Access check – tel: 01228 516280, www.carlisleyouthzone.org

Cockermouth: Leisure Centre
Varied bouldering with natural stonework and Bendcrete. Low cost and good access. Other sports facilities available. Open 08:00 to 22:00 Monday to Friday, 09:00 to 17:00 weekends.
Access check – tel: 01900 823596, www.allerdale.gov.uk

Egremont: Wyndham Sports Centre

A good facility located in the centre of Egremont on the west coast, only half an hour from Wasdale Head. There are practice areas, bouldering, leading walls and a huge roof. Unfortunately no longer open to the public except on a club booking basis.

Access check – tel: 01946 820356.

Ingleton: Inglesport Climbing Barn

Best of the small walls. Very good use of space with leading and bouldering. Regular innovations. Relaxed friendly atmosphere. Cafe and shop nearby. Open 09:00 to 22:00 Monday to Thursday, 09:00 to 17:30 Friday, 08:30 to 18:00 weekends.

Access check – tel: 015242 41146, www.inglesport.co.uk/wall.html

Kendal: The Lakeland Climbing Centre

A magnificent indoor climbing facility with excellent bouldering and leading. Includes a very impressive 23 metre main wall and a huge roof. Located on the Lake District Business Park, across the A6 from Morrison's supermarket. Changing and shower facilities. Open: Winter (September to April) 16:00 to 22:00 Monday, 10:00 to 22:00 Tuesday to Friday, 10:00 to 19:00 weekends and Bank Holidays. Summer (May to August): 10:00 to 22:00 Tuesday to Friday, 10:00 to 17:00 weekends and Bank Holidays.

Access check – tel: 01539 721766, www.kendalwall.co.uk

Keswick: Keswick Climbing Wall and Activity Centre

Located to the east of Keswick at Goosewell Farm. From the A66, approach from "the old road", near Naddle Bridge, following a road towards Castlerigg Stone Circle - the farm is on the right just before this. Bright, airy climbing wall and bouldering wall with a stunning view of Helvellyn out of the main barn doors, you feel you are climbing outdoors no matter what the weather - the Outdoors "Indoors". Open 9:00 – 17:00 Friday to Monday, 9:00 to 21:00 Tuesday to Thursday.

Access check – tel: 017687 72000, www.keswickclimbingwall.co.uk

Penrith: Penrith Leisure Centre – Eden Climbing Wall

An excellent leading wall adjoining the town's swimming pool and leisure centre. Open 9:30 to 21:30 weekdays, 9:30 to 21:00 weekends.

Access check – tel: 01768 863450, www.leisure-centre.com

Where to Stay

This list of Youth Hostels, Campsites and Camping Barns on the eastern side of the Lake District is fairly comprehensive, but there are no doubt more, and fuller details will be available from Tourist Information Offices. This information is current in 2011 but will almost certainly alter and it is probably best to make telephone contact before going to a particular hostel, site or barn.

Youth Hostels

www.yha.org.uk

	Grid Ref	Telephone
Gilsland, Birdoswald	NY 616 664	0870 770 6124
Carlisle, Old Brewery Residences	NY 393 561	0870 770 5752
Dufton	NY 688 251	0870 770 5800
Kendal	NY 514 923	0870 770 5892
Windermere, Troutbeck	NY 405 013	0870 770 6094

Camping Barns

www.lakelandcampingbarns.co.uk

	Grid Ref	Telephone
		01946 758198
Caldbeck, Hudscales	NY 331 375	017687 72645
Kirkby Stephen, Bents Farm	NY 708 065	01946 758 198
Howgills Bunk Barn, Castlehaw Farm, Sedburgh	NY 663 925	015396 21990
Kendal, Wythmoor Farm	SD 588 954	01946 758 198
Broughton-in-Furness, Thornthwaite Farm	SY 242 874	01229 716 340

Campsites

	Grid Ref	Telephone
Caldbeck, Throstle Hall	NY 332 398	016974 68618
Greystoke, Thanet Well	NY 398 350	017684 84262
Berrier, Hopkinson Park	NY 405 288	017684 83456
Penruddock, Beckces	NY 417 277	017684 83224
Brampton, Irthing Vale Caravan Park	NY 522 614	01697 73600
Ainstable, Faugh Head	NY 522 458	016974 72229
Kirkoswald, The Mains	NY 562 398	01768 898342
Lazonby, Lazonby Swimming Pool	NY 552 398	01768 898901
Penrith		
Stone Fold, Newbiggin	NY 475 285	01768 866383
Lowther	NY 526 263	01768 863631

Cliburn, Station House	NY 585 260	01931 714653
Morland, Newby End	NY 599 213	01931 714338
Ousby, Crossfell Caravan Park	NY 619 351	07900 585342
Knock, Silverband Caravan Park	NY 674 275	017683 61218
Dufton, Grandie Caravan Park	NY 688 252	017683 51573
Kirkby Thore, Low Moor	NY 625 260	017683 61231

Appleby

Hawkrigg Farm, Colby	NY 658 205	017683 51046
Appleby, Wild Rose Caravan Park	NY 695 165	017683 51077.
Brough, Augill Caravan Park	NY 810 146	01768 341944

Kirkby Stephen

Takoda	NY 773 095	017683 72587
Pennine View Caravan Park	NY 771 075	01768 371717

Ravenstonedale

Bowber Head Camping Site	NY 742 033	01539 623254
Low Greenside	NY 715 043	01539 625217
Newbiggin On Lune, High Lane Farm	NY 699 058	01539 625416
Raisbeck, New House	NY 642 077	015396 24324

Shap

Bull's Head	NY 564 147	01931 716678
Green Farm	NY 565 144	01931 716235

Sedbergh

Cross Hall Farm, Cautley	SD 689 939	015396 20668
Lincolns Inn Camp Site	SD 631 923	01539 620567
Holme Open Farm	SD 637 908	015396 20654
Garsdale, Yore House Farm	SD 802930	01969 667358
Kendal, Millcrest	SD 526 948	01539 741363
Staveley, Ashes Lane	SD 478 965	01539 821119

Crook

Rather Heath	SD 479 958	01539 821154
Pound Farm	SD 472 953	01539 821220

Windermere

Limefitt Park	NY 414 032	015394 32300
Park Cliffe	SD 388 909	015395 31344
Fell Food Wood	SD 382 873	01539 531014
High Newton,	SD 391 837	015395 31475
Ayside, Oak Head Caravan Park		
Oxen Park, Abbot Park Campsite	SD 313 880	01229 861447

Blawith

Crake Valley Holiday Park	SD 287 897	01229 855203
Birchbank Camping Site	SD 282 875	01229 885277

Above: Richard Tolley takes on the roll of barrow boy for Kirkby Stephen Mountain Rescue team at Murton Crag. **Photo:** Ian Hamilton

Mountain Accidents
by Dr John Ellerton (LDSAMRA)

Procedure for climbers in the Lake District

Mountain rescue in the Lake District is well served by thirteen voluntary teams backed up by special search and cave/mine rescue units. They are equipped to a high standard and work closely with the RAF helicopters and Air Ambulance services. Consequently, only minor casualties should come within the scope of treatment and evacuation by the climber's companions. The rule for all other cases is; to make the casualty safe, to start first aid, and to send for a Mountain Rescue Team.

Sending for Help

A reliable member of the party, with full information about the nature of the injuries and the position of the incident (including, if possible, the map reference) should be sent to find the nearest telephone. He should dial 999, and ask for the Police, who will notify the appropriate team/agency. The sender of the message should stay by the telephone until he receives instructions from the Team Leader. Mobile phones can save a considerable amount of time – please use them to call the Police. Have the mobile phone number handy and keep within reception range (reception is often better on the tops or ridges of the mountains). Do not switch the phone off – the team leader will call back.

Lack of help

You have a difficult decision to make when the casualty is severely injured, possibly unconscious, and you are alone. You should try to summon help from nearby climbers or walkers by shouting, giving the distress call on a whistle (6 blasts repeated regularly), flashing a torch (6 flashes repeated regularly), or sending up a red flare. If there is no response then assess the relative dangers of leaving the casualty, or of failing to get help, and then act decisively in the interest of the casualty.

Emergency precautions and first aid

While waiting for the rescue team, you should check for further danger, and then carry out basic first-aid treatment.

Safety first

Are you and the casualty safe from further danger?

If not, try and make yourselves safe: either by moving, or anchoring yourselves, or both. Is the casualty responsive?

389

Is the casualty's **A**irway open?

If necessary, open it by a simple jaw thrust or lift. If possible, avoid moving the neck after trauma. An open airway is essential if the casualty is unconscious or semi-conscious as reduced consciousness can cause death from asphyxia as the tongue falls back blocking the airway. The position of the casualty, in particular his head and tongue, should be adjusted to open the airway and continually reassessed.

Is the casualty **B**reathing?

Look, feel and listen for breathing. Basic Life Support should be started, if you are trained, when the casualty is unconscious and shows no signs of breathing, and it can be continued until help arrives and where there is a chance of recovery (lightning, drowning, heart attack). It is usually futile in casualties with internal injuries and is probably best to defer in cases of severe exposure/hypothermia until expert help is available. An unconscious and breathing casualty should be put in the Recovery Position if possible. Check the airway is still open.

Is the casualty's **C**irculation adequate?

Stop any bleeding from wounds by elevation and direct pressure with dressings or clothing. The pressure needs to be applied continuously for at least 10 minutes. Raising the legs and/or lowering the head may be appropriate. Internal haemorrhage should be suspected if the casualty has sustained blows to the chest or abdomen or broken the femur (thigh bone). The condition often deteriorates and all steps should be taken to facilitate the rapid arrival of the Mountain Rescue Team and, if possible, a helicopter. A record of the pulse rate and consciousness level is very helpful.

Is the casualty **D**isabled due to damage to head or spine?

Record the casualty's consciousness level – alert, responsive to voice, responsive to pain or unresponsive? Has the spine been damaged? If so, do not move the casualty unless essential for safety reasons. Maintain the head in the normal straight position using your hands.

Check the limbs for fractures

If present, immobilise the limb by the simplest method available. In the case of the arm, pad it and bandage it to the chest, and in the case of the leg, pad it and bandage it to the other leg.

Prevent hypothermia (exposure)

Shelter the casualty from wind and rain. Wrap them in as many layers of clothing as possible and encase them in a 'poly bag' or other impermeable barrier. Do not forget to insulate the head and underneath the casualty.

A **helicopter** may arrive before the mountain rescue team. Extinguish all flames and secure all equipment. The downdraught can knock you over, so get in a safe position. Do not approach the helicopter until clearly signalled to do so by the pilot.

Further points to consider

Large **organised groups** should bear in mind that Mountain Rescue Teams are a finite resource and it is wrong to assume their availability.

The majority of climbers killed in the Lake District as a result of a climbing accident die from a head injury. A **helmet**, whilst not being 100% effective, can make the difference between living and dying.

Whilst **mobile phones** can be very useful in emergencies, any temptation to use them in the hills to call the emergency services in non-emergency circumstances should be resisted. If you are not sure whether it is an emergency or not, please investigate a little yourself first before reaching for your phone.

GPS systems, whilst also useful, are no substitute for carrying a **map** and **compass** and knowing how to use them.

The routine carrying of a suitable **head-torch** would save many needless call-outs.

Lake District Mountain Rescue Teams are made up of unpaid volunteers and rely on charitable contributions. Your consideration and a "Thank you" go a long way to ensure the service continues.

The **Lake District Search and Mountain Rescue Association** (LDSAMRA) acts as an umbrella body for the Lakeland Mountain Rescue Teams. It has a website, which gives contact details for the individual teams, at: http://homepages.enterprise.net/ldsamra

First Ascents

Alternate and varied leads are indicated by (alt) and (var).

North Cumbria & the Eden Valley

Pre-1969	**Headend Quarry** – Long history of usage by groups and individuals. It was first documented in a small guide produced by the BORDER BOTHIES ASSOCIATION.
1969	**Merry Monk** – J WORKMAN, J SIMPSON
1969	**Gadzowt** – A BEATTY, D HODGSON
1970 Dec 19	**Merry Monk Direct** – RJ KENYON, J ALDRIDGE
	Climbed by moving right and then back left. Direct up the corner as now normal, WS LOUNDS, S WILSON, 3rd March 1973.
1970 Dec 27	**Cave Route** – A BEATTY, RJ KENYON (alt.)
1970 Dec 27	**Adam, Eve** – RJ KENYON
1970 Dec 29	**The Crack, Cream Cracker Wall** – RJ KENYON, A BEATTY
1970 Dec 29	**The Mole, Al's Chimney** – A BEATTY
1971 Sep 26	**The Swinger** – A BEATTY, RJ KENYON
1971 Sep 26	**Trundle Wall** – P RIGBY, RJ KENYON (alt.)
1971 Dec 27	**Pseudonym** – A BEATTY
1971	**Cave Corner** – B DIXON
1971	**Silicosis, Pneumoconiosis** – B DIXON, A BEATTY
1972 Jan 2	**One of the World's Many Problems** – A BEATTY, P RIGBY, RJ KENYON, J WORKMAN
1972 Jan 16	**Phred** – B DIXON, RJ KENYON
1972 Jan 16	**Bucket and Spade Job** – RJ KENYON, P RIGBY
1972 Jan 16	**Compost Wall** – RJ KENYON
1972 Jan 22	**Catastrophe Corner** – P RIGBY, RJ KENYON (alt.), A BEATTY
1972 Jan 29	**Insanity Groove** – RJ KENYON, P RIGBY
1972 Feb 5	**Rat Salad** – P RIGBY, RJ KENYON
	Bolted Variation Start, RJ KENYON, 1972
1972 Feb 14	**Sisyphus** – A BEATTY, RJ KENYON, T DALE
1972 Feb 19	**Gumbo Variations** – P RIGBY (unseconded)
1972 Mar 4	**Virtually Part One** – P RIGBY, T DALE, RJ KENYON
1972 Mar 10	**Teragram** – RJ KENYON, P RIGBY, T DALE
1972 Mar 10	**Neanderthal Man** – RJ KENYON, P RIGBY (alt.)
1972 Mar 27	**Jamboree** – RJ KENYON, T DALE
1972 Mar 27	**Moonlight Sonata** – RJ KENYON, T DALE
	Climbed by moonlight!

Above left: Stew Wilson, instrumental in opening up and documenting climbing in the Eden Valley. **Photo:** Ron Kenyon **Above right:** Phil Rigby on first ascent of **Rat Salad** (HVS), in 1972 at Lazonby. **Photo:** Ron Kenyon

1972 Apr 30	**Mij** – RJ Kenyon, J Kilduff
1972 Apr 30	**Barney** – RJ Kenyon, J Kilduff
	Climbed via the left-hand finish. The right-hand finish was added by RJ Kenyon, T Dale and S Laws, 26th December 1972.
1972 Dec 30	**J.J.** – B Miller, RJ Kenyon
1972	**Dirty Old Pillar** – S Wilson, P Hope
1972	**Hernia** – T Dale, A Beatty, P Rigby
1972	**Cobweb** – P Rigby, T Dale
	With aid. Climbed free by T Proctor, A Beatty and B Dixon, 10th August 1974. An impressive ascent, recorded as a photoclimb in *Rocksport* magazine.
1973 May 5	**A Big Hand** – S Wilson, A Yarrow
	The first route on the crag and climbed in front of an appreciative audience.
1973 May 5	**Kingfisher** – S Wilson, A Yarrow
1973 May 12	**Glenwillie Grooves** – S Wilson, A Yarrow (alt)
1973 May 12	**Glenwillie Grooves Direct** – S Wilson, A Yarrow
1973 May 12	**The Bullgine Run** – S Wilson, A Yarrow (alt)
1973 May 12	**Wildcat on the Swallowtail Line** – A Yarrow, S Wilson
	The Crack Finish only. It is not recorded when the full route was done.
1973 May 12	**Ituna** – S Wilson, A Yarrow (alt)
	The ancient name for the River Eden.
1973 May 17	**Flasherman** – A Yarrow, S Wilson (alt)
	Named due to one of the team finding himself in a situation of extreme exposure. The *Direct Finish* was added by P Whillance, 13th March 1975.

Above: Phil Rigby above the River Eden at Lazonby. **Photo:** Tim Dale

Above: Ron Kenyon at Lazonby Crag. His explorations of Eden Valley crags have spanned forty years. **Photo:** Phil Rigby

1973 May 12 **Time And Motion Man** – RJ KENYON, T DALE, S WILSON
    "It was steep, so you had to keep going, hence the name, Time and Motion Man."
    RON KENYON, 'Rock Climbs in the North of England', *FRCC Journal 1981*

1973 May 12 **Nosescratcher** – RJ KENYON, T DALE

1973 May 12 **Joe Soap's Corner** – A YARROW, S WILSON

1973 May 30 **Herbie** – RJ KENYON

1973 Summer **Princess Anne's New Ring** – A YARROW, S WILSON (alt)
    Climbed the day Princess Anne became engaged to Mark Phillips.
    The *Hooked Up* variations were added by D BUSH, 15th July 2010.
    The lower one had definitely been done before.

1973 Summer **Zephyr** – A YARROW, R WHITSOME

1973 Summer **Codpiece** – A YARROW, S WILSON, R MAY (var)
    Two pegs used for aid - first free ascent, J LAMB, 1974.

1973 Summer **Codpiece Left-Hand** – A YARROW, S WILSON

1973 Summer **Barnacle Bill** – RJ KENYON, S WILSON
    Two pegs used for aid - first free ascent, J LAMB, 1974.

1973 Summer **The Monkey Hanger** – S WILSON, A YARROW (alt)

1973 Summer **Stinkhorn** – S WILSON, A YARROW

1973 Sep 30 **FBSJ** – S WILSON, RJ KENYON

1973 Oct 13 **Mandrax** – RJ KENYON, S WILSON

1973 Dec 8 **Douber** – RJ KENYON, T DALE

1973 Dec 9 **The Schnuck** – RJ KENYON, S WILSON, T DALE
    Interest was added when the dead tree used as the only runner,
    slid down the rope towards the terrified belayers huddled on the

Above: Tim Dale in action at Lazonby.
Photo: Phil Rigby

Above: Alan Beatty getting to grips with **Cally Crack** (E2), Armathwaite. **Photo:** Phil Rigby

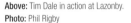

middle ledge. Luckily nobody was hurt.

1973 Dec 22	**Look to the Future; It's Only Just Begun** – RJ KENYON, A MILLER
1973	**Cally Crack** – J LAMB

Named after the Caledonian pub in Carlisle, a climbers' venue.
"The scene of a nasty fall when Mike Hetherington hit the deck 50 feet below – he escaped major injury because his parachute training gave him the ability to land properly." RON KENYON, 'Rock Climbs in the North of England', *FRCC Journal 1981*

1973	**TD Corner** – T DALE
Early 1970s	**Marik** – J SIMPSON, D HODGSON, J WORKMAN

Some aid used - climbed free by RJ KENYON, 1974.

1974 Jan 13	**Inside A Cosmic Orgasm** – P RIGBY, S WILSON
1974 Jan 19	**Mr Woo**, **The Gripe** – RJ KENYON, M SHELDON
1974 Feb 13	**Tigerfeet** – P BOTTERILL, J LAMB
1974 Spring	**Gone** – A YARROW, S WILSON
1974 Jan 12	**Erection** – J LAMB, A LIDDELL
1974 Feb 16	**Blockbuster** – RJ KENYON, AN OTHER
1974 Feb	**Dome Slab** – J LAMB, P BOTTERILL

A photograph of this superb first ascent in *Mountain* gave Armathwaite some national publicity. PETE WHILLANCE made an early second ascent but, whilst top-roping the route, pulled off the spike on the lip which provided the best runner!

1974 Feb	**Cluedo** – S WILSON, S BUTLER
1974 Feb	**Coombs Crack**, **Red Lion** – S WILSON

Top: Jeff Lamb on the first ascent of **Dome Slab** (E6), Armathwaite. **Photo:** Bob Allen *(From **Mountain** No. 41 Jan. 1975)* **Above left:** Carlisle climber Mike Hetherington, whose nocturnal torchlight bouldering sessions at Armathwaite resulted in the naming of Hetherington's Bay. **Photo:** Mark Hetherington **Above right:** Tim Dale, leading and Stew Wilson on an early repeat of **Red Monkey** (E1), Armwathwaite. **Photo:** Ron Kenyon

1974 Feb	**Red Monkey** – M HETHERINGTON	
1974 Feb	**Red Spider** – S MILLER	
1974 Feb	**The Crescent** – J LAMB, M HETHERINGTON	
1974 Feb	**Jelly Terror** – J LAMB, M HETHERINGTON	
	Named after the state of the second on watching the first ascent!	

Above left: Armathwaite pioneer Stew Wilson top-roping **Paper Moon** (E3), Armathwaite. **Photo:** Ron Kenyon **Above middle:** Carlisle's John Moore on an early ascent of **Free 'n' Easy** (E5), Armathwaite – the flares give the date away! **Photo:** Phil Rigby **Above right:** Alan Greig who partnered Pete Whillance on two major additions to Armathwaite. **Photo:** Phil Rigby

1974 Feb	**Solitaire** – A HUNTER (solo)	
1974 Feb	**Paper Moon** – J LAMB	

"The local teams were most astonished one evening when Karl Telfer, a visiting climber from Northumberland, soloed this route on sight." RON KENYON, 'Rock Climbs in the North of England', *FRCC Journal 1981*

1974 Mar 25 **Y-Front** – P BOTTERILL, M HETHERINGTON
A bold on sight first ascent.

1974 May 8 **Free 'n' Easy** – P WHILLANCE, A GREIG
On the Thursday the first ascentionists had to use a point of aid and were seen doing so by MIKE HETHERINGTON, thus they just had to return on the Saturday to do it cleanly so the route was now free but not easy!

1974 Sep 17 **Pickpocket** – P WHILLANCE (solo)

1974 Sep 17 **Wafer Thin** – P WHILLANCE, A GREIG
With side runners in Paper Moon, but still an audacious lead!
Direct Finish added by P WHILLANCE, 18th March 1975.

1974 **The Exorcist** – J LAMB
One of the big ones! Originally called Joiner's Arms which was both the name of a pub in Carlisle and apt as JEFF LAMB was a joiner by profession and had huge arms as a result. A protection peg was placed on the first ascent but LAMB subsequently climbed the route without, as did RON FAWCETT. The peg remains in situ and has performed sterling service!

"But perhaps the most outstanding discovery was found on Armathwaite's Main

Above: Ron Fawcett climbing **The Exorcist** (E4), Armathwaite on a visit to the area in the late 1970s. **Photo:** Ron Kenyon

Above: Ron Kenyon high stepping on **Andy's Slab** (E4), Armathwaite before 'sticky boots'. **Photo:** Ron Kenyon Collection

Buttress. Here Lamb led the fierce overhanging groove in the Central Wall to give The Exorcist (XS), a very difficult climb which no one present could follow (shades of Brown and the Rock and Ice)." Mountain (41, Jan 1975)

1974	**Andy's Slab** – A Hunter
	A great achievement and a route which has seen few convincing ascents hence its other name, **Once In A Blue Moon**.
1974	**Phall** – P Rigby
1974	**The Flake** – S Miller
1974	**The Gebbeth** – A Beatty
1974	**Nightride, Bay Rum, Ged, Trundle Crack, Leaning Crack** – RJ Kenyon
1974	**Steph** – A Hewison, RJ Kenyon
1974	**Rune Wall** – RJ Kenyon, A Hewison
1974	**Kirsten Wall** – A Stark
1975 Jan 18	**Harry's Groove** – RJ Kenyon, J Morton
1975 Feb 2	**Victory V** – J Lamb, M Hetherington, P Botterill, H Loughran
1975 Mar 26	**New Moon** – J Lamb
	This straightened out the original route (P Whillance, 10th September 1974) which came in from the left.
1975 Apr 22	**Cook's Crack** – RJ Kenyon
1975 Apr 22	**Cook's Left Hand, Boomerang, Aborigine** – A Beatty
1975 May 20	**The High Girdle**, Armathwaite – P Whillance
	This bold excursion was also soloed by Whillance, 1st July 1975.

Above: Dave 'Dids' Bowen and Phil Rigby on the immaculate wall of **Fingers** (HVS), Lazonby.
Photo: Ron Kenyon

1975 Jun 19	**Tove Wall** – R PARKER
1975 Jul 26	**Fingers** – P RIGBY
	Pitch 2 only. Pitch 1 was top-roped. K NEAL led pitch 1 in 1979 or 1980.
1975 Nov	**Murton Moggy, Bitter Fingers, Catlike Tread, Deadend**
	Groove – RJ KENYON and members of the EDEN VALLEY MC
1975 Nov	**Keach** – A STARK
1975	**The Scroll** – S MILLER
	This route has been omitted from the guide in order to preserve the fine inscription, a misquote from Izaak Walton's *The Compleat Angler.*
1975	**Grey Duster, Blue Lugs, Jeff's Wall** – J LAMB
1975	**Trilogy** – J LAMB
	With a runner in the tree. Climbed without the tree runner, K LUNT, A WILLIAMSON, 1989.
1975	**Tramlines** – UNKNOWN
1975	**Pickpocket Superdirect** – P BOTTERILL

Above: Jeff Lamb repeating **Titus Groan** (E1), Kings Meaburn, immediately after Phil Rigby had made the first ascent in the mid 1970s. **Photo:** Phil Rigby

Above: Ron Fawcett climbing **The Red Chipper** (E3), Lazonby, on a visit to the area in the late 1970s. **Photo:** Ron Kenyon

1975	**Maid Marian's Way** – P WHILLANCE
1975	**Liang Shan Po** – RJ KENYON, A STARK
1975	**Talking to Trees** – P BOTTERILL
Mid 1970s	**Red Chipper** – J LAMB

A hold had been chipped by persons unknown at the start of the route. It was subsequently hammered smooth and unuseable prior to a clean lead by JEFF LAMB.

Mid 1970s	**Titus Groan** – P RIGBY, A BEATTY
1976 Apr 24	**Meal Ticket, Brown Dirt Cowboy, Felix** – RJ KENYON, MISS S DIXON, R PARKER
1976 Apr 24	**Sunshine Super Sal** – RJ KENYON, MISS S DIXON, R PARKER

Two nuts used for aid - first free ascent, R CURLEY, Summer 1985.

1977	**Blast Off** – P RIGBY, D BOWEN
1977	**The Orbit** – P RIGBY
1978 Jan 15	**Swing Off** – R FAWCETT

Originally top-roped by P RIGBY, 26th September 1971.

1978	**Ace of Wands** – P RIGBY, R KENYON (var), D BOWEN
1978	**Variations on a Swinger** – P RIGBY, D BOWEN

Used a resting point on a nut. First free ascent by K LUNT, A WILLIAMSON, 8th April 1989.

King of the Swingers added by I MAKIN, K LUNT, 30th May 1987.

1978	**Harry's Arête** – RJ KENYON, MISS S THOMPSON

Right: 'Dids' Dave Bowen top roping **Sailing Shoes** (NL), Armathwaite. **Photo:** Ron Kenyon

Above: Dave Armstrong on the **Hetherington Bay** traverse which was used to train steely fingers.
Photo: Dave Armstrong Collection

1979	**Nurts Way** – RJ KENYON
1970s	**Close Encounters**
	A link of two problems, D ARMSTRONG's finger traverse from the right and a traverse from the left to the jug, continued upwards. The *Direct Start* was first climbed by P BOTTERILL or A GREIG.
1970s	**Windmore End** – P DAY and others from Kirkby Stephen did many early ascents. There was also extensive exploration by climbers from Cleveland inspired by KELVIN NEAL who produced a comprehensive guide to the crag, forming the basis for subsequent guidebooks.
1970s	**The Hoff** – Most of the routes were climbed by RJ KENYON, T DALE, P RIGBY, D BOWEN, S WILSON
1970s	**Stormy Petteril, Greta's Climb, John's Climb, Blondie, Out of the Dark** – RJ KENYON, T DALE, S WILSON
	This team were the first to climb at Scratchmere Scar and were responsible for most of the original climbs.
1970s	**The Renwick Bat, Cryptic Crack, The Fenny Thing, The Croglin Vampire, Tabby, Grey Yaud, The Cauldron, Cauldron Wall, Stoney Butts, Black Magic, White Magic, Black Cat** – S WILSON, T DALE, RJ KENYON
1970s	**Starsky, Hutch** – A HEWISON
1970s	**Faulds, Lynedraw, Dunbeath, Aughertree, Snittlegarth, Rash Raiser, Whelpo Way, Thistlebottom, Biggards** – RJ KENYON During preparation of the 1981 North of England Guide.
Late 1970s	**Spadeadam Crag** – Discovered and developed by P HOPE, S WILSON and friends who climbed most of the early routes.
1970s & 1980s	**Cowraik Quarry** – Local climbers were responsible for many

Above: Eden Valley Mountaineering Club members c1972, from left, Dave Powell, Phil Rigby and Al Beatty bouldering at Windmore End. **Photo:** Ron Kenyon

of the early climbs.

1980	**Petit Mal, The Thirty Nine Steps** – S Wilson	
1981	**Titus Alone** – JP de Rohan	
	Soloed in wellies! Originally a top-rope route.	
1981	**Herne** – P Botterill	
	Originally called **Smear** but not recorded at the time – the name Herne was bestowed by the second ascentionists.	
1982	**The Navvy, On The Footplate, Colonel Biffo** – RJ Kenyon, S Wilson	

1983 *Summer* **Murton Scar**: a concentrated effort was made by a strong team from Appleby consisting of Robin Curley, Chris Thwaites and Noel Stanfield produced the following impressive tally of routes. There must be something in the local water as a few years later Leo Houlding also attended Appleby Grammar School!

Sunshine Super Sal (first free ascent), **Morgan's Lane, The Haunted Smear** – R Curley

Mind Over Matter, All Along The Watchtower – C Thwaites

Bigus Dickus – N Stansfield

Incontinentia Buttocks – R Curley, N Stansfield

Red Hot Spankers, Earl Street, Earl Street Direct and **Body Rock** – R Curley, An Other

1983   **Peanuts** – R Curley

There has been some confusion about who did the first ascent, however, it would appear likely that Robin Curley bagged this fine and difficult line.

Into the Light was added by K Lunt in 1985.

Above: Karl Lunt on the first ascent of **Perilous Journey** (pitch 2) (E3), Lazonby in 1986.
Photo: Chris Crowder

1984	**Brough Scar** – Although mentioned in the 1980 guide, no developments were forthcoming until 1984 when a small band of very young, very keen lads, inspired by **Robin Curley**, paid a visit to the crag and developed it over the next twelve months.
1985 Jun 2	**Phantom** – K Lunt, N Frowe
1985 Aug 22	**Kojak, The Wand, Creepshow, Toil and Trouble** K Lunt (solo)
1985 Sep 5	**White Spirits** – K Lunt (solo) Clipping gear with a cow's tail.
1985 Oct 12	**Grey Malkin** – K Lunt, M Tomlinson, AN Other
1985	**Blanks' Expression** – L Blanks
1986 Mar 15	**Fear Is The Key**, **Mystery Achievement** – K Lunt, C Crowder
1986 Apr 11	**Lip Service** – C Crowder, K Lunt
1986 Apr 11	**Electric Avenue**, **Savage Rib** – K Lunt, C Crowder
1986 Apr 12	**Suspended Animation** – C Crowder, K Lunt (alt.)
1986 Apr 12	**Sahara Crossing** – C Crowder, K Lunt An early attempt on The Fearful Void.
1986 Apr 14	**Technical Ecstasy** – K Lunt (unseconded) Second attempt following a near groundfall from the final moves.
1986 May 27	**Perilous Journey** – C Crowder, K Lunt (alt.)
1986 Aug	**Kaleidoscope Eyes** – M Tomlinson
1986 Aug	**Smiling Faces** – M Holden, D Holden, M Tomlinson
1986 Sep 7	**Scorpion** – K Lunt, N Frowe, M Carter
1986	**Moondance** – S Wilson, Mrs M Wilson, A Williamson
1986	**The Green Knight** – S Wilson, Mrs M Wilson
1986	**Gwalchmai** – S Wilson, J Wilson, T Suddaby
1986	**John's and Frog's Route** – J Wilson, J Hughes

Above: Karl Lunt on the first ascent of **Like An Arrow** (E2), Hebblethwaite Hall Gill in 1987. **Photo:** Geoff Dawson

Above: Karl Lunt on the first ascent of **Venom** (E3), Spadeadam Crag in 1988. **Photo:** Andy Williamson

1986	**Cook's Apron** – D HETHERINGTON, S WILSON
1987 Feb 7	**Crescent Arête** – R PARKER
1987 May 3	**Snowball, Far Above the Splat Mat, Cellnet, Red Square Dare** – G DAWSON, K LUNT
1987 May 3	**Herbal Abuse, The Neighbourhood Bully, The Right Stuff, The Cockpit** – K LUNT, G DAWSON
1987 May 30	**I Can't Breakdance!** – K LUNT, I MAKIN
1987 Jun	**Windkey** – P CARLING, J WILSON, S WILSON
1987 Aug 2	**Stained Class** – K LUNT, S WILLIAMSON
1987 Sep 6	**Andy's Arête, A Week Before The Beast, Rain Stopped Play, Most Sincerely, Moss Trooper, Steppin' Out, Room 101, Pump It Up** – K LUNT, A KAY
1987 Sep 13	**Shark's Fin Soup** – A KAY, K LUNT
1987 Sep 16	**Gothic Horror** – A KAY, K LUNT
1987 Sep 16	**Nemesis Towers** – K LUNT, A KAY
1987 Sep	**Viennese Oyster** – G BROWN, H LOUGHRAN
1987 Oct 1	**The Fearful Void** – K LUNT, A KAY
	An apt name, taken from the title of the book by Geoffrey Moorhouse about his attempt to traverse the Sahara; as much an examination of inner feelings as a journey!
1987 Oct 1	**Eye in the Sky** – K LUNT, A KAY
1987	**One Hand Clapping** – G BROWN (solo)
1988 Apr 1	**Back and Biting** – K LUNT, J STRINGFELLOW
1988 Apr 6	**Snakelet, Snake Charmer** – K LUNT (solo)

Above: Bill Lounds making an early solo of **The Horror** (E3) at Lazonby. **Photo:** Phil Rigby

1988 Apr 6	**Venom, Hissing Sid Vicious, Black Adder, Backstreet Crawler** – K LUNT, A WILLIAMSON
1988 Apr 9	**Hesitation, Jam Today** – K LUNT (solo)
1988 May 12	**Demolition Dancing** – K LUNT, MISS S OLIVER
1988 Aug 12	**Afterlife** – K LUNT (solo)
1988 Sept 11	**Machoman** – K LUNT, N IBBERSON
	Originally climbed on nuts and one peg for aid and called **Microman** by T DALE, P RIGBY (var), 13th December 1972.
1988 Sep 11	**Footfall** – K LUNT, N IBBERSON
1988 Oct 29	**Rattle And Hum, Red Barchetta, The Toe, Sunflower** – K LUNT (solo)
1988 Oct 29	**No Comebacks, Get Close, Home Sweet Home, Don't Worry, Be Happy** – K LUNT (solo)
1988 Nov 26	**Double Jeopardy, The Flange** – K LUNT
1988 Nov	**Headmaster Ritual** – K LUNT
1988 Dec 31	**Neptune** – S GRIEVE (unseconded)
1988	**The Small Assassin** – K LUNT
1989 Apr 4	**Pavane** – K LUNT, M TOMLINSON
1989 Apr 8	**The Horror** – K LUNT, A WILLIAMSON
	Originally top-roped by WS LOUNDS, T DALE, S WILSON, P RIGBY, 3rd March 1973.

Right: Karl Lunt making the first ascent of **The Professionals** (E2), Helbeck Wood Crag in 1989. **Photo:** Tom Phillips

Armathwaite – the "Not Led" Routes

Early explorations at Armathwaite involved ground up ascents with no pre-inspection – adventurous stuff considering the soft friable nature of the rock. However, with its adoption as a training ground for some of the county's best climbers, it became acceptable to inspect harder routes by abseil and top-rope practice them prior to a clean lead. Due to their seriousness, some of these climbs were in fact never led and were recorded in the 1992 guide as "Not Led". A few such climbs have since been led and their details are in the first ascents list above and below; the routes listed immediately below are the remainder. Needless to say this is a list of challenges for the future and a lead of any of them would be a fine achievement.

The "Not Leds" span a fifteen year period from the mid '70s to ca 1990 and were confined to Armathwaite and Scratchmere Scar – the FRCC feel they should stay that way and that future claimants should restrict themselves to routes that they have actually led!

1974	**Rise and Shine** – P BOTTERILL or J LAMB
	The lower arête only was led by R PARKER, 7th Febuary 1987 and claimed as **Swing Out Sister**. It was soloed shortly afterwards by P CARLING.
1975	**Sailing Shoes** – A HEWISON
1975	**Erection Arête** – J LAMB
1970s	**Limpet Lil** – P BOTTERILL
1977	**Moving Pictures** – S WILSON, D BOWEN
1986 Aug	**Astral Wall** – M TOMLINSON, M HOLDEN
1986	**The Field of Dreams** – S WILSON, J WILSON, T SUDDABY
1986	**Cook's Tour** – D HETHERINGTON, S WILSON
1987 Jan 31	**Smear Or Die** – A GREIG, R PARKER
1987 Feb 1	**The Black Russian** – R PARKER, A GREIG
1987 Sep	**Indian's Revenge** – G BROWN
1987	**Devil Moon** – A GREIG, R PARKER
1987	**Plain Sailing** – A GREIG
1989 Sep	**Mr Bundy's Best Friend** – G BROWN

Not Leds where further details are not known:

Variation Finish to Andy's Slab

Bad Moon Rising

Overdose (Scratchmere Scar)

Left: Karl Lunt on the first ascent of **Rocket to Russia** (E1), Helbeck Wood Crag, in 1989.
Photo: Tom Phillips

1989 May	**The Ring of Confidence** – K Lunt, T Phillips
1989 Jul 5	**Why Flymo When You Can Napalm?** – S Grieve (unseconded)
1989 Sep 10	**Rabbit on the Windscreen, The Hollow Karst, Deterrent, Superpower** – Tom Phillips, Karl Lunt
1989 Sep 10	**Crossfire, Silkworm, Stealth, The Professionals, Fight or Flight** – Karl Lunt, Tom Phillips
1989 Sep 10	**Judgemental Jibe** – Tom Phillips (solo)
1989 Sep 10	**Privates on Parade** – Karl Lunt (solo)
1989 Sep 23	**Sergeant Rock, Fylingdale Flyer, Judge for Yourself, Trench Warfare** – Tom Phillips, Karl Lunt
1989 Sep 23	**Shoot to Kill, Lethal Weapon, Rocket to Russia** – Karl Lunt, Tom Phillips
1989	**Windmore End, Far Right Area** – K Lunt and T Phillips with L Fallen in some ascents
	Extensive exploration resulted in **Viva Garibaldi!, Rock And A Hard Place** and free ascent of **Rebel Without a Pause** amongst others.
1980s	**Bouldering to right of Scratchmere Scar** – S Wilson
1980s	**Gont** – S Wilson and C King – independently and at about the same time.
1980s	**The Black Streak, Scratch** – P Botterill
1980s	**Tamalin, Bechers Brook, Rubstic, Rubstic Direct, Alverton** – RJ Kenyon
1980s	**Sue's Route** – Miss S Thompson, RJ Kenyon
1980s	**Angel in the Centrefold** – S Wilson, S Ferguson
1980s	**The Helm** – N Conway
	Previously top roped.
Late 1980s	**The Windeye** – P Carling, S Wilson
1990 Mar	**Strangeways, Chill Factor** – K Lunt
1992 Jun 14	**Time Being, Soft Target** – G Dawson, K Lunt
1992 Jun 14	**Grand Designs** – K Lunt, G Dawson
1992 Oct 10	**Rottweiler, Winalot, Distemper** – K Lunt
1993 May	**Phallacy, Phall Direct** – A Margerson, I Lowis
1993 May	**Just for Shirl** – A Margerson
Early 1990s	**Leo's Line** – Leo Houlding
Early 1990s	**Young at Heart, Creepers Keepers, Rattle Up, Angerton, Warnell Way** – P Ross, C Bonington, P Greenwood and friends
1994 or after	**Mistral** – L Garnett (solo)
	The solo ascent moved right at top. Previously top-roped and named by K Lunt, 13th July 1994.

Right: Karl Lunt on the first ascent of **Viva Garibaldi!** (E2), Windmore End, in 1989.
Photo: Tom Phillips

Above: Mark Hetherington making an early top-rope ascent of **Beyond The Thunder Dome** (E5), Armathwaite. **Photo:** Mark Hetherington Collection

1995 Jun 11   **Mellow** – C King, T Mawer
     Top-roped and named by P Williams in the 1970s.

1995   **66 The Highway Speaks** – A Dougherty

1996 Mar 10   **Blinkered Vision** – RJ Kenyon, A Heron

1996 Jun 13   **Trouble Without a Cause** – S Crowe (solo)
     Right Trouble Without a Cause variation added in 2005
     by J Greave.

1996   **Apple Sponge** – P Soulsby, D Weatherly

1996   **Apple Crumble, Apple Pie** – D Weatherly, P Soulsby

1997 Mar 7   **Diamond Lil** – C King, A Hewison
     Top-roped and named by S Wilson, 1974.

1997 Mar 7   **Soft Touch** – C King, A Hewison
     Top-roped and named by A Greig, 1987.

1997 Apr 29   **Beyond The Thunder Dome** – C King, RJ Kenyon, P King
     Top-roped and named by R Parker, A Greig, 1987.

1997 May 27   **The Famous Grouse, Schrodinger's Cat** – K Lunt,
     Miss A Sharman

1997 Oct 26   **Celadon** – K Lunt (unseconded)

1997 Oct 26   **Ten Years After** – K Lunt, M King

1998 May 16   **Meat is Murder** – C King, T Butler
     Top-roped and named by M Holden, D Holden, M Tomlinson,
     1986. The final of a series of outstanding leads at Armathwaite from
     Chris King, all after top-rope practice. Needless to say they are
     serious undertakings but maintain the challenge of the crag -
     no need for bolts here, all that's required is talent and a long neck!

1998 May 16   **Duckling Drop** – C King, T Butler

1998   **Lastra Wall** – A Dougherty (solo)

Above: Rising star: Leo Houlding, aged 11, with his father, Mark, at his home crag **The Hoff**.
He would go on to make major additions to King's Meaburn, as well as a few elsewhere.
Photo: Phil Rigby

1999 Aug 8	**Bonington's Sardine Solution, Sound as a Trout** – B Devenish, P Cotton	
1999 Aug 8	**Young Turbots Go For It, Turbot Don't Dyno** – P Cotton, B Devenish	
1999 Sep 3	**Zephyr, Chinook** – K Lunt	
1999 Sep 4	**Samoon, Scirocco** – K Lunt	
1990s	**Barry's Arête** – B Lindsley, K Avery	
1990s	**The Wind Cries Mary, Blowin' in the Wind, Heanz, Imbalanced Pressure, Pressure Crack, Aelion, Fern Wall** – A Dougherty	
1990s	**Main Wall Traverse** – S Wilson, AN Other	
2000 Aug 28	**Scrogbank Ravers** – L Houlding	
2000 Aug 28	**Can You Feel It?** – R Curley, L Houlding	
	Appleby's finest team up before the Scrogbank Rave.	
2000	**Good Dog Glen** – S Wilson, M Wilson	

Above: Chris King who in the latter half of the 1990s made the first leads of five Armathwaite top-rope test pieces, **Mellow, Diamond Lil, Soft Touch, Beyond The Thunder Dome** and **Meat is Murder**.
Photo: Stephen Reid

2002 Oct 5	**Raindance** – C King, RJ Kenyon	
2003 Oct 19	**Borderliner** – C King, M Kenyon, RJ Kenyon	
2003	**Fresh Breeze** – A Dougherty, C Dougherty, P Johnson	
2003	**Mungo is Angry**, **Mungo Direct**, **Pot Black**, **Neanderthal Crack**, **Neneh Cherry**, **Black Cherry** – J Kettle	
2003	**Teenage Kicks** – P Simpson	
2004 Apr 22	**Titus Again** – C King, S Prior, S Brown	
2004 May	**Hurricane Force Direct** – A Dougherty	
2004 Oct 4	**Fossil Arête** – G Uney	
2004 Nov 9	**Savage Simian** – A Little, T Cornish	
2004 Dec 4	**Janet of the Apes** – A Little, T Cornish	
2004	**Coral Arête**, **Continuous Crack**, **Blank Wall**, **Corner and Wall**, **Phreatic Crack**, **Phreatic Twin**, **Fingers Wall** – A Dougherty, C Dougherty	
2005 May	**Murenger** – J Clarke, J Holden	
2005 Jul 27	**Cassandra** – RJ Kenyon, M Willett, B Lloyd	
2005 Aug 9	**The Buzz** – RJ Kenyon, M Kenyon	
2005 Aug 9	**Verteris Outlook** – RJ Kenyon, M Kenyon, Miss C Kenyon	
2005 Aug 9	**Mike's Overlap**, **Mike's Arête** – M Kenyon	
2005 Aug 15	**Shining Through** – BJ Clarke, B Ledson	
2005 Aug 16	**The Baggins Effect** – RJ Kenyon, M Kenyon, B Lloyd, Miss C Kenyon	
2005 Aug 16	**Well Head**, **Harebells**, **Wild Thyme** – RJ Kenyon	
2005 Sep 23	**First of Many** – N Atkinson, G Uney	
2005 Dec 8	**Wilkes's Wander** – D Upton, Wendy Graham, C Peckham	
2006 Jan 4	**Sidewinder** – C King, SJH Reid	
2006 Jan 4	**Indian Rope Trick** – SJH Reid, C King	
2006 Apr 12	**Rose Amongst Thorns** – BJ Clarke (solo)	
2006 Apr 21	**Thorn Corner** – BJ Clarke (solo)	
2006 Apr 23	**Egmont** – S Broatch, BJ Clarke, J Simpson	
2006 May 24	**Cool Runnings** – M Kenyon	
2006 Jun 2	**The Greave Speaks** – J Greave	
2006 Jun 2	**Cool Man** – M Kenyon	
2006 Jun 10	**Aisgill Experience** – C King, RJ Kenyon	
2006 Jun 17	**Worker for the Wind**, **Underneath the Arches**, **Beside the Arches**, **Endless Storm**, **Force 7 Coming in Strong** – A Dougherty	
2006 Jun 23	**Limekiln Recess routes** – A Dougherty	
2006 Jun	**The Wall Beyond routes** – A Dougherty	
2006 Sep 23	**Steppin' Up**, **Flying Rabbits**, **Spider's Dinner** – M Kenyon	
2006 Oct 15	**The Grit Beyond routes** – A Dougherty, K Flint	
2006 Oct 29	**Legion Slab** – RJ Kenyon	
2006 Oct 29	**Nightshift**, **Nightlight** – J Greave, RJ Kenyon	
2006	**Fistful of Garnetts** – L Garnett	
2006	**Right on 66** – J Greave	
2006	**Lost on 66** – J Greave (solo)	

2007 Mar 17	**The Aspirant** – J Kettle	
2007 Apr 14	**The Lollypop** – RJ Kenyon	
2007 Jul 31	**Mighty Midget** – RJ Kenyon, M Kenyon	
2007 Jul 31	**Layaway Kenny** – M Kenyon	
2007 Oct 15	**Striation Crack** – BJ Clarke	
2007	**The Unseen Message** – RJ Kenyon, M Kenyon	
2007	**Seat of Power** – M Kenyon	
2007	**Paddigill** – RJ Kenyon, M Kenyon, C Kenyon	
2008 Mar 1	**Puss in Boots** – BJ Clarke, Tanya Coates	
2008 Apr 13	**Manic of a Different Breed** – RJ Kenyon, Miss C Kenyon	
2008 May 3	**Life's Problems** – M Kenyon	
2008 May 3	**High Squeeze** – P Ridgwell, J Harling	
2008 May 26	**Shady Hollow** – BJ Clarke	
2008 May	**Just for Kicks** – M Kenyon, Miss C Kenyon, RJ Kenyon	
2008 May	**What Care the Wind, Months of Rage** – M Kenyon (solo)	
2009 Mar 29	**Catwalk** – R Kenyon, Miss C Kenyon	
2009 May 25	**Julian Bream** – P Cotton (unseconded)	
2009 May 25	**A Surfeit of Lampreys** – Melanie Cotton, P Cotton	
2009 Jun 7	**Fox and Pheasant** – R Kenyon, I Scobie, J Smith	
2009 Jun 27	**Resisting Chiptation** – D Robinson, M Kenyon	
2009 Jun 27	**The Sands of Time** – R Kenyon, D Robinson, E Parker, M Kenyon	
2009 Jun 27	**Two Pints and a Packet of Crisps** – E Parker, M Kenyon, R Kenyon, D Robinson	
2009 Oct 11	**Buffalo Bill** – J Farnworth, E Parker, RJ Kenyon	
2009 Oct 29	**Big in Japan** – J Hughes, Miss Tracy Dixon	
2010 Mar 2	**Perfect Weather to Fly** – D Bush	
2010 Mar 14	**Itchmere Nose** – C Ford	
2010 Apr 10	**Headbutt the Bed** – D Bush, L Bush	
2010 Apr 14	**Megamoose** – D Pattinson	
2010 Apr 20	**Midget Gem** – D Bush (solo)	
2010 May 9	**Sequence Dance** – M Magus	
2010 Jun 5	**Swing Right, Hayturner** – RJ Kenyon	
2010 Jun 8	**Two Step, Upmanhowe** – M Kenyon	
2010 Jun 8	**Swing Left, Swinging Gate, Tewfitt's Struggle, Spurrigg Pillar, Todd's** – RJ Kenyon	
2010 Jul 3	**Helm Arête** – M Kenyon	
2010 Jul 3	**El Presidento Robbo** – JH Robinson, RJ Kenyon	
2010 Jul 3	**The Wider Sea** – A Davis, Miss MG Brown, RJ Kenyon	
2010 Jul 5	**New Fair Invasion, Here's to the Coalition, Bongate Bogey, Hooray for Harold** – A Davis, E Parker	
2010 Jul 7	**Helm Bar** – RJ Kenyon, E Parker	
2011 May 10	**La'al Wall** – G North	
2011 Aug 25	**Extended Traverse** – SJH Reid, R Armitage	
2012 Mar 15	**Scrapyard Challenge** – SJH Reid, C King	

South Cumbria & South Lakes Limestone

1960-ish   **Born Free** – F Booth, J Duff, M Goff
Originally climbed with aid and started further left than today's line.
First free ascent by E Cleasby, M Lynch, C Brown, 1975.

1966 Nov   **The Fertility Variation** to the Girdle Traverse, Humphrey Head
– M Goff, D Marshall. Originally called **West Wall Traverse**.

1966   **Virility** – K Woods, AH Greenbank

1967 Oct 20   **Noda** – M Goff, J Duff
Two points of aid used.

1967 Oct 29   **Fusion** – M Goff, F Booth
First free ascent by A Phizacklea, J Topping, August 1986.

1968   **Girdle Traverse** – M Goff and members of Lancaster MC

1968   **Hammerlock** – M Goff
First free ascent by A Brindle, A Moore, 1988.

1968   **The Book of Invasions** – F Hunsperger, A Dunn (maybe)
(A2). Reduced to one point of aid by D Cronshaw, D Knighton,
2 Jun 1979. Final aid removed by E Cleasby, 1982, on freeing
Prometheus Crisis.

1968   **Air City** – F Hunsperger, A Dunn (maybe) (A2).
First free ascent by D Cronshaw, D Knighton, 29th September 1979.

1968-ish   **Sunflake** – AH Greenbank

Pre 1969   **Stag**, **Direct Route**, **Chimney Route**, **Moose**, **Cracked Wall**,
Easy Chimney, **Ridge** – A Hassall (most probably)

Pre 1969   **The V** – A Hassall (most probably)
Golf variation added by K Lunt, R Wilkinson, 23rd October 2007.

1972 Jun   **Captain's Crack** – A Evans

1972   **Pioneers' Cave** – L Ainsworth, D Cronshaw

1973   **Central Gully** – A Evans

1973   **Stride Pinnacle** – D Cronshaw, L Ainsworth, B Lodge

1974   **The Veil** – L Ainsworth, D Cronshaw
Direct Start added by T Walkington, D Bates, B Rogers, 1985.

1974   **Starshine** – L Ainsworth, D Cronshaw

1974   **Sun God** – D Cronshaw, L Ainsworth

1974   **Moonchild** – R Fawcett, A Evans, D Parker
*"There is, however, a drawback. The crag is on private land and the owners are
hostile. Surprisingly, walkers are welcomed, but climbers are considered beyond
the pale, for a variety of spurious reasons."* Table thumping in *Mountain*
(41, Jan 1975)

1974   **Lunatic** – P Livesey, J Sheard
*"Livesey also points out that the landowners' objections to climbing on this crag
(see Mountain 41) may have been prompted by the destruction of about forty*

Right: Pete Livesey on the first ascent of **Lunatic** (E3), Chapel Head Scar in 1974. **Photo:** John Sheard

Above: Chapel Head lads Dave Cronshaw, left and Ed Cleasby. **Photo:** Al Phizacklea Collection

trees when the crag was being opened up." Humble pie eating in *Mountain* (42, Mar/Apr 1975)

1974 **Great Gully** – K Myhil, A Evans

"Controversy continues to swirl about Chapel Head Scar, a worthwhile cliff which, together with other nearby areas, could become Lakeland's answer to Tremadoc. The impression left by the initial gardening (described by some as being unnecessarily ruthless) is proving a major obstacle to an amicable access agreement…" Al Evans commented: *"Without the gardening the crag would have been worthless as a climbing ground but accusations of vandalism have been wildly exaggerated."* More comment in *Mountain* (55, May/Jun 1977)

"Without this gardening the crag would have been worthless as a climbing ground. But gardening on that scale is no longer necessary or desirable. The accusations of vandalism bandied about up to now have been wildly exaggerated, even in the climbing press." What Al Evans actually wrote, *Crags* (6, ca Feb/Mar 1977)

1974 **Pathfinder** – A Evans, D Parker (A1)

First free ascent by P Botterill, S Howe, March 1985.

1975 **Ivy League** – I Greenwood, D Knighton (1pt of aid)

The climb had been done previously with with a lot more aid by an unknown team. First free ascent by T Walkington, 1982.

1975 Mar 25 **Cyborg** – E Cleasby, M Lynch

1975 Apr 6 **Cross of Lorraine** – E Cleasby, M Lynch, C Brown

1975 Nov 29 **Icicle** – TW Birkett, I Greenwood

1975 Nov **Cliff's Route** – C Brown, D Goodwin, D Jewel

1975 Nov **Steppin' Out** – I Greenwood, TW Birkett

1977 Jan **Puppy Dog Pie** – D Cronshaw, L Ainsworth

1977 Feb 25 **Fast Breeder** – A Parkin, E Cleasby (alt)

1977 Apr	**Half Life** – E Cleasby, I Postlethwaite	

Above: Les Ainsworth, one of the first explorers of South Lakes limestone with new routes at Mill Side Scar, White Scar and Chapel Head Scar in the early '70s.
Photo: Brian Cropper

1977 Apr 30 **Gully Wall** – WS Lounds, P Sanson

1977 **Atomic Bong** – E Cleasby, A Parkin

1977 **Back to the Future** – A Hyslop, Miss J Hyslop A2. First free ascent by J Dunne, April 1991. **Direct Variation** added by J Gaskins, 2005.

1977 **Brain Salad Surgery**, **Broken Zipper** – M Robinson, D Parker

1978 Dec 26 **Aqualung** – D Cronshaw, L Ainsworth

1978 **War of the Worlds** – R Fawcett

1978 **Dune** – E Cleasby
One point of aid used. Aid eliminated by A Phizacklea, J Topping, 30th August 1986.

1978 **The Left Hand of Darkness** – M Danson, A Cock, P Butterworth

1978 **Triggerfinger** – P McVey, M Danson

1978 **Hoad Road** – M Danson

1979 Apr 13 **Android** – E Cleasby, P McVey
One point of aid used. Climbed to the tree on Atomic Bong. Completed with the original finish by E Cleasby, A Phizacklea, I Greenwood, 14 April 1979. First free ascent by D Knighton, 1979. *"In the early days would-be pioneers were faced with an irascible gamekeeper, whose shotgun caused instant compliance with his orders. The cliff had a slow rise to fame until Ron Fawcett produced Moonchild followed shortly afterwards by Pete Livesey with Lunatic. The actions of the Yorkshiremen spurred the Kamikaze Kid – Ed Cleasby – into action. He decided to top their efforts on the highest unclimbed part of the cliff – Great Buttress. He climbed it with the aid of a tree which was so flimsy that he tied it to the cliff with a lengthy of frail tent guy-line and then had to tie his leg to the tree so that he could place the cliff's first bolt."* Trevor Jones, *Cumbrian Rock* (Pic Publications, 1988)

1979 Jul 29 **Interstellar Overdrive** – D Cronshaw, D Knighton
One rest point.

1979 Aug 4 **The Rocinante** – D Cronshaw, D Knighton

1979 Aug 15 **Chain Reaction** – D Knighton, D Cronshaw

1979 Aug 18 **The Omega Factor** – D Knighton, D Cronshaw

Above left: Ed Cleasby on the first ascent of **Android** (E4), Chapel Head Scar in 1979.
Above right: Dave Cronshaw on the first ascent of **Interstellar Overdrive** (F6c), Chapel Head Scar in 1979. **Photos:** Al Phizacklea.

1979 Sep 30	**The Prometheus Crisis** – D Knighton, Miss A Widowson
	Pitch 1 only. Pitch 2 added by D Knighton, D Cronshaw, J Gridley in October the same year using one point of aid. First free ascent by E Cleasby, 1982.
1979 Oct 7	**Strongbow** – I Greenwood, A Phizacklea
1979	**TMA** – D Knighton, D Cronshaw (alt)
1979	**Garden of Eden** – E Rogers
1980 Jan	**Torn Curtain** – D Knighton, D Cronshaw, Miss A Widowson
1980	**The Malacia Tapestry** – D Knighton, B Woodhouse
1980	**Apollo's Exit** – M Danson, I Williamson
1981 Jan	**January** – I Greenwood, Miss A Widowson
	The top pitch only. The starting corner had been climbed previously as **Pleasant Corner**.
	September Arête Variation – D Cronshaw, L Ainsworth, 20th September 1997.
1981 Sep 20	**Wild Winds** – A Phizacklea
	Solo with a knotted rope alongside.
1981 Dec 13	**The Turin Shroud** – D Cronshaw, D Knighton
1982 Apr 12	**Cadillac** – E Cleasby, A Phizacklea
1982	**Fossil Groove** – I Greenwood
1982	**Fossil Crack** – I Greenwood

Right: George Smith on the first ascent of **The Route of All Evil** (F7a+), Chapel Head Scar in 1983. **Photo:** Al Phizacklea

1983	**Enter the Neutron** – I Conway, R Baker
1983 Sep 11	**The Route of All Evil** – G Smith, A Phizacklea

"George Smith, who had recently done the first ascent of Route of All Evil, met Martin 'Basher' Atkinson for the first time at an Ulverston Club dinner. Martin asked George about the route with the intention of repeating it. George, at 6'4", looked down at Martin, at 5'8", and said "But you're too short to do that route!" That spurred Martin to not only repeat the route with ease, but he stamped his authority on it by adding a harder direct finish, **The True Path** (M Atkinson, M Danson, 29th October 1983, since superseded by Eraser Head)" Al Phizacklea reminisces.

1979-83	**Two Overhang Route** – I Greenwood (solo)
	Cartmel Groove variation added by L Ainsworth, 1987.
1979-83	**Missing Words** – I Greenwood (solo)
1984 May 9	**The Firing Squad** – A Phizacklea, R Knight

"Another limestone cliff, Humphrey Head, was developed right next to Morecambe Bay, but unfortunately it was crowned with sixty feet of vertical grass and loose rock which made belaying at the top impossible. Ace climber-photographer Al Phizacklea decided on drastic action and armed himself with a hired electric generator and bolt-placing equipment and placed thirteen in one day. They were four and a half inches long and half an inch thick, with stainless steel hangers to offset the battery effect of sea water. Most of them were strategically placed to be used as belays at the top and this helped the Lake District to have a seaside cliff like Wales. Phizacklea waited tensely for the reaction." Trevor Jones, **Cumbrian Rock** (Pic Publications, 1988)

"Bolt Placed in Lakeland Rock". Headline of an article by Bill Birkett, *Climber*, October 1984.

Mountain Scene

LAKESCENE   BILL BIRKETT

Bolt Placed in Lakeland Rock

Al Phizacklea climbed "Firing Squad", E3, 6a, 80 ft. at Humphrey Head (see Lancashire Guide) placing a BOLT runner in Cumbrian Limestone. This really goes against the massive trend to clean climbing; an ethic particularly strong in the Lakes. The consensus of opinion is generally against this "despicable act" but there are also some who consider it to be the new face of rock climbing. In his favour, perhaps, is the fact that he has made a route out of a particularly unprotectable/undesirable piece of rock.

Above: Controversy! **Photo:** Al Phizacklea

Right: Paul Cornforth on the first ascent of **Super DuPont** (F7c), Chapel Head Scar in 1985.
Photo: Al Phizacklea

Above: Al Phizacklea who placed the first bolts in Lakeland limestone and added the superlative **Wargames** to Chapel Head Scar in the mid '80s. **Photo:** Al Phizacklea

Above: Quick on the draw: Paul Cornforth shows off his bolt gun. **Photo:** Paul Cornforth Collection

1984	**Up Town** – G GIBSON
	The arrival of GARY GIBSON, a well known prolific new-router shocked the locals into more activity.
1984	**Kathleen** – P SHORT, A TOWSE
1985 Jan 5	**Comedy Show** – D BATES, T WALKINGTON
1985 Jan 6	**Oddbods** – D BATES, T WALKINGTON
1985 Jan 11	**Winter Pincher** – T WALKINGTON, D BATES
1985 Jan 11	**Gully Wall Direct** – D BATES
1985 Mar 11	**Born to Run** – J BIRD, D SEDDON
1985 Mar	**Countach** – P INGHAM, P BOTTERILL
1985 Oct 25	**Wargames** – A PHIZACKLEA
1985 Oct 27	**Perverse Pépère** – P CORNFORTH, P McVEY, A PHIZACKLEA
	The bolt arrives at Chapel Head, ushering in a new dawn of possibilities.
1985 Oct 29	**Bleep and Booster** – S HUBBARD, A MITCHELL
	The **Direct Start** was added after retrobolting in 1996/7 by K PHIZACKLEA and S MERRY.
1985 Nov 13	**First Blood** – P CARLING, M GLAISTER
1985 Nov 20	**Super DuPont** – P CORNFORTH
	"Paul Cornforth audaciously produced Super DuPont (E5 6c) the first of that technical standard on the cliff, but more important, at last here was a Cumbrian climber able to technically match the Yorkshire predators." TREVOR JONES,

Cumbrian Rock (Pic Publications, 1988)

1985 Nov 21	**Darth Vader** – A Mitchell
1985 Nov 24	**Driller Killer** – P Ingham, P Cornforth
1985 Dec	**Grass Roots** – G Sutcliffe, P Carling
1985	**Different Strings** – R Southall, T Thomson
1986 Feb 27	**La Mangoustine Scatouflange** – P Cornforth
1986 Apr 23	**Telegraph Road** – P Carling, M Glaister
1986 May 14	**Poetry in Commotion** – J Bird
1986 May 19	**Idle Times** – D Bates
1986 May 20	**A Vision of Things Gone Wild** – A Mitchell, D Bates
1986 May 21	**A Fistful of Steroids** – J Bird
1986 May 21	**Grave New World** – D Seddon, J Bird

Sadly, an almost prophetic name: Dave Seddon, a popular local climber, was killed soloing in 1989.

1986 Jun 2	**Pits Stop** – J Bird
1986 Jun 17	**Crimes of Passion** – J Bird, F Booth
1986 Jul 4	**Spectral Wizard** – J Bird, N Conway

Bar Six Variation added by N Conway, 4th April 1987.

1986 Jul 19	**Beers for Fears** – D Seddon
1986 Aug 3	**Warm Push** – M Greenbank
1986 Aug 5	**Super Duper DuPont** – P Cornforth

"… A very sustained E6 6c, his fourth major line on this wall." Al Phizacklea, *Mountain* (112, Nov/Dec 1986)

1986 Aug 15	**Phantom Zone** – P Ingham
1986 Aug 19	**The Job** – P Pritchard, P Kelly
1986 Aug 23	**Le Flange en Decomposition** – A Phizacklea, S Hubbard
1986 Aug 23	**Sylvester Strange** – J Bird, C Lewis

Originally named **Sylvester Straits** – it is uncertain why or when the name changed.

1986 Sep 3	**Stan Pulsar** – S Hubbard
1986 Sep 6	**Shot by Both Sides** – J Topping, A Phizacklea
1986 Sep 7	**Sniffin' the Saddle** – A Phizacklea, J Topping
1986 Sep 7	**Humphrey Hymen (Met a Sly Man)** – P Cornforth
1986 Sep 13	**Electric Warrior** – A Mitchell
1986 Sep 20	**The Heinous Penis** – A Phizacklea, P Ingham
1986 Oct 4	**Maboulisme Merveilleux** – P Cornforth

"There was a ludicrously overhanging challenge to the left of Great Gully which obsessed Cornforth. During one attempt at the end of a big roof a hold broke off and he fell into space. He found the missing hold, abseiled down and glued it back into place. Then Pat McVay on the same line broke another hold off, and again Cornforth glued it back. On one attempt Paul even jumped to get a critical finger jam but failed. Eventually he was successful with Maboulisme Merveilleux (E7 6c), the first of that standard produced by a local climber in the whole of Lakeland." Trevor Jones, *Cumbrian Rock* (Pic Publications, 1988)

1986 Oct 11	**Zantom Phone** – P Ingham
	Originally started up Sun God but straightened by J Gaskins, 21st July 1991.
1986 Oct 11	**Cosmic Dancer** – A Mitchell, P Ingham, P Cornforth
	Alternative Start added by C Matheson, K Phizacklea 13th August 1999.
1986 Oct 16	**Perverted Start** – P Ingham
1986 Dec 7	**Crumblefoot** – G Sutcliffe, P Carling
1986 Dec 13	**Blue Screw** – P Carling, S Wilson
1986	**Kathleen's Nightmare** – N Conway
1986	**Toirdealbach** – M Liptrot
1987 Feb 24	**Videodrome** – P Ingham
1987 Mar 1	**Strange Times** – K Lunt, G Dawson
	There was evidence of previous activity in the form of old pegs and belay stakes.
1987 Mar 1	**Out on a Limb** – K Lunt, G Dawson
1987 Mar 1	**Like an Arrow** – K Lunt, G Dawson
1987 Mar 1	**Bitter Creek** – G Dawson, K Lunt
1987 May 18	**9½ Weeks** – J Bird
1987 Jun 16	**Stretchy Perineum** – P Cornforth
1987 Jun 21	**Agent Provocateur** – A Mitchell, P Cornforth
1987	**The Witherslack Flange Finish** – P Cornforth
1986-87	**Elk** – First ascentionist not known
1988 Feb	**Introducing the Hardline** – M Lovatt, D Kenyon
1988 Jun 28	**Prime Evil** – A Mitchell, S Sutton
1988 Sep 17	**Tricky Prick Ears** – P Cornforth
1988	**Jess** – L Ainsworth, Miss A Ainsworth
1989 Mar 31	**Live Rounds** – R Graham, L Steer
1989 Mar 31	**Shooting the Load** – R Graham, L Steer
	Superseded **Humphrey Cushion** by A Phizacklea, J Topping, P Cornforth, September 1986.
1989 Apr	**3-2-1** – E Rogers, K Forsythe
1989 Aug 31	**A Song for Europe** – P Cornforth
1989 Nov 25	**Hollow Lands** – M Radtke, J Metcalfe
1990 Jun 1	**Mite** – K Lunt, T Phillips
1990 Jun 1	**Midget** – K Lunt, T Phillips
1990 Jun 1	**Morsel** – K Lunt, T Phillips
1990 Jun 1	**The Mighty Micro** – K Lunt, T Phillips
1990 Jun 1	**Respect Your Elders** – T Phillips, K Lunt
1990 Jun 29	**Calling Mr Hall** – P Cornforth
1990 Sep 12	**Cement Head** – J Bird
1991 Feb	**Reefer Madness** – I Vickers, D Cronshaw
1991 Apr 16	**Slightly Shoddy** – A Hyslop
1991 Apr 21	**Leather Pets** – A Hyslop

1991 May	**Sniffin' the Saddle Direct** – R Graham
1991 May	**Stymen** – R Graham
1991 May	**Pork Pie** – R Graham
1991 Jun 28	**Mustang** – R Graham, E Rogers
1991 Jul 16	**Eraser Head** – J Bird
	The upper half had previously been climbed as **The True Path** by Martin (Basher) Atkinson, M Danson, 29th October 1983.
1991 Jul 16	**Guloot Kalagna** – P Cornforth
1991 Jul 20	**Mid–Air Collision** – A Hyslop
	A new lower section, linked to **Flight Path** (A Mitchell, June 1986) to create another independent line.
1991 Aug 4	**Ropearse** – S Halford
1991 Aug 14	**Meet the Wife** – M Lardener
1991 Aug	**Jelly Head** – J Bird, A Tilney
1991 Sep 1	**Unrighteous Doctors** – D Birkett
1991 Nov 25	**Born Again** – J Bird
1991 Dec 27	**Zzzz!** – A Hinton, J Shepherd, K Lunt
1991 Dec 27	**Geryon** – K Lunt, A Hinton, J Shepherd
1991 Dec 27	**Pingora** – K Lunt, A Hinton, J Shepherd
1991 Dec 27	**Spike** – J Shepherd, A Hinton, K Lunt
1991 Dec 27	**Amazon** – J Shepherd, A Hinton, K Lunt
1991	**Poetry in Motion** – A Tilney
1991	**Humphrey Bogart** – K Forsythe
1992 Jan 11	**Uclid** – J Shepherd, K Lunt
1992 Jan 11	**Big Job** – J Shepherd, K Lunt
1992 Jan 11	**The Slickrock Trail** – K Lunt, J Shepherd
1992 Apr 5	**First Past the Post** – K Lunt, J Shepherd
1992 Apr 5	**Party Politics** – K Lunt, J Shepherd
1992 Apr 5	**Crusher Run** – J Shepherd, K Lunt
1992 Apr 5	**Type One** – J Shepherd, K Lunt
1992 Apr 5	**Cat 955** – J Shepherd, K Lunt

Above: John Shepherd and Andrew Hinton on the first ascent of **Amazon** (E2), Slape Scar, in 1991.
Photo: Karl Lunt

1992 Apr 5 **D6** – J Shepherd, K Lunt
Recount Variation,
D Platt , R Larkin ,
9th April 2000.

1992 Apr 5 **Poll Position**
– J Shepherd, K Lunt

1992 Apr 5 **Slape Victim**
– J Shepherd, K Lunt

1992 Apr 5 **RB22** – J Shepherd,
K Lunt

1992 May 30 **The W** – B Davison

1992 Jun 10 **Surfing with the Alien**
– J Gaskins

1992 Jun 23 **Treeline Traverse**
– T Phillips, K Lunt

1992 Jun 23 **Little Yosemite Rib**
– T Phillips, K Lunt

1992 Jun 23 **The Colostomy Kid** –
K Lunt, T Phillips

1992 Jun 23 **The Badger** – T Phillips,
K Lunt

1992 Jun 23 **Scaredy Cat** – K Lunt, T Phillips

1992 Sep 4 **Cool Your Jets Mum** – S Halford and his Mum

1992 Sep 7 **Humphrey Dumphrey** – I Greenwood

1992 Sep 16 **Doctor's Dilemma** – J Bird

1992 Oct **Reefer Madness** – S Halford, D Gribbin

1992 **Shades of Mediocrity** – S Wood

1992 **Gilbert Cardigan** – K Phizacklea

1992 **For When the Tree Falls** – D Birkett

1992 **More Games** – D Birkett

1992 **Tufa King Hard** – A Burnell

1993 Jun 24 **The Insular Peninsula** – A Phizacklea, JL Holden, A Rowell
The **Direct Start**, now incorporated into the climb, was added by
A Phizacklea, JR Martindale, JL Holden, 28th July 1993.

1993 Jun 27 **Black Gold** – A Phizacklea, JL Holden

1993 Jun 28 **Baedecker for Metaphysicians** – JL Holden, JR Martindale

1993 Jul 5 **Gold Digger** – JL Holden, JR Martindale

1993 Jul 5 **Neibelheim** – JR Martindale, JL Holden, A Rowell

1993 Jul 5 **Welcome to Barrow, Gateway to Oblivion** – A Phizacklea,
JL Holden

1993 Jul 5 **Paranoid Man** – A Rowell, JR Martindale, A Phizacklea,
JL Holden
Probably a record of some sort: John Holden left his house at 17:30
and was in the pub by 21:00, having done four new routes.

Above: Keith Phizacklea who added **Gilbert Cardigan** and **62 West Wallaby Street** to Chapel Head Scar in the 1990s **Photo:** Rob Matheson

1993 Jul 9	**The Last Train to Millom** – A Phizacklea, JL Holden
1993 Jul 20	**Goodbye Cruel World** – A Phizacklea, JL Holden, A Rowell
1993 Jul 22	**The Glassbead Game** – JL Holden, A Rowell
1993 Jul 28	**Hunding** – JR Martindale, JL Holden, A Phizacklea
1993 Jul 31	**Grace Under Pressure** – R Southall, T Thomson
1993 Jul	**Tormented Shower** – J Bumby, I Williamson
1993 Jul	**Summer Lightning** – I Williamson, J Bumby
1993 Aug 1	**La Villa Strangiato** – R Southall
1993 Aug 14	**Bypass to Nowhere** – A Phizacklea, B McKinley
1993 Aug 14	**Caught by the Fuzz** – A Phizacklea, B McKinley

The police were called to investigate reports from local inhabitants about *"some nutters throwing themselves off the quarry top"*. The *"nutters"* managed to convince the police that they were actually competent climbers – quite an achievement in itself!

1993 Aug 22	**Arrested Development** – A Rowell, A Phizacklea
1993 Aug	**Anniversary Waltz** – I Williamson, G Jones
1993 Aug	**Anaconda Adams** – I Williamson, G Jones
1993 Sep 25	**Power Windows** – T Thomson, R Southall
1993	**Bornville** – S Halford
1994 Mar 29	**Englebert Humphreding** – I Greenwood
1994 June 5	**Permanent Waves** – T Thomson
1994 Aug 28	**Le Grand Traverse** – S Crowe, A Earl
1995 Jan	**Firebird** – K Phizacklea
1995 Jan	**Proton** – K Phizacklea
1995 Feb	**Integrali** – D Donnini, K Phizacklea
1995	**The Green Route** – K Phizacklea
1996 Jan 19	**Worlds Apart** – D Cronshaw, L Ainsworth
1996 Jan	**Slim Groove** – D Cronshaw, L Ainsworth
1996 May 19	**Caress of Steel** – T Thomson
1996 Jun 5	**Sad But True** – S Whittall, K Phizacklea
1996 Jul 27	**Sidewinder** – B Davison, N Green
1996 Aug 8	**Natural Science** – R Southall, T Thomson
1996 Aug 25	**Zona Norte** – M Lovatt, S Wilcock
1996 Aug 29	**Big Strides** – N Green, B Davison
1996 Sep 8	**Men at Work** – M Lovatt, Tim Whiteley
1996 Sep 22	**Ten Years Gone** – M Lovatt, S Wilcock
1996 Nov	**White Groove** – D Cronshaw, L Ainsworth
1997 Feb 8	**War Hero** – Stevie Whittall, K Phizacklea, A Phizacklea
1997 Jun 29	**Sir Edgar's Crack** – D Cronshaw, L Ainsworth
1997 Jul 8	**Mr Self-Destruct** – J Gaskins
1997 Jul 13	**Oktoberfest** – D Cronshaw, L Ainsworth
1997 Jul	**Easy Groove** – L Ainsworth
1997 Jul	**Broken Groove** – L Ainsworth
1997 Jul	**Icarus** – D Cronshaw, L Ainsworth

1997 Jul	**Stone Rose** – D CRONSHAW, L AINSWORTH
	Election Special Variation, D PLATT , R LARKIN , 9th April 2000.
1997 Jul	**On Line** – D CRONSHAW, L AINSWORTH
1997 Sep 6	**Right–Hand Man** – D CRONSHAW, L AINSWORTH
1997 Sep 19	**Where Bolters Fear to Tread** – D CRONSHAW, L AINSWORTH
1997 Sep 20	**Wolfman** – D CRONSHAW, L AINSWORTH
1997 Sep 20	**Adela** – D CRONSHAW, L AINSWORTH
1997	**62 West Wallaby Street** – K PHIZACKLEA
1998 May 14	**Late Scoop** – J MASON, MISS S VIGANO
1998 May 14	**Loose Pinnacle** – J MASON, MISS S VIGANO
1999 May 15	**Crystal Dancer** – D CRONSHAW, L AINSWORTH
1998 May 27	**Mindfields** – J GASKINS
1998 Aug 1	**Au** – D CRONSHAW, L AINSWORTH
1998 Aug 2	**The Pipe** – D CRONSHAW, L AINSWORTH
1999 May 15	**Goldsmith** – D CRONSHAW, L AINSWORTH
1999 Jun 12	**Midas Touch** – D CRONSHAW, L AINSWORTH
1999 Aug 8	**Ealasaid** – R BARR, R BAKER
1999 Oct 17	**Green Light**, **Traffic Light**, **Amber** – R LARKIN
1999 Oct 17	**Slapester** – D CRONSHAW, L AINSWORTH
1999 Nov 4	**Halloween Outing**, **The Art of Limestone Rock Painting** – R LARKIN, P OSBORNE
1999 Nov 4	**Pagan Ritual** – R LARKIN
1999 Nov 4	**Critical Friend** – P OSBORNE, R LARKIN
2000 Aug 20	**Undercut** – B DAVISON
2000 Aug 20	**K9** – B DAVISON
2000 Aug 20	**It's My Party** – B DAVISON, N JONES, J WALKER
2000	**Axiom** – J GASKINS
2004 Aug 7	**Witherslack Alice** – A TOWSE, P SHORT, D SHORT
2004 Aug 7	**Head Like a Hole** – J GASKINS Still the hardest climb on the South Lakes limestone over half a decade later.
2006 Aug 13	**Jump for Joy** – B DAVISON, N WHARTON
2006 Aug 13	**Tin Roof** – B DAVISON, N WHARTON
2007 Oct 23	**Cracked Moose** – K LUNT, R WILKINSON

Above: John Gaskins, responsible for the hardest routes ever done on South Lakes limestone, including **Axiom** (2000) and **Head Like a Hole** (2005). **Photo:** John Gaskins Collection

2008 Feb 17	**Ostrakon** – K Lunt, A Madden	
2008 Feb 17	**Rose Tinted** – K Lunt, A Madden	
2008 Mar 30	**Soft Option, Idolatry** – K Lunt (solo)	
2009	**Milly** – N Wharton, R Chaldecott	
2009	**Pip** – R Chaldecott, N Wharton,	
2011 May 15	**The Gold Standard** – A Phizacklea, JL Holden	
2011 Oct 28	**The Borg** – I Cooksey, K Phizacklea	
2011	**Doctor Evil** – John Freeman	

A massive rebolting operation at Chapel Head Scar took place in 2005/2006 and was carried out by a team of volunteers, the most active of whom were Ian Cooksey, Toby Denny, Keith Phizacklea, Alan Steele and Rob Knight. The supply of bolts and lower offs by the BMC was organised by local BMC representatives, David Staton and Colyn Earnshaw. Following on from this, the Cumbria Bolt Fund was established to replace old bolts (many of them well over 25 years old) on crags around Cumbria and this has gone on, under the leadership of Dan Robinson and Ron Kenyon, to oversee bolt replacement at Scout Scar and Mill Side Scar. In 2011/12 the FRCC donated £1000 from guidebook profits to the fund. If you climb on bolted rock, please contribute to the fund. Further details are available at www.cumbriaboltfund.co.uk.

Left: Rebolting operations at Scout Scar in 2007.
Photo: Ron Kenyon

Unfortunately the routes with no known first ascentionists or date of first ascent in this guide are too numerous to list: any information or claims would be appreciated and can be recorded at www.frcc.co.uk

Index

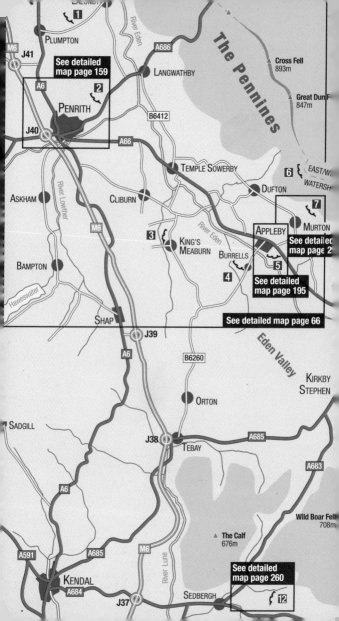